Beyond Sketches of Spain

Beyond Sketches of Spain

Tete Montoliu and the Construction of Iberian Jazz

BENJAMIN FRASER

OXFORD
UNIVERSITY PRESS

OXFORD
UNIVERSITY PRESS

Oxford University Press is a department of the University of Oxford. It furthers
the University's objective of excellence in research, scholarship, and education
by publishing worldwide. Oxford is a registered trade mark of Oxford University
Press in the UK and certain other countries.

Published in the United States of America by Oxford University Press
198 Madison Avenue, New York, NY 10016, United States of America.

Library of Congress Cataloging-in-Publication Data
Names: Fraser, Benjamin, author.
Title: Beyond sketches of Spain : Tete Montoliu and the construction of
Iberian jazz / Benjamin Fraser.
Description: [1.] | New York : Oxford University Press, 2023. |
Includes bibliographical references and index.
Identifiers: LCCN 2022027555 (print) | LCCN 2022027556 (ebook) |
ISBN 9780197549285 (hardback) | ISBN 9780197549308 (epub) |
ISBN 9780197549292 | ISBN 9780197549315
Subjects: LCSH: Montoliu, Tete—Criticism and interpretation. |
Jazz—Spain—History and criticism.
Classification: LCC ML417.M8487 F73 2022 (print) |
LCC ML417.M8487 (ebook) | DDC 781.650946—dc23/eng/20220613
LC record available at https://lccn.loc.gov/2022027555
LC ebook record available at https://lccn.loc.gov/2022027556

DOI: 10.1093/oso/9780197549285.001.0001

1 3 5 7 9 8 6 4 2

Printed by Integrated Books International, United States of America

For Ruth and Howard, side-by-side on the piano bench.

Contents

Acknowledgments

Listening to a single vinyl recording by Tete Montoliu inspired this book. Only a few years ago I found his album *Catalonian Folksongs* in my dad's record collection, which was heavy on piano jazz and also included releases by Dave Brubeck, Chick Corea, Bill Evans, Erroll Garner, Herbie Hancock, Keith Jarrett, Thelonious Monk, Art Tatum, and McCoy Tyner. My immersion in that vinyl collection as a young listener is likely just as important as my more recent journeys through it.

Jazz performers and musicologists will certainly want for more detail in my descriptions of Tete's style, performances, and compositions—but I have intended for these descriptions to be suited for either general readers or scholars from cultural studies, urban studies, and disability studies. I have written this book as a passionate listener of jazz rather than as a musician. During my youth I never had the opportunity to take jazz lessons nor did I take to reading music, though I learned enough through classical piano lessons and in rudimentary saxophone at school to move on to the guitar, bass, and drums. Recently, however, I began learning jazz piano on my own. Garner and Monk remain among my favorite jazz pianists, and I have enjoyed working out passable versions of "Ruby, My Dear," "Blue Monk," "Round Midnight," and "Misty," among other tunes. I remain grateful to my piano-playing parents, piano teachers, former bandmates, and friends in music for the memorable engagements with music that have brought me no shortage of joy over the years.

This book is not truly a jazz biography, though it does contain a significant amount of Tete Montoliu's biographical information. Instead, it is an interdisciplinary journey that approaches the musician's life and jazz work through a series of distinguishable themes: Tete's connection to Barcelona, his congenital visual impairment, and his contributions to jazz—understanding the latter as a form of musical culture influenced by modern urban life. I am thankful to many colleagues from Iberian cultural studies whose interdisciplinary scholarship in these areas has been an inspiration: among them are Ed Baker, Mari Paz Balibrea, Silvia Bermúdez, Enric Bou, Malcolm Compitello, Justin Crumbaugh, Bob Davidson, Encarna Juárez-Almendros,

Susan Larson, Eduardo Ledesma, Araceli Masterson-Algar, Jorge Pérez, and Stephen Vilaseca.

In 2018 I found two more Tete Montoliu albums at the iconic record store PDQ (now closed and the site razed) in Tucson, Arizona, and this book began to seem like more of a reality. *Catalonian Fire* (1974) and *Tete!* (1974) were released on the SteepleChase label out of Copenhagen, both were recorded by the Tete Montoliu Trio—featuring Albert "Tootie" Heath and Niels-Henning Ørsted Pedersen—and both had the unmistakable stamp of modern jazz. With a lyricism reminiscent of Evans, with finger-work recalling Tatum, and with off-kilter Monk-like phrasings, Tete seemed to me to deserve a spot at the top of the list. I became obsessed with getting my hands on as many of Tete's vinyl releases as possible. Using the Discogs app, I was able to purchase a number of hard-to-find recordings from sellers in North America and Europe. I was able to find more albums in record stores in London, Barcelona, and Brussels while traveling during the summer and fall of 2019. I thank Mari Paz Balibrea of Birkbeck, University of London, for inviting me to lead a workshop on urban culture there in July 2019, which provided me with the additional opportunity to browse for vinyl while escaping from the Tucson heat. Likewise, I thank University of Arizona's College of Humanities Dean Durand for financial assistance that made my trip to Barcelona possible.

Perhaps most important among the sources I consulted are two books by Miquel Jurado consisting largely, but not exclusively, of extensive interview transcripts featuring Tete's own words: *Tete: Quasi autobiografia* (Barcelona: Pòrtic, Proa, 1998) and *Tete Montoliu* (Barcelona: Ajuntament de Barcelona/Diàlegs a Barcelona, 1992). In addition, I often relied on the comprehensive account provided by Jordi Pujol Baulenas in his book *Jazz en Barcelona, 1920–1965* (Barcelona: Almendra Music, 2005), which itself returns again and again to Tete Montoliu's jazz work, though briefly and only in passing. Publications by music scholars Iván Iglesias and Juan Zagalaz also deserve special mention.

While finalizing this book, I was fortunate enough to visit a permanent exhibit, accessible via appointment, featuring some 200 objects donated by Tete's family to the Organización Nacional de Ciegos Españoles (National Organization of Spanish Blind Persons, or ONCE) in Barcelona. I am extremely grateful to Josep Pitarch Rodríguez, who is Cap de la Unitat de Cultura i Esports at ONCE, for facilitating my visits to the exhibit during late October 2019. Because that exhibit includes Tete's own piano, it was amazing for me to have the opportunity to run through the opening two-finger crawl to "Blue Monk"—one of the pianist's favorite Thelonious Monk compositions—on the very same keys that Montoliu himself had played.

In particular, I found very helpful the exhibit's inclusion of five large tomes that consolidate published newspaper articles, interviews, and homages dedicated to Tete Montoliu. These bound books include clippings dating back through the early 1950s in a number of languages (Spanish, Catalan, English, French, and German, among others), clippings that have been crucial in solidifying my understanding of Tete's underappreciated transnational reputation. Many of those clippings provide further details or quotations that I am sure will interest some readers. In some cases—and this is particularly the case with the earlier clippings—it was not feasible to track down the full original publication information. Still, I cite from these published pieces where relevant, and I provide the additional designation—"ONCE"—to indicate that the citation's source is to be found in the binders of periodical clippings. For consistency, and due to incomplete publication information, these ONCE sources appear only in the book's endnotes and not in the full references list at the end of the book. I am grateful also to Montserrat García-Albea Ristol for her encouragement and communications with me as I finalized the book, and to Nils Winther, founder of the SteepleChase label, for his interest in the project and for providing me with the cover image from the *Tete!* album (Photo by Lissa Winther © SteepleChase Productions ApS). All translations from Catalan and Spanish that appear in parentheses are my own.

I am very grateful to Oxford University Press, to Lauralee Yeary of OUP, and to the anonymous readers whose suggestions have vastly improved this book's organization and argument. I published an overview of Tete's life and jazz work in *Catalan Review* (2020), including remarks on the interdisciplinary approaches employed, which have been refined and expanded here. I am grateful to William Viestenz and Aurélie Vialette, and to the anonymous reviewers who provided helpful feedback on that original article. General thanks also go to Bob Davidson at University of Toronto for his encouragement of my forays into Catalan studies. For this project I am indebted to David Bolt, editor of the *Journal of Literary and Cultural Disability Studies*, who provided me with a crucial reading list on relevant work from disability studies on music and the social construction of blindness. My gratitude goes to Nieves González-Fuentes and the Department of Romance Studies at UNC-Chapel Hill for providing me with the invaluable opportunity to deliver an invited lecture on this book's subject in February 2020. Finally, I could never have written this book without the support of my wife and partner in vinyl music, Abby Fuoto, who indulged my repetitive and obsessed listening sessions most Sundays from 2018 to 2020 when we might have otherwise been listening to the post-rock band Russian Circles.

Selected Tete Montoliu Vinyl Discography

Tete Montoliu once said that "El disc compacte és inhumà, com és inhumana la perfecció" (The compact disc is inhuman, just as perfection is inhuman). The following discography thus includes only those vinyl recordings whose close and repeated listening brought this project to fruition. Of course, it is not without some gaps. The prolific nature of Tete's recording career means that it is difficult, not to mention cost-prohibitive, to assemble a complete collection of his vinyl discography. The fact that his reputation was established transnationally—across various recording labels, national industries, and performing partnerships—has presented an obstacle to forming even this partial list. I found it difficult to get a hold of recordings that were both affordable and of sufficient quality. Another obstacle is that some of the albums that were quite popular in the late 1980s and 1990s have only been released on compact disc.

Readers should be cautioned that this list is not exhaustive, but rather a trace of the listening practices that have shaped this book. This selected vinyl discography nonetheless represents a significant quantity of musical material, totaling almost fifty recordings made across four decades. In a number of cases, Tete's albums were first issued years or even more than a decade after they had been recorded. Whether an original release or a re-release, items are organized here by their original recording date. The purpose of this is for readers to be able to follow the artistic development of the modern jazz pianist's career through his recorded performances, rather than parse out the specific decisions that led to a given Spanish, European, or American release on vinyl at a given time. Other jazz recordings mentioned in the book are documented in a separate section that appears after the final references list.

Finally, it should be noted that in the body text of this book all dates given in parentheses refer to the original recording year of a performance, while release dates are mentioned without parentheses in prose. For example: "On *Jazz Flamenco* (1956) by Lionel Hampton and His Orchestra, Tete Montoliu's contribution remains uncredited; the album cover for the 1957 American release did not feature his image." With very few exceptions, the titles of all songs discussed throughout the book reflect their original spelling on the physical vinyl releases listed here.

1950s

1956   *Jazz Flamenco*, Lionel Hampton and His Orchestra
        Madrid, Spain, RCA-Victor, LPM-1422
1958   (7") *Tete Montoliu y su cuarteto*
        Barcelona, Spain, SAEF, SP-1000

1960s

1961   *The European All Stars 1961*
        Berlin, Germany, Sonorama L-67
1963   *Kirk in Copenhagen*, Rahsaan Roland Kirk
        Chicago, USA, Mercury, MG 20894
1964   *King Neptune*, Dexter Gordon Quartet
        Copenhagen, Denmark, SteepleChase SCC-6012
1965   *A tot jazz*, Tete Montoliu Trio
        Barcelona, Spain, Concèntric 5701-SZL
1965   *A tot jazz 2*, Tete Montoliu Trio
        Barcelona, Spain, Concèntric FSR-4001
1965   *Núria Feliu with Booker Ervin*, Tete Montoliu Trio
        Barcelona, Spain, Edigsa CM-119
1966   (7") *Calafat*, Tete Montoliu Trio
        Barcelona, Spain, Concèntric, R-13
1967   (7") *Elia Fleta / Tete Montoliu Trio*, Tete Montoliu Trio
        Barcelona, Spain, Concèntric 6043-ZC
1967   (7") *Israel, Come Rain or Shine*, Tete Montoliu Trio
        Barcelona, Spain, Concèntric 6064-ZC
1968   *Piano for Nuria*, Tete Montoliu Trio
        Black Forest, Germany, MPS 30-53177
1968   *Ben Webster Meets Don Byas*, Tete Montoliu Trio
        Black Forest, Germany, MPS 30-20658
1969   *Tete Montoliu interpreta a Serrat*, Tete Montoliu Solo
        Madrid, Spain, Discophon SC 2050
1969   *Lliure jazz*, Tete Montoliu Trio
        Barcelona, Spain, Discophon DM-5274-01

1970s

1970   *Soul's Nite Out*, Lucky Thompson, Tete Montoliu Trio
      Barcelona, Spain, Ensayo ENY-35

1971   *Body and Soul*, Tete Montoliu Trio
      Munich, Germany, Enja 4042

1971   *That's All*, Tete Montoliu Solo
      Copenhagen, Denmark, SteepleChase SCS 1199

1971   *Lush Life*, Tete Montoliu Solo
      Copenhagen, Denmark, SteepleChase SCS-1216

1971   *Songs for Love*, Tete Montoliu
      Madrid, Spain, Marfer 30-217-S

1972   *Gentle Ben*, Ben Webster, Tete Montoliu Trio
      Barcelona, Spain, Ensayo ENY-301

1972   *Recordando a Line*, Tete Montoliu Trio
      Barcelona, Spain, Discophon (S)4335

1974   *Temas latinoamericanos*, Tete Montoliu Trio
      Barcelona, Spain, Ensayo ENY-302

1974   *Catalonian Fire*, Tete Montoliu Trio
      Copenhagen, Denmark, SteepleChase SCS-1017

1974   *Music for Perla*, Tete Montoliu Solo
      Copenhagen, Denmark, SteepleChase SCS-1021

1974   *Tete!*, Tete Montoliu Trio
      Copenhagen, Denmark, SteepleChase SCS-1029

1974   *Vampyria*, Jordi Sabatés, Tete Montoliu Duo
      Barcelona, Spain, EDA LP-13

1975   *Brasil*, Tete Montoliu
      Barcelona, Spain, Ensayo/Impacto EL-142

1975   *Vereda tropical*, Tete Montoliu Trio
      Barcelona, Spain, Ensayo/Impacto, EL-153

1975   (7") *Tete Montoliu*
      Barcelona, Spain, Belter 00-104

1975   *Tate a Tete at La Fontaine*, Buddy Tate Quartet/Quintet
      Copenhagen, Denmark, Storyville SLP-4030

1976   *Tête à Tete*, Tete Montoliu Trio
      Copenhagen, Denmark, SteepleChase SCS-1054

1976   *Words of Love*, Tete Montoliu Solo
      Copenhagen, Denmark, SteepleChase 11-0066

1977   *Meditation*, George Coleman, Tete Montoliu Duo
        Wageningen, Holland, Timeless JS-113

1977   *Yellow Dolphin Street*, Tete Montoliu Solo
        Wageningen, Holland, Timeless SJP-107

1977   *Secret Love*, Tete Montoliu Trio
        Wageningen, Holland, Timeless SJP-111

1977   *Boleros*, Tete Montoliu
        Madrid, Spain, Ensayo ENY-305

1977   *Catalonian Folksongs*, Tete Montoliu Solo
        Wageningen, Holland/New York, USA, Timeless Muse TI 304

1979   *Tete Montoliu al Palau*
        Barcelona, Spain, Zeleste/Edigsa UM 2057-58

1979   *Live at the Keystone Corner*, Tete Montoliu Trio
        Wageningen, Holland, Timeless SJP-138

1979   *Lunch in L.A.*, Tete Montoliu
        Los Angeles, USA, Contemporary 14004

1980s

1980   *I Wanna Talk about You*, Tete Montoliu Trio
        Copenhagen, Denmark, SteepleChase SCS-1137

1980   *Catalonian Nights, Vol. 1*, Tete Montoliu Trio
        Copenhagen, Denmark, SteepleChase SCS-1148

1980   *Boston Concert*, Tete Montoliu Solo
        Copenhagen, Denmark, SteepleChase SCS-1152/3

1981   *Steps Up*, Eddie Harris Quartet
        Copenhagen, Denmark, SteepleChase SCS-1151

1984   *Carmina*, Tete Montoliu Trio
        Hollywood, California, USA, JazzIzz JIR 4003

1986   *The Music I Like to Play, Vol. I*, Tete Montoliu Solo
        Milan, Italy, Soul Note 21180

1986   *The Music I Like to Play, Vol. II*, Tete Montoliu Solo
        Milan, Italy, Soul Note 21200

Note on Theodor W. Adorno and Jazz Criticism

Because this interdisciplinary exploration of Tete Montoliu's life and work assumes no previous knowledge, a primer of sorts may be useful. I anticipate that readers may include specialists in Iberian studies for whom jazz is a secondary concern, scholars with interests in disability and music who may be relatively unfamiliar with the Iberian context, students of popular culture in its numerous global manifestations, or jazz aficionados who may be more interested in musical biography than in historical or theoretical debates. Those readers who are already well versed in the cultural theorizations of jazz music will certainly be aware of the polemic nature of the essays on jazz written by German philosopher and cultural critic Theodor W. Adorno (1903–1969). Still, it is important to introduce general readers to Adorno's much-discussed writings, because they reflect certain misunderstandings regarding jazz in Europe that must be dispensed with if we are to properly assess Tete Montoliu's musical work and legacy.

Though jazz criticism has long demonstrated the fallacious nature of many of Adorno's conclusions on the subject, he nevertheless posed a crucial question in his writings: What is jazz? That is, what is the nature of the musical culture associated with jazz? To what degree can one identify the essence or the roots of the music as they are expressed even in the widest range of performances and recordings? This questioning is particularly important given our investigation, here, of the transposition of the musical form from the United States to Europe. If we are to gain a sense of how jazz can function as critique, and of how Tete Montoliu reshaped the nature of that critique to suit his local, regional, national, and European contexts, general readers must first dispense with many of the common misperceptions, problematic perspectives, and outright errors that run throughout Adorno's early to mid-twentieth-century essays on popular music. Rather than delve extensively into Adorno's texts, I limit myself to a few brief characterizations of his approach and some remarks on how his thought has been discussed and received. The information condensed into this note will nonetheless prove useful as readers once again encounter passing references to Adorno in the introduction and selected chapters of this book.

Adorno launched a substantial critique of the role of popular music within the circuits of contemporary capitalism in essays such as "On the Social Situation of Music" (1932), "Farewell to Jazz" (1933), "On Jazz" (1936), "On the Fetish-Character in Music and the Regression of Listening" (1938), and "Perennial Fashion—Jazz" (1953). The conclusions and the tenor of these writings have prompted many readers to ask, as Robert W. Witkin does in the title of his publication, "Why Did Adorno 'Hate' Jazz?" While it is clear enough that Adorno systematically downplayed the value of jazz music, there are nuances related to the positioning and scope of his writings that merit close attention. Among those nuances are his comments related to the artistic structure of popular music, and ultimately also his misrepresentation of one of the hallmarks of jazz criticism—that is, Adorno's direct contestation of the fact that the origins of jazz lie in African American music.

Among other remarks in Adorno's essay "On Jazz" there are these: "The extent to which jazz has anything at all to do with genuine black music is highly questionable; the fact that it is frequently performed by blacks and that the public clamors for 'black jazz' as a sort of brand-name doesn't say much about it, even if folkloric research should confirm the African origin of many of its practices."[1] For Adorno, the roots of European jazz were to be found, not in African American culture but, quite puzzlingly, in a transnational US-European military culture. Adorno seeks to support his claim that "march music" is the base of jazz music by calling attention to a handful of details that deserve mention. First, he argues, jazz of the 1920s and 1930s ostensibly made prominent use of the Sousaphone.[2] This large musical horn was named after American "march composer" John Philip Sousa, who had been a member of the US Marine band and in the 1890s had played a role in J. W. Pepper's creation of the tuba-like horn.[3] The Sousaphone was indeed a prominent instrument in marching bands, due to the ease with which it could be carried. Second, Adorno states that the saxophone—also a prominent instrument in jazz—was created by the Belgian instrument maker Adolphe Sax in the 1840s and was "borrowed from the military orchestra."[4] And third, he writes, "the entire arrangement of the jazz orchestra . . . is identical to that of a military band."[5] This book's introduction returns to—and diverges from—Adorno's thoughts on the origins of European jazz in discussing the music's cultural significance in Nazi Germany and Fascist Spain.

In theorizing the ills of what he coined as *Kulturindustrie* (the culture in-dustry), Adorno sought to update and expand upon the Marxian concept of alienation, now for a twentieth-century society. In the nineteenth century, Karl Marx had theorized the way in which modern people were alienated from the products of their labor, from each other, and from themselves. Yet Marx was unable to foresee certain changes, among these that the hallmark rationalization of an industrialized society would greatly impact modes of musical production that had previously been relatively autonomous to ad-vanced capitalism. In short, music would become standardized in tune with the capitalistic regularization of industrialized labor.

There is an important observation to be made here regarding the prolif-eration and eventual digitization of the musical object as commodity. This shift has both confirmed Adorno's anti-capitalist critique and also rendered it somewhat banal. Such banality is not paradoxical, by any means. Instead, it is consistent with the alienation and colonization of everyday life that ac-celerated in post–World War II Europe.[6] The musical object—for example the musical recording, as Adorno discusses in essays such as "The Curves of the Needle" (1927) and "The Form of the Phonograph Record" (1934)—is one particular expression among a much wider range of practices that can be described as evidence of consumer-culture commoditization. Interest in these practices has already driven cultural studies analyses by generations of scholars studying the postwar twentieth century. Neither is this a new idea for contemporary consumers, who have become somewhat anesthetized to the practice of musical consumption. Such consumers, of course, remain alienated from the spontaneity of musical production itself. That is to say, by and large, they do not produce music as much as they consume it.

Adorno already made this point in "The Curves of the Needle," where he writes: "It is the bourgeois family that gathers around the gramophone in order to enjoy the music that it itself—as was already the case in the feudal household—is unable to perform."[7] With the development of the cul-ture industry, he writes in "On the Social Situation of Music," "the aliena-tion of music from man has become complete."[8] Despite arguments that the Internet has made it easier than ever before to record and distribute one's own musical production—arguments that must still grapple with the profit-making character of such digital mediation—the musical object remains a prevalent residue and a persistent reminder of this modern alienation. Sales of vinyl records have ebbed and flowed with the decades, and have even been resurging in the twenty-first-century marketplace, along with other selected items that David Sax has highlighted in his book *The Revenge of Analog* (2016). Simultaneously, of course, music is commoditized digitally though many other processes, among them the sound file, the subscription streaming service, and the concert video. It is also key to make clear that Adorno's simplistic but nonetheless enduring specification of "jazz" as the sole stand-in for all nonclassical musical composition cannot be sustained in our contemporary twenty-first-century context.[9] Indeed—whether or not we elect to classify them as "popular"— classical recordings, and the classical musical object more broadly considered, are equally a commoditized form in our twenty-first-century society.[10]

Adorno's critique of aesthetics included a broad categorization of what the theorist called "the two spheres of music."[11] Scholars Gillian Rose and Max Paddison have examined this aspect of Adorno's thought in light of his insights into the culture industry as a whole. It is possible that this instance of dualistic thinking alone reveals that he "was content to give way to his own irrational prejudices in the most uncritical and unreflective manner."[12] Adorno's perspective distinguishes "popular music," which adapts to com- modified exchange and distribution processes, from "serious music," which resists this adaptation.[13] One might label these categories as "uncritical music" and "critical music," understanding also that "critical music" over time may become "uncritical" due to shifts involving social context and use.[14] Yet no matter which set of terms is used, it is hard to believe that such a binary approach could ever fully account for the nuances of contemporary musical production and consumption.

Accounts of Adorno's theorizations have frequently emphasized the se- verity of his conclusions regarding the culture industry. In what is admit- tedly a deterministic viewpoint, he did not allow for popular music forms to be critical practices. Adorno also effectively ignored the value of the music's enjoyment by listeners.[15] The links that Adorno established between music and society, based on the social reality of alienation, are not nuanced enough to allow for anything but a model of popular music as escapism.[16] Certainly there is no small degree of truth contained in his remarks. That is, there is indeed an ideological condition that frames how popular music is engaged by listeners living in modern society.[17] Yet to imagine that there can be no other coexisting or competing understandings of listening practices is to elide all the contradictions inherent in a Marxian approach to everyday life.[18] Similarly, to do so would be to ignore long-standing debates within the field of cultural studies. Adorno's dualistic model of serious/critical music and popular/uncritical music, whether it was justifiable in the context of his larger theory or not, is insufficient if we are to understand what became of postwar European music in general, let alone what modern jazz specifically was to become. Moreover, it is impossible to sustain today the high-modernist defense of that classical music form which Adorno had aspired to contrast with the example of "jazz" in his writings. While it was relatively easy for him to sustain a hard distinction between classical music and popular music vis-à-vis the musical marketplace, it proves to be more difficult for the twenty-first-century reader to do so.

Beyond Adorno's remarks on the intersections of music and the culture industry of capitalism, one finds very little detail in his description of jazz—or at least very little that cannot also be applied to other twentieth-century musical genres as varied as country, dance, electronic, goth, hardcore, hip-hop, house, industrial, metal, pop, punk, rap, rock, slowcore, trance, and so on. While his point is that popular music is a homogenized form, his approach is equally flat. In popular music's regularization of drums, he hears only evidence of the rationalization of industrialized society; in its steady beats, he perceives solely an evacuation of critique.[19]

Some scholars have drawn attention to the inaccuracy of some of Adorno's statements. For example, while Adorno bemoaned what he characterized as the regularized structure of the thirty-two-bar tune, critics have shown this to be a blatant mischaracterization of much of the jazz music of his day.[20] He also deemed elements of popular music unworthy of consideration merely for having appeared in earlier forms of composition. For instance, in the essay "Farewell to Jazz," Adorno dismissed what others referred to as the syncopation evident in some popular music styles. He considered such syncopation to be derivative of earlier innovations in classical music, rather than an innovation to be explored in its own right.[21] He praised Stravinsky for the way in which the classical composer borrowed from jazz, and yet he pointed to Duke Ellington's classically influenced compositional style merely as further evidence that jazz should be seen as a simplified and uncritical commoditization of classical music.[22]

Adorno's approach to popular music is weakened by its lack of nuance. This lack of nuance is more evident the more deeply one considers its assumptions regarding aesthetics. The location of jazz within social structure, for the philosopher, ran parallel to the structure of its artistic form. That is, the music's loose structure, in his view, further reflected its co-optation by capitalist ideology. In the essay titled "On Jazz," he asserts that the syncopation, improvisation, and immediacy of the music were little more than an attempt to "deceive" listeners.[23] Refusing to celebrate the space created in the music for and by improvisation, Adorno denigrated jazz improvisation as mere ornamentation, or what he even called a "mask" for the music's regressive character. This regressive character meant that it was impossible for the music to be part of critical practice, and this lack of critique was reflected in the music's compositional subdivision into what were interchangeable parts.[24] The interchangeable and commoditized structure of jazz was, he felt, most evident in the "the practice of American popular music whereby each variation, or '*chorus*,' is played with emphasis on a special instrumental color, with the clarinet, the piano, or the trombone as quasi-soloist." As Adorno continued to remark, "This often goes so far that the listener seems to care more about treatment and 'style' than about the otherwise indifferent material, but with the treatment validating itself only in particular enticing effects."[25]

The practice of listening to popular or uncritical music such as jazz was, for Adorno, a necessarily passive enterprise he referred to as "regressive listening."[26] At the same time that he denigrated the regressive music itself, he took listeners to task for not knowing how to listen to music. Specifically, they were engaged in the practice of "deconcentration," an activity characterized by a lack of willingness to fully concentrate on the sound and structure of music. His assertion that jazz is "fine for dancing but dreadful for listening"[27] conveys the same disparagement of "commercial jazz" that would place the blame for the popular music form's seemingly objectionable standardization at the feet of specific performers, rather than acknowledge the expectations of the industry in which they must live and work. While not itself drawn from Adorno's own comments, one example would be the unfair characterizations of jazz great Erroll Garner as being merely a "cocktail pianist." Concealed in this sort of remark is Adorno's premise that such popular music is great only if you are not paying too much attention to it. (Of course, it probably does not help things that Garner released an album titled *Cocktail Time* in 1950.) An overemphasis on the deleterious effects of "commercial jazz" is yet another way in which the deterministic fatalism of Adorno's perspective on popular music expresses itself in his aesthetic theory. He leaves no room in the cultural sphere for nuance, enjoyment, or *jouissance*.[28]

Situating jazz music within the discourse of urban modernity, as will occur in chapter 2 of this book, reveals the reductive logic at work in Adorno's description of popular music as unredeemable. While the culture industry is undoubtedly a valuable perspective on industrialized modernity, it can be distinguished from Georg Simmel's insights into the overstimulation that increasingly came to characterize urban life. Simmel's essay "The Metropolis and Mental Life" (1903) famously applied Marxian principles to urbanized turn-of-the-century Europe and asserted that the modern urban subject must adopt a blasé attitude to cope with the visual stimuli and aural cacophony of the city. Contemporary research into modern urban culture has drawn attention to the ways in which a strong tradition of thinking modernity through tropes of detachment could be productive rather than purely negative. This tradition highlighting "productive" detachment can be said to link the work of Simmel with celebrations of urban wandering by both Charles Baudelaire and Walter Benjamin, and even the concept of "civil inattention" theorized by Erving Goffman.[29] No doubt there are connections between industrialization and urbanization, which are true partners in forging the social patterning understood by the term *modernity*.[30] Yet while the culture industry and practices of urban detachment can and should be grouped together among these same overarching modern shifts toward industry and the mega-urb, Adorno's theories on popular music lack the nuance embedded in the ideas of these other theorists. What he does not acknowledge is that listening, performing, and consuming music are, in the context of postwar everyday life, inherently complex activities. Cultural theory since Adorno has been clear that the tension between commoditization and resistance in the cultural sphere continues to reflect the core contradictions embedded in capitalist modernity.[31]

This does not mean, however, that we should discard Adorno's idea of "regressive listening" altogether. There is an important lesson to be learned here regarding how the commoditization of music begins to drive certain shifts in both production and consumption of the musical object among mass audiences in the twentieth century. Adorno employs the example of popular "hot" jazz pieces that were designed to be "just like" what came before them and yet also "original."[32] No doubt this was, and certainly still remains, the formula for creating a popular music hit. However, his conclusion was unnuanced and deterministic. He explicitly compared modern listeners to children, writing that, "[a]gain and again and with stubborn malice, they demand the one dish they have once been served."[33] In his assessment, such listeners were categorically uninterested in being educated about either the technique or the meaning of music.[34] "To make oneself a jazz expert or hang over the radio all day, one must have much free time and little freedom," wrote Adorno.[35] Of course, the twenty-first-century reader knows all too well that popular music across all of its subgenres must "be 'just like' what came before and yet 'original,' " whether they have danced to it, heard it on the radio, played it on vinyl records, or subscribed to a streaming service. The fact remains that, as Robert Witkin suggests, Adorno denounced jazz without first taking the time to understand it.

It is because "Adorno never learned to listen to jazz" that he thus falls too easily into positions that are untenable.[36] Along with denigrating the spontaneity and improvisation of jazz, he also wrote off the practice of musical quotation as part of the music's purportedly regressive and childish language, when instead he might have understood it as evidence of creativity or part of an organic, playful, and even self-referential musical practice.[37] While his indictment of the upper-class German appropriation of jazz was quite clear in his critique of *Kulturindustrie*, Adorno nonetheless systematically maligned musical fandom and the popular bonds it might have held for those he referred to as "enthusiasts."[38] His characterizations of regressive listener types—including "the gas station attendant who hums his syncopation ingenuously while filling up the tank"—revealed a misanthropic strain as much as it pointed to the fetishistic character of regressive listening.[39]

It is a mistake to think that Adorno was writing about the same object "jazz" that we today understand as "jazz."[40] His analysis of the culture industry's commoditization of music was specifically constructed in parallel to the rising international popularity of jazz music during the 1920s and 1930s. As such, it was limited in scope. It has been asserted that in his remarks on popular music he "sometimes seems to make little distinction between popular songs (*Schlager*), jazz, and 'light music' (*leichte Musik*)."[41] As a consequence, the views he expressed on jazz are somewhat uninformed and imprecise, and, as critics have noted, they undergo a process of ossification early on from which they are never rescued. Thus, it is no surprise that in his later essay "Perennial Fashion—Jazz" (1953), his views on jazz have not evolved. Paddison suggests that Adorno's work still reads as willfully ignorant of new developments even well into the 1960s.[42] This situation undoubtedly informs and limits the German philosopher's thinking, such that one easily understands why critics have read his dismissal of jazz as prejudicial.[43] It is one thing for Adorno to suggest, in Paddison's words, that 1920s and 1930s popular jazz lacks "a second level of reflection, a critical self-reflection, [which] is necessary at the level of the structure of the music to enable it both to distance itself from social tendencies and to take a critical stance against those tendencies."[44] And yet it is another thing entirely to apply that critique to the forms of jazz produced and consumed after the emergence of bebop and rock-and-roll.[45]

Critics are right to question how Adorno's theories could possibly shed light on landmarks performances and recordings such as Miles Davis's *Kind of Blue* (1959), Ornette Coleman's *Free Jazz* (1960), or John Coltrane's *My Favorite Things* (1961).[46] The latter alone is evidence enough for making the case that musical quotation can indeed mark a pathway to the avant-garde jazz composition. It is evident that, as the separation between jazz and popular music becomes clearer in the 1950s and 1960s, the decline in the mass appeal of jazz allows it "to emerge from the grip of the culture industry and to develop, as a cultural process, its own forms of resistance."[47] In a certain sense, these considerations are consistent with Adorno's own theories of serious/critical musical forms that elude and resist mass appeal. Moreover, they are vital to keep in mind, given how Tete Montoliu positions himself in the transnational landscape of modern jazz. To wit, Dustin Bradley Garlitz—in a section of his thesis that he titles "Zeroing in on Adorno's Misconceptions of the Jazz Establishment"—introduces the possibility that Adorno might have liked modern jazz, or at least that he might have appreciated those artists who are most direct in their use of the music for dissent.[48] I choose to imagine that one such artist would have been US-based jazz saxophonist Rahsaan Roland Kirk, with whom Tete played and recorded at the Jazzhus Montmartre in Denmark's capital city for the release *Kirk in Copenhagen* (1963)—more on this in chapter 2.

Witkin insists that Adorno's conclusions may be relevant only to the context of 1920s and 1930s popular jazz,[49] which may excuse some of the theorist's misconceptions regarding the structure and social import of popular music. Yet Adorno's comments contradicting the African American origins of jazz music are more difficult to ignore. While the German critic believed it was possible to separate jazz music from its origins in the Black American experience, in this book I invoke the assertion made by Fumi Okiji—author of *Jazz as Critique: Adorno and Black Expression Revisited* (2018)—that jazz is inseparable in principle from the notion of Black expression. While Adorno asked the pertinent question "What is Jazz?," it is Okiji who has provided the answer: jazz is critique rooted in the US Black experience. Drawing on Okiji's reflections and adapting them to reconfigure the study of a key figure in European jazz, the chapters of this book are informed by a cultural studies method that entangles Tete's biography with the notion that jazz music can function as a minority language. As the example of Tete

Montoliu demonstrates, the Black American origins of jazz are not erased by its transnational European invocation, nor are they irrelevant when considering the contributions of a white European musician to the modern jazz form. The question that the present book asks is whether the critique and the language of jazz can be put to use by musicians in other places and times. While exploring the life and work of Tete Montoliu cannot definitively answer this question, I believe that reflecting on his legacy can inspire us to think through what it means for European musicians to practice jazz as a language of critique and as a way of gathering in difference.

Introduction

No musician did more to shape Iberian jazz than pianist Vicenç Montoliu i Massana, who was known simply as "Tete." *Beyond Sketches of Spain: Tete Montoliu and the Construction of Iberian Jazz* explores the artist's life, musical production, and international reception within a cultural studies framework. In addition to offering a multifaceted portrait of an outstanding musician, it confirms—in the European context—three interconnected points made by Paul Austerlitz. These are: (1) that jazz remains "an art that is intimately tied to national identity in the United States," (2) that jazz is "inextricable from its African-influenced base," and (3) that jazz is "a major current of transnational culture."[1] This book moves beyond mere sketches of Spanish nationhood, challenges conventional scholarly narratives, and recovers links between the United States, Barcelona, Catalonia, Spain, and Europe in the investigation of an impressive and often overlooked transnational modern jazz legacy.

Tete Montoliu (b. March 28, 1933, d. August 24, 1997) enjoyed a well-deserved international reputation in Barcelona, within Catalonia, across Spain, and even throughout Europe. Though recognition of this fact has been slow to develop among Anglophone audiences, it is nonetheless patently obvious in Spanish and Catalan circles of music and musical criticism. Miguel Arribas García underscores Tete's reputation within the capital city of Catalonia, stating that he was "[l]a figura principal del jazz moderno o bebop en Barcelona" (the principal figure of modern jazz or bebop in Barcelona).[2] Saxophonist José Luis Gutiérrez confirms that Tete is widely understood to be the main highlight of jazz in Spain under the Franco dictatorship.[3] Music scholar Xavier Moreno Peracaula writes about the exportation of the Catalan jazz pianist's fame outside of Spain, stating that saxophonist Pedro Iturralde, who made his name with flamenco jazz, and Tete Montoliu "have been the Spanish jazz musicians with the most projection outside the country."[4] And finally, speaking to the scale of European jazz as a whole, promotor Julio Martí Moscardó has stated definitively that Tete "era el mejor pianista de jazz que ha habido en Europa jamás de jazz – jazz, de be-bop" (was the best jazz pianist—of bebop jazz—that there ever was in Europe).[5]

In the process of exploring Tete Montoliu's life, musical work, and impact, this book simultaneously works toward a number of additional critical goals. First and foremost, it offers a correction. Tete's legacy poses a real challenge to a whole tradition of American jazz historiography that, as E. Taylor Atkins affirmed in *Jazz Planet*, "has consistently failed to look overseas for jams of consequence."[6] Likewise, to explore Tete's jazz work is also to correct for certain tendencies within the existing English-language scholarship on Spanish culture of the Francoist dictatorship. While the amount of scholarship synthesizing history, politics, and literature during this period is immense, it is only in the twenty-first century that researchers based in humanities departments have begun to investigate musical practices in sufficient depth.[7] A relative critical neglect of Spain's musical cultures of the 1950s through the 1970s manifests in a collective lack of knowledge about the jazz pianist, whose complete vinyl and CD discography includes some one hundred releases. To emphasize Tete's significance for modern jazz as a whole is thus simultaneously to contribute to increasing interest in Spain's twentieth-century cultural history. With all this in mind, chapter 1 explores in depth a handful of landmarks in the transnational musical landscapes of European jazz, while chapter 2 explores the intersection of jazz with the modern urban experience.

This book also challenges the notion of a monolithic Spain. The usage of the phrase "Iberian jazz" in this book's title is intended to emphasize what Joan Ramon Resina has called "a peninsular plurality of cultures and languages pre-existing with the official cultures of the state."[8] The methodological approach of "Iberian studies" thus stands as a challenge to conventional Spanish studies. Renewing interest in the linguistic and cultural heterogeneity that has long shaped territories located within the Spanish state, this critical formation interrogates the nuanced and often fraught relationships between hegemonic Castilian (Spanish) language and power and contemporary expressions of the Galician, Basque, and Catalan languages and cultures.[9]

The notion of *catalanitat* (Catalan-ness) is central to understanding the context of Tete Montoliu's musical production. This is to recognize that "for many Catalans the adjective 'Spanish' excludes any reality distinct from centralist, 'Castilian' and typically, *castizo* [pure Spanishness] or *flamenco*."[10] While it can indeed be said that "the exhibitions of Catalan and Spanish identities in public is fairly common and not always antagonistic,"[11] neither is it difficult to identify times, places, and circumstances where such antagonisms have been present. Tete's own statements regarding his strong Catalan identity, his relationship with the city of Barcelona, his purposeful engagement with traditional Catalan musical themes, and his connections with popular Catalan song traditions distinguish his music from what might otherwise be called "Spanish" jazz. Blending music with history and politics, chapters 1 and 3 employ the modern jazz pianist's legacy as a catalyst that pushes readers beyond narrow understandings of Spain.

Furthermore, this study contributes to the need to acknowledge that "disability is everywhere in music."[12] Tete was a person who experienced total visual impairment from birth, someone who was often labeled as congenitally blind. Though his experiences as a person living with visual impairment were an important part of his musical identity and became inseparable from his international reputation, this fact has not yet been approached within a sophisticated critical framework. Just such a framework can be found in the interdisciplinary field of disability studies, considering most carefully the work of David Bolt, Georgina Kleege, and Rod Michalko, who give critical attention to the social and cultural construction of blindness.[13] Chapter 4 distinguishes the material experience of visual impairment from the notion of disability as a social relationship and pursues both themes in discussing Tete's musical biography, cultural context, marketing, and reception.

In addition to being a crucial figure for destabilizing traditional jazz narratives, diversifying scholarship on Spanish jazz, and recognizing the importance of disability for music studies, Tete Montoliu enjoyed unparalleled fame in European circles. He thus becomes an almost paradigmatic case of the way in which jazz artists tend to achieve a status on par with other prominent literary and cultural figures. In lieu of a conclusion, this book's concise epilogue takes on Tete's wider cultural notoriety by sifting through literary narratives, documentary and fiction films, and even a graphic novel in which he appears. Drawing from a range of interconnected disciplinary discourses, including jazz studies, Iberian cultural studies, urban studies, and disability studies, this book's subject finally emerges for readers of English as worthy of the recognition he enjoyed among audiences in Catalonia, Spain, and across Europe.

It is important to keep in mind that Tete Montoliu came of age as a musician in a Spain shaped by war and conflict, still unable to grapple fully with the persisting racialized dimensions of its imperial and dictatorial histories. This introduction thus references both the Spanish Civil War (1936–39) and the early years of the dictatorship of Francisco Franco (1939–75) as key coordinates for understanding the social context of Tete's life and the significance of his engagement with the Black American jazz form as a white European musician. Rather than delve exhaustively into these historical conflicts, which have received a robust historical treatment elsewhere,[14] the sections that follow emphasize Tete's own experiences, his family, his childhood, his musical influences, and the transnational encounters that occurred in parallel to his musical apprenticeship. Readers are introduced to anecdotes that convey the effects of war and the early dictatorship on musical culture in Spain, brief vignettes of American musicians who influenced Tete, notes on the composition and activities of his early bands, and references to prominent Black intellectuals from the United States who were important witnesses to Spain's war-torn twentieth-century geography.

Tete's Musical Biography

Vicenç Montoliu Jr. was born in Barcelona on March 28, 1933, as the only child of Ángela Massana i Coma and Vicenç Montoliu y Melià. His uncle gave him the nickname "Tete," and it stuck.[15] Music was extremely important in his family. Tete's grandfather played the clarinet, directed the Banda de Montsó, and pushed Tete's father to play music from a young age. At age seven, Vicenç Sr. moved with the family to Barcelona, where he studied at the Conservatori Superior de Música. By 1929 he was already a professional musician and was touring with the Banda Municipal all around Europe, including a performance during the Universal Expo of Berlin. He played the oboe, English horn, alto sax, clarinet, violin, and the bandoneon, and he formed L'Orquesta Montoliu, or the Conjunto Montoliu, which achieved a great reputation.[16] Vicenç Sr. was one of the most active musicians of prewar Catalonia.[17]

As it was with many Catalans, Tete's father was forced to leave Spain for France after the civil war, but he snuck back over the Pyrenees as soon as he was able.[18] When he turned up once again in Barcelona, which was now governed by the fascist dictatorship of Francisco Franco, he was quickly denounced as a traitorous red. In the Francoist tribunal that ensued, however, no clear judgment was reached, and he was released. Miquel Jurado writes of this trial: "Com que no hi havia unanimitat i, possiblement, com que no el consideraven un element perillós (un músic semblava que comportava poc perill per a la dictadura feixista) va ser posat en llibertat" (Since there was no unanimity and, possibly, because they did not consider him to be a dangerous element [a musician seemed to pose little danger to the fascist dictatorship] he was released). Soon Vicenç Sr. was back playing music with the Banda Municipal, and later the orchestra of the Gran Teatre del Liceu.[19] Tete reports that his father never played music in the house, and from the pianist's reflections one gathers that he seems to have often been gone, traveling to and from performances elsewhere. Yet, on Sundays, Vicenç Sr. would take him to the Palau de Belles Arts, so that his son could listen to him play with the municipal band.[20]

Tete was the child of not just one, but two musicians. His mother, Ángela, had made a name for herself as a competitive swimmer, and she also played the ukulele, as well as tangos on the piano.[21] Once the civil war broke out in the mid–late 1930s, she would take her son to the silent movie screenings held for the soldiers on a military base. Tete would have been only around three or four years old at the time. Despite his young age, or perhaps because of it, these experiences made quite an impression on him. As was the fashion, the silent films were shown with accompanying live music, and as Tete later recounted, "El pianista de la banda hi posava la música a base de *rag times* i coses per l'estil. En aquelles sessions de cine mut vaig començar a comprendre aquella música i a enamorar-me'n. Aquell piano i els discos de la meva mare van ser els que em van impulsar definitivament a dedicar-me a la música i concretament al piano" (The band's pianist played music based on rag times and things like that. In those silent movie sessions I started to understand and fall in love with that music. That piano and my mother's records were what definitely pushed me to dedicate myself to music and specifically to the piano).[22]

At home, Tete would spend the days listening to his mother's recordings of Fats Waller and Duke Ellington,[23] a listening practice that would have a lasting impact. To wit, he later recorded Ellington's "Sophisticated Lady" a few times, releasing it on both on *Lunch in L.A.* (1979) and *Meditation* (1977), for example—the latter as a duo with George Coleman on sax. He also recorded the renowned bandleader's "Come Sunday" on *Yellow Dolphin Street* (1977) and on his *Boston Concert* (1981) album, and he also performed the song as part of his renowned performance at Barcelona's Palau de Música, which was released as a double LP *Tete Montoliu al Palau* (1979). "Come Sunday" was distilled from Ellington's famed suite titled *Black, Brown and Beige* (1943), which had been performed at Carnegie Hall, and its lyrics were understood to evoke both the religious faith and social struggles of the African American community. "Satin Doll" was a favorite that Tete performed with saxophonist Dexter Gordon multiple times in 1964, and that was also included on the Concèntric label release *Tete Montoliu Presenta Elia Fleta* (1966).[24] On the album *King Neptune* (1964), where Tete played as a member of the Dexter Gordon Quartet, the song stretches into the thirteenth minute as "Gordon and Montoliu work together as hand in glove," according to the liner notes by Ib Skovgaard. Other compositions Montoliu performed that were borrowed from the Duke Ellington band writing team (in which Billy Strayhorn and Juan Tizol deserve special recognition) included "Lush Life," "Take the 'A' Train," "Caravan," "Perdido," "I Got It Bad (and That Ain't Good)," "In a Mellow Tone," "C Jam Blues," "In a Sentimental Mood," "It Don't Mean a Thing," "Cotton Tail," "Prelude to a Kiss," and "Mood Indigo."

It is well known that Duke Ellington was an incredibly important figure in the spread of American jazz to Europe. Yet, although he toured extensively in France and through several other countries, it is difficult to find evidence that he performed, or even thought about performing, in Spain from the 1930s through the end of the 1950s.[25] Ellington did perform with Ella Fitzgerald in Barcelona and Madrid at the beginning of 1966, and a concert film exists of a performance by Ellington's orchestra that was recorded on November 24, 1969, in Barcelona's Basilica Santa Maria Del Mar.[26] Beyond the fact that Ellington's music was readily accessible to Tete through his mother's record collection, and through the performances of other jazz artists visiting Barcelona, however, the bandleader and composer is also a fitting model for the Catalan pianist's transnational invocation of jazz. To start, the Duke was insistent that his music was international.[27] In the words of jazz critic Stanley Crouch, in his forty years of touring internationally, "Ellington learned that his versions of rhythm and tune were international languages and that those languages were capable of bringing whatever he knew of the human universe into any room in which he and his musicians were playing. Those foreign lands and societies were brought to the bandstand, sooner or later, their spirits wrestled or coaxed into melody, harmony, tonal colors, and rhythm."[28] Tete's biography provides ample evidence that he understood jazz to be an international language, as it was for Ellington before him. Not only that, Montoliu also maintained merely one degree of musical separation from the bandleader—for example, playing and recording with the Duke's band member and ongoing collaborator saxophonist Ben Webster, most famously on the album *Gentle Ben* (1972). Webster once said of Tete that "té un *swing* com cap altre pianista blanc a tot Europa" (he has a swing like no other white pianist in all of Europe).[29]

Thomas "Fats" Waller is an equally important point of reference for those seeking to make sense of Tete's musical trajectory. Like Fats, who began to play at age six, Tete was also a child prodigy.[30] Waller was not merely a charismatic performer. He was a composer in his own right who brought together influences from multiple styles, including blues, ragtime, and classical music—a mix that echoes in any survey of Tete Montoliu's influences and recordings. Ted Gioia suggests in *The History of Jazz* that Fats Waller did more than any other musician from his day "to bring the Harlem style to the attention of the broader American public,"[31] and Waller's influence on Tete demonstrates that there is also a transnational dimension to the spread of his piano style. In certain original compositions by Montoliu, one hears echoes of Waller's ambitious compositional style. For example, while working a long stint in England in the late 1930s, Fats had written a six-part piece he titled "London Suite." Montoliu, for his part, composed his own "Catalan Suite." As described by Chris Sheridan in the context of the "New York story of jazz" on the liner notes for the album on which "Catalan Suite" appears (*Tête à Tete*, 1976), Tete's composition consists of "five traditional Catalonian songs which segue together imperceptibly to form a cohesive whole"; Sheridan adds that, "throughout, the ghosts of Catalonian minstrels are jostled by equally vivid spirits of Harlem pianists."[32] If the "London Suite" by Waller "reflects the critical action of transatlanticism" via "its mix of stylistic markers of 'hot' jazz with melancholic 'sweet' music, which references European classical music," then much the same description can be offered regarding the musical hybridity of Montoliu's composition.[33] Also of interest is that Waller complained about the clear market preference for "primitive" jazz in Europe, which he had to cater to even when he was hoping to play in a softer or introspective mood.[34] Montoliu's battles with the market expectations for ball music and tropical jazz in Spain, when he wanted to play the newer and less popular forms of bebop, present yet another parallel with the Harlem pianist's musical biography.

Fats Waller himself can be taken as quite a modernizing force in the music. He can be thought of as a pianist who moved jazz forward when other stride players still clung to their ragtime roots.[35] Importantly, keeping Tete's own improvisational style in mind, Fats was one of the first stride pianists to introduce some improvisational elements into his songs during the middle-eight sections of his thirty-two-bar songs.[36] "Honeysuckle Rose" was perhaps the Fats Waller song that most stuck with Montoliu throughout his career, though there is also Tete's performance of "Jitterbug Waltz" with David Murray in Madrid on May 15, 1990. The Catalan pianist first recorded "Honeysuckle Rose" with his trio and guest vocalist Elia Fleta in 1966, and he had learned to play the Harlem pianist's "Alligator Crawl" in his earliest years. He was able to play the song by ear when he was only eleven, notes Miquel Jurado, and, in fact, Tete learned to play all of the Fats Waller songs in his mother's collection of vinyl recordings.[37] Also at eleven years old, Tete began buying his own records with a twenty-*peseta* allowance from his parents, which would get him one newly released record per week.[38] He gravitated toward foreign recordings, and throughout his life he would bring titles that were unavailable in Spain back into the country from his travels.

Among the instruments in Tete's childhood home was a foot-pumped harmonium that was small enough for him to bring it with him from one room to another.[39] He used the instrument to imitate songs he heard on the radio, and around age eight, in 1941, he debuted his skills in a children's music contest hosted by Ràdio Barcelona.[40] After this, his parents changed out the harmonium for a piano.[41] This was at the height of fascist enthusiasm in Spain.[42] Jazz music still thrived in localized pockets of the city despite the harsh conditions of the early postwar period.[43] Even in 1941, Barcelona managed to hold two Hot Jazz festivals featuring "los principales conjuntos de la capital catalana: las orquestas Martín de la Rosa, Gongo, Ramón Evaristo y Plantación, el dúo de piano Matas-Roqueta, el terceto Barreto, el Cuarteto Masmitjá, el Quinteto Hot Club, y las cantantes Conchita Leonardo y Rina Celi" (the principal bands of the Catalan capital: the orchestras of Martín de la Rosa, Gongo, Ramón Evaristo and Plantación, the piano duo Matas-Roqueta, the Barreto Trio, the Masmitjá Quartet, the Hot Club Quintet, and the singers Conchita Leonardo and Rina Celi).[44]

Tete's remarks in interviews reveal that he associated jazz with Black American musicians from a young age. He remembers how his obsession with the transnational culture of jazz music manifested itself in ways that are both problematic and instructive: "Quan anàvem pel carrer amb la meva mare i vèiem un negre, sempre l'aturàvem per preguntar-li quin instrument tocava, però mai no trobàvem cap músic" (When we walked down the street with my mother and we saw a black man, we always stopped to ask him what instrument he played, but we never found a musician).[45] This anecdote expresses the degree to which young Tete was interested in a musical language that, importantly, he associated with Black American musical culture. He describes attending a concert by US saxophonist George

Johnson in 1946 and for the first time wanting to be able to speak English.[46] He once said that "[e]l inglés es el idioma del jazz, como el castellano es el idioma del flamenco" (English is the language of jazz, just as Castilian is the language of flamenco).[47] Yet jazz, for Tete, was more than a musical language.[48] It set him on a path that propelled him, in linguistic terms, out of the fraught Castilian Spanish-Catalan binary that structured life under Francoism. As this book's continued references to his jazz work bear out, Montoliu felt at home in the alternative sociality he experienced in jazz—a gathering that for him was defined by musical, linguistic, cultural, national, and racial difference.

Another influence on Tete during his early years was Carlos Wesley Byas,[49] otherwise known as Don Byas. The US tenor saxophonist visited Spain in the 1940s and spent time in both Madrid and Barcelona. Scholar Iván Iglesias credits Byas with being part of the awakening of Spanish interest in bebop.[50] The sax player had performed with Lionel Hampton, Count Basie, Don Redman, and Andy Kirk, but he came to Tete's attention while he was playing with Bernard Hilda's orchestra at the Copacabana terrace on the Diagonal in the Catalan capital.[51] Byas soon became a staple of the Barcelona jazz scene. Tete would later remark that "així com a París o Amsterdam o Londres o a Berlín es van quedar tots els músics americans del món, nosaltres només en vam tenir un, que va ser el Don Byas, i prou" (while all the American musicians in the world stayed over in Paris or Amsterdam or London or Berlin, we only had one, which was Don Byas, and that was enough).[52] The pianist insists that he was introduced to jazz by his mother's Duke Ellington and Fats Waller records, and not by Byas,[53] but the musician's influence and physical presence in Tete's life during his formative years is notable nonetheless.

The timing of Don Byas's stay in Barcelona allowed a lasting connection to be forged with the teenage pianist. In the words of Rafael Pérez Vigo:

Hay un hecho de mucha importancia que ocurre en 1947. Nos referimos a que Don Byas decide apadrinar a Tete Montoliu, que era el más sobresaliente músico de jazz español, y empieza a enseñarle el lenguaje y los rudimentos del nuevo estilo que estaba de moda en Estados Unidos, es decir, el be-bop. En muy poco tiempo, Montoliu creó un cuarteto de jazz dedicado a difundir la música be-bop.[54]

(There is a very important event that occurs in 1947. We refer to Don Byas's decision to take under his wing Tete Montoliu, who was the most notable Spanish jazz musician, and he began to teach him the language and the basics of the new style that was in fashion in the United States, that is, bebop. In very little time, Montoliu formed a jazz quartet intent on spreading bebop music).

During this time, Tete was reportedly attending a number of jam sessions throughout the city—accompanied, not by his father, but rather by local pianist Damià Cots. At these sessions, he met Byas, and they quickly formed a friendship. "A Byas li va caure bé, el nen blanc i cec que volia ser músic de jazz, i la simpatia va augmentar considerablement després de tastar els guisats de la seva mare. A partir d'aquella experiència Byas es va convertir en un habitual de la llar dels Montoliu, a la qual anava pràcticament cada dia per dinar" (Byas took to him well, the white and blind boy who wanted to be a jazz musician, and his affection grew considerably after tasting his mother's stews. From that point on, Byas became a regular at the Montoliu home, which he would visit practically every day for lunch).[55] Though Byas spoke neither Catalan nor Spanish, Tete says that he learned many things about jazz from him.[56] From the conversations that Miquel Jurado and Tete have documented in publications like *Tete: Quasi-autobiografia*, one gets the feeling that Byas was not merely a musical influence but also a sort of father figure for Tete. Thus, it must have been gratifying that, some twenty years later, the pianist would record with him and Duke Ellington's famous saxophonist bandmate on the album *Ben Webster Meets Don Byas* (1968).[57]

In the late 1940s and early 1950s, Tete was already very active in his own bands and was very much influenced by a number of US jazz artists. "Tete Montoliu y su Conjunto" was an early sextet whose repertoire included hits by the "King of Swing," Benny Goodman, such as the song "Dos Gardenias." What followed was a new group dedicated exclusively to jazz called "El Quartet Be Bop," which featured Tete along with guitarist Jordi Pérez, bassist Jerry de Larrocha, and drummer Juli Ribera. Tete described the band by saying, "El Quartet Be Bop érem quatre senyors intel·lectuals una mica repugnants que estàvem en contra de tot, però molt especialment dels defensors del jazz clàssic com Hugues Panassié o Alfredo Papo" (Those of us in the Be Bop Quartet were four off-putting intellectuals who were against everything, but especially against those like Hughes Panassié or Alfredo Papo who defended classic jazz).[58] Their interest in the new style of bebop brought the group no shortage of conflict. The discourse of bebop was frequently racialized, as evident in Tete's reflection that "[l]a mare de Jordi Pérez em va acusar una vegada de fer sortir el seu fill amb negres i depravats" (Jordi Pérez's mother once accused me of making her son hang out with blacks and degenerates).[59] El Quartet Be Bop lasted until the end of 1954, when Tete and Pérez went to Holland and Ribera went to Paris. The band's peak accomplishment was playing a concert at the Casal del Metge de Barcelona at 11 p.m. on March 18, 1952—a concert that Jurado describes as "el primer concert de *be bop* autèntic ofert per músics espanyols" (the first authentic *bebop* concert put on by Spanish musicians).[60]

Tete's success in Barcelona brought him other opportunities, and he began traveling to play gigs in other cities. At one point, he was playing at the American Bar in Madrid at the same time that his father was also playing in Madrid with the band of Jaime Camino. One night, the singer Pilar Morales was performing with Camino's band, and Tete subsequently fell deeply in love with her. Pilar and Tete were married in Barcelona on April 5, 1956. The very next day the *Diario de Barcelona* featured a full article announcing the marriage. Its subtitle read: "El novio es ciego de nacimiento y la novia tiene la piel de color" (The groom is blind from birth and the bride has colored skin).[61] Jurado comments that because Pilar was two years older than Tete, not to mention Black and from Cuba, this was enough for the relationship to not be viewed positively in Francoist Spain. As a consequence, Tete had to deal with racist remarks from his friends and family.[62] In his own words, "Jo em considerava un defensor dels drets dels negres i no podia suportar el racisme amagat. . . . A Barcelona ningú no era racista, però que jo em casés amb una negra era un escàndol" (I considered myself a defender of the rights of black people and could not stand hidden racism. . . . In Barcelona [presumably] no one was racist, but that I married a black woman was a scandal).[63] The pianist's own comments on the matter reveal the persistent, deeply rooted, and contradictory attitudes on race that would so puzzle Richard Wright during his visits to Spain, as discussed later in this introduction.

Soon after meeting, Tete and Pilar recorded 78s together under the name "Tete Montoliu y su Conjunto Tropical," an act that included Jorge Candela. They also shared a brief tour at the end of 1956, and performed together at the Café Terrasse in Zurich. The latter gig allowed Tete the opportunity to attend a performance at Congress Hall that included Lester Young, Miles Davis, Bud Powell, and the Modern Jazz Quartet.[64] Pilar may have felt she sacrificed her musical career so Tete could pursue his; their relationship worsened toward the end of 1974, and they subsequently divorced.[65] Much later, in 1995, the pianist married Montserrat García-Albea, though they had reportedly first met in 1973 while he was playing at the Whisky Jazz and the Balboa Jazz clubs in Madrid.[66] While he and Montserrat had no children, Tete and Pilar did have a child together, named Núria, who was born on June 26, 1957.[67] Tete's album *Piano for Nuria* (1968), which included the original composition "Blues for Nuria," is a clear tribute to the love he had for his daughter. It is equally a testament to the musical nature of the passion that brought her parents together. And as discussed in a later chapter, the song also demonstrates the way in which Tete Montoliu's approach to modern jazz was a performance of the unevenness, overstimulation, dissonance, and chaos that defined urban identity.

Anti-Jazz Attitudes and Transnational Encounters in Spain

The soundscapes of Black American jazz that Tete Montoliu experienced as a child listening to his mother's vinyl records, and later as a young musician immersed in Barcelona's jazz circuits, were not consistent with the anti-jazz attitudes pervasive in his postwar Spanish dictatorial milieu. Due to his early exposure to American jazz music and musicians, the young pianist was forging a very different understanding of Blackness than the one propagated by Spain's racialized imaginary, one that had become deeply embedded in the conservative, dictatorial society of the postwar period.

Anti-jazz attitudes, of course, had emerged in Spain prior to the civil war and the Franco dictatorship. In early twentieth-century writings, for example, "black music" was already being imagined as a moral threat or corrupting force.[68] These Spanish attitudes in turn had their roots in deeply rooted sociopolitical dynamics whose acknowledgment is crucial to understanding the marginalization of jazz. Spain's imperial history of slavery and colonization, fueled by the prolonged bloody wars of the Reconquista, forged a racialized imaginary that continues to shape discourse on inequality, Blackness, and immigration in Iberia today.[69] For instance, in *Rocking the Boat: Migration and Race in Contemporary Spanish Music* (2018), Silvia Bermúdez crafts a careful account of the role played by deeply rooted racial hierarchization in the production and reception of Spanish popular music since the 1980s. Building on previous scholarship, she joins scholars such as Jerome C. Branche in asserting the continuing power of a "written tradition that over five hundred years has reified the negative connotations assigned to the Spanish words *negro/negra*."[70] The racialized dimensions of Spain's extensive imperial and colonial histories undoubtedly hold consequences for investigations into jazz, though it would take us too far afield to represent that literature here with any degree of depth. Most appropriate, given the task at hand, is to explore the way in which these histories reassert themselves implicitly in twentieth-century discourse.

Tete's engagement with American jazz forms occurred in parallel to transnational encounters that brought noted US Black intellectuals of the mid-twentieth century to Spain. These physical visits were only one part of the complex links between African Americans and Spain that Rosalía Cornejo-Parriego terms a "symbolic cartography."[71] As the contributions to Cornejo-Parriego's edited volume *Black USA and Spain: Shared Memories in the Twentieth Century* (2020) bear out, the intellectual, cultural, and political aspects of this symbolic cartography were mutually constitutive, and subsequently influenced the activities of "Spanish teenagers participating in the collective experience of consuming African American music."[72] Tete Montoliu was one such Spanish youth, of course, and his engagement with the jazz form over the course of a lifetime ultimately serves as a reinforcement of the impact this symbolic cartography had on future generations.[73] The writings of Langston Hughes, who traveled to the country during the civil war in the late 1930s, and Richard Wright, who did so later during the dictatorship in the late 1950s, highlight pertinent and contradictory elements of the country's racial landscape. Though it is considered only briefly, this important background can push readers to imagine Tete Montoliu's embrace of jazz music against the background of Francoism's hegemonic racialized landscapes as the marked and perhaps even defiant practice that it was.

Langston Hughes traveled to Spain as a reporter for the *Baltimore Afro-American* in 1937—in the midst of the Spanish Civil War. Since he spoke Spanish, he was asked "to cover for that paper the activities of Negroes in the International Brigades," troops who were fighting with the Spanish Republic against Franco and the military uprising.[74] He penned a number of prose writings on the subject, and even came to be recognized by some as a transplanted Spanish poet, given the work he produced during 1937–38.[75] Among his prose writings from that period are those with titles such as "Negroes in Spain," "Prelude to Spain," "Bombs in Barcelona," "Sweet Wine of Valencia," and "Breakfast in Madrid." In the piece titled "Harlem Swing and Spanish Shells," Hughes wrote of Madrid during the Francoist bombings of the city. A group would gather and listen to records as a way of drowning out the sounds. They usually played classical recordings by Beethoven, Brahms, or Wagner, Hughes reported, "[b]ut when I appeared with a box full of swing music, folks would call for Benny Goodman, Duke Ellington, Lunceford or Charlie Barnet."[76] In the essay he titled "General Franco's Moors," Hughes discussed the North Africans fighting on the side of fascism as "colonial conscripts" of Spain's civil war, and he quoted from people of many nationalities who insisted that "there was not the slightest trace of color prejudice in Spain."[77] The question, of course, is whether readers should accept these reports without challenging them. The truth is much more complex.

Hughes was very aware of the irony that those who were "victims themselves of oppression in North Africa—[were] fighting against a Republic that had been seeking to work out a liberal policy toward Morocco." This irony drove the poem with which he concluded his essay. The poet addressed this "Letter from Spain" to the Black American members of the Lincoln Brigade who crossed the Atlantic to fight against fascist troops during the Spanish Civil War.[78] Here, as in his other writings, Hughes was also attentive to the transnational dimensions of what has been called the "Spain-Africa nexus" or the Afro-Atlantic.[79] As did W. E. B. Du Bois, he articulated the possibility of a transnational Black modernity, one that Spaniards specifically were seen as having been prevented from realizing.[80] Here it is useful to note that Du Bois famously referred to the "black Spaniard" as an important part of the international struggle for justice.[81] Notwithstanding the contradictions of Black North African troops being conscripted to fight on Franco's side in the civil war, it is important that Hughes's writings link Blackness, and—through the anecdote related above—even jazz music, with Republican resistance to the fascist uprising.[82]

Richard Wright traveled to dictatorial Spain three times during 1954–55, and recounted his experiences in the travel memoir *Pagan Spain* (1957). Note that, because "Franco's government censors banned many New Negro writers," this travelogue written by a canonical Black American writer was not translated into Spanish until 1970, in the final five years of the dictatorship.[83] Unlike Hughes, Wright did not speak Spanish, and thus perhaps struggled more to make sense of the cultural and racial landscape he experienced. Like Hughes, however, Wright was equally quick to point out that the Spanish military's uprising and Franco's rise to power were facilitated not merely by the conservative segments of Spanish society, but also by Black troops from North Africa. He went on to identify what has been described as the "repressed black heritage" of Spaniards.[84] In the process, however, he engaged in what critics have seen as primitivizing, exoticizing, and exceptionalizing notions about Spain.[85] On the same page that Wright quoted Gertrude Stein's statement that "Spain is primitive," he repeated—offhand and perhaps without an appropriate degree of skepticism—the notion that the Pyrenees, "some authorities claim, mark the termination of Europe and the beginning of Africa."[86] The irony here was one Wright seemed not to be aware of—i.e., that he was ultimately treating Spain as colonizing Western powers treated Africa. If these two transnational encounters are any guide, Blackness in Spain during the years of Tete's early life was subject to complex and even contradictory meanings.

Equally complex and contradictory was the way in which the dictatorship of Francisco Franco used culture and music "intensively and systematically," but often stopped short of the sustained prohibitions against jazz that one might expect to encounter in the historical record.[87] Musicologist Iván Iglesias has brought the regime's ambivalent attitudes toward jazz music to the attention of the twenty-first-century reader. Generally speaking, "Jazz was officially identified with black American music and defined as the antithesis of Spanish music."[88] As Iglesias explores, critics of the early 1940s such as Francisco Padín and Eduardo López Chavarri were dedicating themselves to a campaign promoting "Spanish" music against jazz, which they perceived as a foreign and invasive form of popular music.[89] By mid-1942, at the height of the Franco regime's fascist fervor, writes Iglesias, it was forbidden to broadcast "the so-called black music, swing, or any other kind of compositions whose lyrics are in a foreign language."[90] That said, however, after 1943 both the press and the regime itself began to position themselves as tolerant of, if not also interested in, American music and culture—perhaps hoping to ingratiate themselves to the Allied countries of World War II.[91] Overall, the anti-jazz rhetoric of music critics nonetheless softened, though it did not disappear entirely.[92] Post-1945 it was difficult to find evidence of explicit condemnation of Black music by the dictatorship.[93] After 1946, jazz-specific publications reappeared, along with the Hot Clubs of Barcelona and Madrid, which had found it difficult to operate in the early years of Francoism.[94]

Even though the regime's official ban of jazz was short-lived, however, resistance to Black music ran deep in the conservative strata of postwar Spanish culture. The alternative sociality of jazz music was a potential threat to fascist Spain in much the same way that it was to Nazi Germany.[95] Scholarship on music in Nazi Germany has noted the perception there that jazz was an "American-black-Jewish" product. As a consequence, the music was scorned both for how it sounded and for what it represented—its modeling and celebration of hybridity was a threatening notion to any dictatorial regime.[96] The cultural geography of Spain mirrored that of Germany somewhat, in the sense that retrograde concepts of purity and cohesion were similarly instrumental to the self-image of the Francoist dictatorship. These concepts found their way into the ideologically fascist proclamation that dictatorial Spain was "Una, Grande, y Libre" (One, Great, and Free). This transnational comparison deserves further consideration in that it assists us in characterizing Tete Montoliu's engagements with the jazz form as being wonderfully out-of-synch with the hegemonic, politicized, and racialized musical culture into which he was born.

By contributing to the jazz tradition he had very early on come to associate with the United States, Tete's focus was not on developing a European musical form. Instead, he was intent on contributing to the development of the African American jazz form in the context of Europe. This is a crucial distinction when one considers Theodor W. Adorno's attempts to brand white European jazz as entirely distinct from Black American jazz. In the book *Anti-Music: Jazz and Racial Blackness in German Thought between the Wars* (2018), Mark Christian Thompson makes clear that Adorno emphasized just such a hard distinction between German jazz and jazz in the US context.[97] Thompson also tackles Adorno's insistence on "what he felt to be the myth of the music's African American origin."[98] Perhaps unsurprisingly, given Adorno's argument that the roots of jazz music of the 1920s and 1930s was to be found in militaristic "march music"—owing to the prominent role of the Sousaphone and the saxophone in marching bands—the German theorist considered that jazz could "be easily adapted for use by fascism."[99] Adorno had identified a racializing and primitivizing discourse surrounding the upper-class appropriation of jazz music in interwar Germany, a discourse that Thompson characterizes as more broadly representative of European listening practices.[100] By insisting that jazz was, in Thompson's words, "a commodity born on the battlefields of World War I and exploited by the culture industry in Germany," rather than a music originating in the Black experience, Adorno sidestepped the subject of race and erased the contributions of African Americans to the musical form in its transnational European variant.[101]

Fumi Okiji's *Jazz as Critique: Adorno and Black Expression Revisited* (2018) is a lucid correction of the excesses of Adorno's theories. The book is not a mere rebuttal of Adorno's perspective, but instead entails a criticism, recalibration, and extension of the German philosopher's insights. Okiji suggests that the theorist may have been unable and unwilling to see the value of jazz because he was intent on preserving what she calls "the exceptionalism of Austro-German and critical formalism."[102] High-modernist that he was, it is hard to dismiss this allegation. Both Okiji and Thompson make compelling cases that the Black experience simply "does not figure" in, and is "wholly inconsequential" for, Adorno's theory.[103] This is not true with respect to Tete Montoliu's legacy, in which the musician's acknowledgment of the Black American roots of jazz was essential. Tete was fond of recognizing this musical debt in various ways, and he did so quite directly, as in an interview where he declared: "Admito la raíz negra de la música que toco y que resulta fundamental" (I acknowledge the black roots of the music I play, and which is fundamental).[104] As later chapters of this book bear out, Tete's jazz work itself not only foregrounded its musical debt to Black American culture, it also aspired to a form of critical practice that had been modeled in the jazz culture of those Black US musicians whom the pianist either revered, emulated, or performed with, a list that would include Anthony Braxton, Billy Brooks, Don Byas, George Coleman, Miles Davis, Duke Ellington, Booker Ervin, Dexter Gordon, Al Grey, Johnny Griffin, Lionel Hampton, Eddie Harris, John Heard, Albert "Tootie" Heath, Billy Higgins, Bobby Hutcherson, Elvin Jones, Rahsaan Roland Kirk, Thelonious Monk, Sonny Rollins, Archie Shepp, Sonny Stitt, Buddy Tate, Art Tatum, Art Taylor, Fats Waller, Doug Watkins, and Ben Webster.

To emphasize the notion of jazz as critique, Fumi Okiji reinvests in the notion of jazz as artistic expression that Adorno had disparaged and ignored.[105] Where the German philosopher saw jazz as an unredeemable manifestation of capitalistic ideology, Okiji asserts jazz as a critique and "a critical reflection."[106] Her goal is clearly stated: "I propose that jazz is also capable of reflecting critically on the contradictions from which it arises— indeed, that it is compelled to do so."[107] For her, the polyphony of jazz is recognized as a productive force, and the musical practice demonstrates "a gathering constituted by the play, the wrestling and cooperation, of disparate parts."[108] Rather than denigrate the individual jazz solo or performance, she underscores the persistence and generative potential of jazz collaboration, or what she calls "localized pockets of genuine community."[109] This genuine community also has a temporal dimension, as reflected in her extended acknowledgment of the way in which different performers have over the years brought their own "idiosyncrasy" to well-known standards such as the Johnny Green composition "Body and Soul."[110] Moreover, she regards the blues—undoubtedly part of the Black American cultural landscape informing jazz—as equally a communal and non-individualistic musical form.[111] In the process she recovers jazz work from Adorno's insistence that it be understood as an inferior mode of composition precisely by emphasizing its performative dimensions. In all these ways, Okiji's text establishes the criteria by which this book sets out to assess Tete Montoliu's contributions to modern jazz.

Jazz as Gathering in Difference

Most important for any appraisal of Tete's jazz work is Fumi Okiji's understanding that jazz—performing jazz, recording jazz, and even listening to jazz—can be understood as a model for "gathering in difference."[112] This notion of difference as performative, relational, and dialectical is evidenced in her statement that "[t]he musicians are 'at play in themselves,' but they are also at play with the image of concept the world has of them."[113] This remark is important because it is explicitly related to the concept of double consciousness. Okiji cites this notion from its appearance in *The Souls of Black Folk* by Du Bois, who wrote that the double consciousness experienced by African Americans involves "looking at oneself through the eyes of others."[114] There may be reason enough to extend this notion to a transnational and intersectional understanding of the important role of difference in jazz work, one that makes room, for example, for Tete's own embodiment of alterity when considered against the norms of his surrounding Spanish culture. That is, for the present purposes, the most radical application of Okiji's daring assertion that "an alternative sociality" is operative in jazz work would extend, by means of its primary dialogue with the Black experience, to still other forms of alternative sociality. The specific nature and context of Tete Montoliu's critical jazz practice creates a compelling justification to reimagine this phrasing of double consciousness not as a "looking" but as a "listening to oneself through the ears of others." To modulate this description of double consciousness from the visual to the aural—these are not just visual and aural metaphors but also visual and aural modalities—not only allows us to adapt Okiji's premise to the jazz work of a Catalan pianist who experienced visual impairment from birth, but also allows us in principle to extend the idea of jazz-as-critique to a wide range of global spaces and various ways of being-in-music.

Adopting an intersectional stance on social marginality in transnational contexts strengthens our understanding of how Tete's experiences might be understood to resonate with the place-rooted double consciousness that Du Bois had explored in *The Souls of Black Folk*. The pianist was both a Catalan living and working in what was, for most of his lifetime, a dictatorial and fascist Spanish state and a visually impaired person immersed in a hegemonic sighted culture. These lived experiences of otherness or alterity impacted his musical production and the way in which it might be understood. This in turn helps reframe how scholarship might address notions of difference and cultural identity in European jazz. To take seriously the investigation of jazz in Europe means moving beyond the assumptions that it is a monolithic practice or else a musical landscape completely disconnected from African American traditions. Tete Montoliu approaches jazz musical culture as a way of participating in a minority language. He adapts that participation toward a form of critique that echoes in some ways its US-based origins but diverges from them in its Catalan positioning.

Undoubtedly, when Tete played the piano he was intending to participate in jazz as critique. In this sense, his musical practice should be seen as transnational adaptation of the critique set forth by Black American jazz artists. Subsequent chapters of this book thus continue to advance the argument that Tete's musical legacy should be described as a coterminus, transnational variant of US modern jazz. This account, which represents a transnational application of Okiji's arguments, is certainly at odds with Adorno's understanding of European jazz. The question is, what might it have meant for a white musician in dictatorial Spain to come to be recognized as "Un grande de la música negra" (One of the greats of black music), as one newspaper headline put it in the late 1960s?[115] Tete's gravitation toward the modern jazz form can only be understood by acknowledging the denigration of Black music that pervaded the dictatorial Spanish culture of his formative years—evident also, for example, in the relative lack of enthusiasm in the press regarding the jazz work of Black musicians visiting from the United States during the dictatorship.[116]

Chief among any such considerations is the fact that the Catalan pianist's jazz biography provides evidence of a quite immersive and, for him, seemingly transformative inculturation in Black American musical circles.[117] To borrow a phrasing from Fumi Okiji, Tete Montoliu demonstrated admiration of and attention to "the potential of the African American distinction from which the music originated."[118] The pianist never forgot where the jazz form came from—nor did he ever let his listeners or critics forget—such that he could be remembered as not only "el millor pianista de jazz català, sinó també una de les figures més destacades del jazz europeu, comparable amb altres genis singulars que des del Vell Continent han entrat en el món de la música afroamericana" (the best pianist of Catalan jazz, but also one of the most out-standing figures of European jazz, comparable to other unique geniuses who from the Old Continent have entered into the world of African American music).[119] Even if Montoliu's musical message is not synonymous with that of Anthony Braxton, Rahsaan Roland Kirk, or Archie Shepp—three artists whose radical Black expression remains a superb example of American jazz's ability to function as both implicit and explicit critique[120]—the Catalan pi-anist nevertheless positioned himself in an adjoining musical and social space. Tete's fashioning of this adjacent critical space both acknowledged and drew strength from jazz's roots in African American musical practice. What should emerge from reading *Beyond Sketches of Spain* is thus a much more complex evaluation of European jazz than scholarship has pursued to date—one that foregrounds rather than obscures the music's connection with Black American expression.

1

Sketches of Flamenco

At the same time that this chapter continues to introduce readers to Tete Montoliu's life, musical work, and impact, it also challenges certain transnational assumptions regarding Spanish jazz. It is important to attend to ways in which the listening practices of mid-twentieth-century Anglophone audiences were shaped by the popular jazz market. In particular, it is by dispensing with misrepresentations of the connection between jazz and flamenco that readers can move beyond mere sketches of Spain and begin to appreciate the full complexity of Iberian jazz. This effort is further supported by Montoliu's own strong opinion that "Mezclar flamenco con el jazz es como mezclar las almejas con el chocolate. Es una mezcla imposible de digerir" (Mixing flamenco with jazz is like mixing clams with chocolate. It is a mixture that is impossible to digest).[1]

There are two long-standing assumptions held by critics and listeners that have proven to be obstacles to the recognition of Tete's transnational jazz contributions. The first assumption concerns Spain's purported lack of jazz. As legendary British-born jazz critic Leonard Feather famously put it in an old chestnut that likely dates from the 1960s, Spain was often conceived as a desert for jazz.[2] Even as late as 1987 it was still possible for Max Harrison to write in the liner notes for the pianist's solo release *The Music I Like to Play, Vol. I* that "what is unusual about Vincente 'Tete' Montoliu is that he is from a country which even now shows less jazz consciousness than most others in Western Europe." In the twenty-first century, impressive scholarship on the long history of jazz in Spain certainly exists. It is just that little of this scholarship is currently accessible to the English reader.[3] Individual chapters of interest to scholars of Iberian music can indeed be found in edited volumes such as Bruce Johnson's *Jazz and Totalitarianism* (2016) and Sílvia Martínez and Héctor Fouce's *Made in Spain: Studies in Popular Music* (2013). Yet, by and large, readers must make do with passing references to Iberian jazz artists, such as those appearing in established European jazz histories like *Eurojazzland* (2012), edited by Luca Cerchiari, Laurent Cugny, and Franz Kerschbaumer. Precisely because none of the contributions to *Eurojazzland* focus on Spain, it is all the more striking that Cerchiari mentions Spain and Tete Montoliu specifically on the book's first page, where the Catalan pianist is named in a list of the "most important European jazzmen ever."[4]

A second key misconception regarding Spanish jazz is that it was limited to the "flamenco jazz" style associated with American artists whose seemingly exotic musical landscapes promised to bring Anglophone listeners closer to understanding aspects of Iberian culture.[5] In fact, those US-Iberian collaborations that were most prized by jazz critics contribute to this musical tradition, as evident in this chapter's investigation of two important recordings. Given its widespread recognition and enduring fame, *Sketches of Spain* (1960) by Miles Davis and Gil Evans is an unavoidable and emblematic point of reference. Perhaps slightly less well known, but no less important, are Tete Montoliu's contributions on three tracks recorded with Lionel Hampton's orchestra for the album *Jazz Flamenco* (1956). This encounter with Hampton sparked Tete's increased notoriety in Europe, eventually leading to his selection by jazz critics for the *European All Stars 1961* concert and album release. By 1962 he was already being regarded as the "máxima figura del jazz europeo" (greatest figure in European jazz).[6] While a select group of listeners may have been familiar with Tete's early work and reputation, it is hard not to conclude that the persisting identification of Spain with flamenco and bullfighting in the transnational imagination impeded his wider reception in Anglophone jazz markets.

Sketches of Spain, Francoism, and Regressive Listening

When asked to identify examples of Spanish jazz from the 1950s to the 1970s, Anglophone listeners may first point to landmark albums of so-called flamenco jazz recorded by American jazz artists—not only *Sketches of Spain* (1960) and *Jazz Flamenco* (1956), but also *Olé* (1961) by John Coltrane, for example. There are notable jazz albums recorded by Spanish artists in the late 1960s and early 1970s to consider, with guitarist Paco de Lucía's *Fuente y caudal* (1973) and saxophonist Pedro Iturralde's *Flamenco-jazz* (1968, with Paco de Lucía) likely being among those releases with the most prominent international impact.[7] Yet Tete Montoliu's contributions deserve equal, if not more, attention than these milestones, given the strong transnational jazz connections he cultivated during these decades and sustained over the course of his career. By considering how international audiences were primed to expect a certain kind of jazz coming out of Spain, we can understand better why Tete's musical reputation was slower to develop in transnational English-language jazz criticism than it deserved to be.[8]

This discussion harkens a return to Theodor W. Adorno's remarks on "regressive listening"—one of the German theorist's more salient ideas, as introduced in the note that preceded this book's introduction. A general premise of Adorno's critique of the culture industry was that once the musical object became a popular cultural product, consumers began to expect that it would express a carefully calibrated relationship between what was familiar and what was new. Regressive listeners craved only the sort of music with which they were already familiar. Infusing this understanding of regressive listening with a transnational dimension can help listeners to understand that Tete Montoliu's muted international reception was related not to a lack of talent, but rather to the lack of a pre-existing audience.[9] So-called regressive listeners in international circuits would have expected a flamenco jazz style coming out of Spain, not the work of a modern jazz artist who drew on the legacy of Harlem's piano greats and, later on, performed and recorded Catalan folk songs. Montoliu gave them formidable keywork matching that of Art Tatum, melodic improvisation akin to Keith Jarrett's, lyricism recalling that of Bill Evans, and strikingly dissonant original compositions echoing those of Thelonious Monk in the modern jazz idiom. Because of this, rather than stand out from the US jazz musicians alongside whom he played in Europe—artists such as Anthony Braxton, Dexter Gordon, Rahsaan Roland Kirk, and Archie Shepp—his sound blended in with theirs to a substantial degree. And because the identification and marketing of European jazz was slow to develop—with the European Jazz Foundation formed only in the late 1960s[10]—Tete's music was largely known only by very few who were paying close attention. For quite some time this group may have only included artists and companies in Spain, listeners with access to releases by European record labels—above all the Danish label SteepleChase—and selected critics who, for one reason or another, decided to take more than a passing interest in European jazz.

For many listeners, the line between flamenco jazz and Latin jazz may itself be blurred. Jazz pianist Chick Corea—with whom Tete recorded the album *Lunch in L.A.* (1979) during one of a handful of stints in the United States—demonstrated this on *My Spanish Heart* (1976), which blends both Spanish and Latin American musical elements and employs the word "Spanish" to refer to musical styles and peoples from both continents. This usage is something that was relatively common at the time in American English and that, in addition, relates to the earlier history of jazz. As identified by American jazz composer and pianist Jelly Roll Morton, the importance of a "Spanish tinge" in jazz can be traced back to early twentieth-century developments in New Orleans.[11] Yet this phrase usually only provided an indirect link with Spain proper. "Spanish tinges" in jazz music were themselves a recognition of Spain's influence in the development of syncretic musical practices in the Americas. As such they spoke more directly to what now might be called Latin traditions rather than to anything specifically Spanish per se, and should themselves be placed within the context of the Black diaspora.[12]

One of the most important jazz albums to invoke Spain specifically, and to spark the US imagination regarding Spanishness, was *Sketches of Spain* (1960) by Miles Davis, arranged and conducted by Gil Evans. There should be no doubt regarding this album's appeal: it is a masterful arrangement, a work of undeniable musical quality, and ultimately a landmark recording in the history of jazz. For his part, Tete Montoliu listed it among his favorite jazz albums of all time.[13] The album featured five tracks—"Concierto de Aranjuez," "Will O' the Wisp," "The Pan Piper," "Saeta," and "Solea"—of which the first is certainly the most famous.[14] This version of "Concierto de Aranjuez" has been regarded as an "exceptional adaptation" of a tune by the Valencian composer Joaquín Rodrigo, a musician who—like Tete—had experienced visual impairment from a young age.[15] If jazz critic Stanley Crouch's account is any indication, the album and its accompanying liner notes shocked listeners at the time into thinking of jazz in transnational terms. Crouch once reflected that the way those notes "described Miles Davis and the deep song of Spanish culture struck a mortal blow against my unintended provincialism. I was impressed because I had never thought of a jet-black Negro like Miles Davis being connected to anything beyond the world of Negroes in America."[16]

Interestingly enough, Tete is himself partly responsible for events that led to the banning of the *Sketches of Spain* album under the Franco dictatorship. Montoliu had purchased it while abroad, as he so frequently did, given the lack of foreign jazz albums even in cosmopolitan Barcelona. Due in part to his childhood piano teacher Petri Palou, a connection between Tete and Joaquín Rodrigo had developed. One day, Rodrigo called Montoliu on the telephone. Tete had this to say about that phone call and what happened next: "[S]abia que jo tenia el disc i em va demanar de sentir-lo. Vaig anar amb el disc a casa seva. El va escoltar i va denunciar la Societat d'Autors americana perquè no li havien demanat permís per fer-ne la versió. I el disc es va prohibir fins que li van donar els milions que tocava" (He knew that I had the record and he asked me to hear it. I went with the record to his home. He listened and denounced it to the American Artists' Society because they had not asked his permission to make the version. And the record was banned until he received the millions he was due).[17]

While *Sketches of Spain* was a worthy musical release, it also helped to construct certain expectations among listeners who were enjoying the international market for flamenco jazz. Here it is important to adopt a skeptical position when assessing whether or not the album's success in the jazz market is due to an authentic musical or cultural connection with Spain. From this position, the Davis-Evans album is not merely a landmark recording in its own right, but is also a landmark recording in the history of constructed listenership. Its success cannot be separated from the superficial way in which it constructed musical landscapes that Anglophone listeners would hear as bearing a connection with Andalusian folk culture.[18]

The language used by jazz critic Nat Hentoff to pitch the album to US consumers in the liner notes accompanying *Sketches of Spain* was laden with tropes of the exotic and the authentic:

> A brooding, dramatic Spanish sound and feeling pervades all the work on this album, particularly in *Concierto de Aranjuez* and *Saeta*. What is most remarkable is the surprising authenticity of phrasing and timbre with which he plays. It is as if Miles had been born of Andalusian gypsies, but, instead of picking up the guitar, had decided to make a trumpet the expression of his *cante hondo* ("deep song"). And Evans also indicates a thorough absorption of the Spanish musical temper which he has transmuted into his own uncompromisingly personal style.

These notes are far more than mere product packaging. They are a window into deeper considerations regarding the transnational production and consumption of jazz at the time of the album's release.

First and foremost, Hentoff's seemingly casual remarks convey how embedded the idea of jazz music as a transnational language had become by 1960. To play jazz was to bring an African American idiom into engagement with a broader sociocultural world. The liner notes asserted that Spain could be part of this international dialogue—a relatively new idea for mid-century Anglophone listeners. Terms denoting national jazz markets—like "Italian jazz"—were not yet in vogue in the Anglophone lexicon, and even jazz performed in Europe tended to display more of a connection with "Latin" music than with European folk traditions.[19] Yet by the start of the second half of the twentieth century, Spain had been brought more directly into the wider jazz consciousness through an entanglement of musical and political concerns. This entanglement was on display in the visits of American intellectuals such as Langston Hughes and Richard Wright to Spain, as elaborated in the introduction. It is fair to wonder whether Davis and Evans would have even been prompted to record *Sketches of Spain* were it not for the fact that the Spanish Civil War and the Francoist dictatorship that followed had directed the collective attention of the United States toward the Iberian peninsula.[20]

The flamenco references in the album's liner notes can tell us quite a bit about regressive listener expectations at the time. Hentoff makes a point of the fact that Miles Davis had already recorded flamenco jazz tunes such as "Blues for Pablo" from *Miles Ahead* (1957, with Gil Evans) and "Flamenco Sketches" from *Kind of Blue* (1959). By the late 1950s, American listeners in particular had been primed for jazz releases asserting Spain's connection with flamenco. These listeners would have likely taken to a certain transnational sociocultural parallel—that is, to the fact that, as Peter Manuel has written, "both flamenco and jazz have socio-historical roots in the subcultures of marginalized subaltern minorities, that is, Andalusian Gypsies and Afro-Americans, respectively."[21] Hentoff's liner notes played into this likelihood and the transnational solidarity such a connection would bring to mind ("It is as if Miles had been born of Andalusian gypsies").[22] It will thus be disappointing for some to realize that, as Peter Manuel states definitively in an article from the *Journal of Jazz Studies*, the tune "Flamenco Sketches" in fact "has nothing to do with flamenco."[23] Juan Zagalaz acknowledges that the album is exceptional, but concludes that "aunque está presente en casi todas las conversaciones sobre la existencia (o inexistencia) del Jazz-Flamenco, se trata, realmente, de un nuevo disco de Miles Davis que emana creatividad, calidad y jazz con aromas ibéricos, lúgubres, y en partes, procesionales" (although it is present in almost all conversations about the existence [or non-existence] of Jazz-Flamenco, it is a matter, really, of its being a new album by Miles Davis that emanates creativity, quality and jazz with aromas that are Iberian, gloomy, and in parts, processional).[24] These accounts suggest precisely how evocative merely the mention of the word *flamenco* itself could be for certain jazz listeners. Consistent with Adorno's descriptions, such regressive listeners would have been looking for music that was largely familiar to them, while also boasting an additional element, an "aroma," they could consider to be "new." Stanley Crouch's verdict—that once "Davis's trumpet voice is removed, in fact, a good number of Evans's arrangements sound like high-level television music"[25]—stands as testament not only to Miles Davis's virtuosity, but also to the relative banality of the orchestral structures against which he distinguishes himself on *Sketches of Spain*.

At the time, the beginnings of an identifiable market for Spanish jazz were being established. The profitability of this international jazz market hinged on the superficial identification of Spain with flamenco in the popular imagination more than it did any specific musical elements or historical connections. Those listeners willing to delve deeper into this superficial identification are forced to confront contradictions in the historical appropriations of flamenco. That is, there are both normative, hegemonic uses of the genre and also playful uses, engaged in contestation and resistance to power. For example, while the Franco dictatorship seized upon Andalusian identity and culture as a form of self-legitimization, as discussed further below, there was also a form of flamenco singing developed by Antonio Mairena that became associated with opposition to the Francoist regime.[26] Yet, in truth, no such deeper investigation would prove to be necessary for the regressive listeners whom Adorno describes so well. While flamenco could function as an ambivalent signifier in political terms, for international consumers prepared to receive it as a generalized symbol of Spanish nationhood, it could be received as a self-evident cultural trope.

The willingness of Anglophone jazz aficionados to consume flamenco-branded jazz without probing any deeper echoed the way in which the Franco dictatorship itself appropriated flamenco as part of its co-optation of elements of Andalusian identity. As Iberian studies scholar Jo Labanyi has explored in the introduction to the edited volume *Constructing Identity in Contemporary Spain: Theoretical Debates and Cultural Practice* (2003), the very idea of national culture "is also accompanied by the mythification of folk culture as an expression of the national 'soul.'"[27] Flamenco's association with the "national soul" of Spain has been ambivalent. It originated as a music and dance form in Andalusia in the nineteenth century and was the product of multiple pre-existing influences that can be traced to Romani migrations, North African occupation of the Iberian peninsula, and Sephardic Jewish traditions. Yet, as has happened with other appropriated cultural forms, it experienced a process of change that largely evacuated these elements of the cultural geography from which it emerged. As Michelle Heffner Hayes writes in her book *Flamenco: Conflicting Histories of the Dance* (2009), "During the twentieth

century, flamenco became one of the most visible symbols of Spanish national identity in the international community, largely due to the attrac-
tion of the tourist-oriented spectacles in Spain and abroad."[28] The Romani
traditions underlying flamenco as both music and dance were associated first
with Andalusia in southern Spain, and then with Spanish nationhood as a
whole—both under the Franco dictatorship and also in the transnational jazz
imagination. The pathway by which the origins of flamenco in historically
marginalized Romani communities became associated with an Andalusian
identity that was presumed to be internally homogeneous, and was later identified with the culturally uneven geography of Spain itself, is a puzzling one,
to be sure.[29] This shift in processes of cultural representation, of course, says
less about flamenco itself and more about the pathways of cultural appropriation through which such national representations are constructed. The
specific question of what it meant to Anglophone consumers that a group of
American musicians had invoked flamenco in their album *Sketches of Spain*,
however, can be partially answered by exploring the Francoist dictatorship's
nuanced use of Andalusian flamenco representations.

The political or ideological meanings of flamenco, Gerhard Steingress has
suggested, have stemmed largely from the uses that intellectuals interested
in it have made of the form.[30] It is important that, before flamenco came to
be associated with Spain as a whole, it was already subjected to sustained
attempts to construct an Andalusian regional identity. Prior to the efforts of
Spanish composer Manuel de Falla and poet and playwright Federico García
Lorca to tie flamenco to a progressive ideology in the early twentieth century, it was deemed largely reactionary and was associated with conservative elements of society.[31] Once modern Andalusian regional identity was
more-or-less established during the early twentieth century,[32] the Franco
dictatorship was then able to elevate this particular identity and its attendant,
if constructed, cultural expression to a national scale. One must keep in mind
that Francoism imposed a single state form that intended to unite the disparate regions of the Spanish territory by erasing any trace of cultural, linguistic, religious, or political difference. Established linguistic and cultural
identities—such as those embraced in the Catalan and Basque regions—
were precisely those populations that Franco's armies sought to eradicate
in the Spanish Civil War. These regional identities were virtually erased
from the public sphere under the Francoist dictatorship's violent expurga-
tion of linguistic and cultural difference.[33] By contrast, however, "Andalucía
aportaba unos valores culturales populares lo suficientemente inofensivos

para convertirlos en 'representación nacional' de toda España" (Andalusia offered popular cultural values that were harmless enough to be turned into a "national representation" of all of Spain).[34]

Appropriated and co-opted by Francoism to some degree, the comparative inoffensiveness of Andalusian identity found expression and even exploitation in censor-approved Spanish postwar cinema. In the wake of the severe censorship instituted by Franco's dictatorship, one of the most successful film genres by the late 1940s was the curious fusion of Andalusian-themed folkloric musicals known as *españoladas*. In her book *White Gypsies: Race and Stardom in Spanish Musicals* (2012), Eva Woods Peiró investigates how these films turned on tropes of an exoticized Spanish nation. Such tropes had been in play since the eighteenth century, and "they typically reduced Spain to flamenco and bullfighting."[35] The presence of Romani representations in Spanish film under the dictatorship, along with their coding as near-white, was a strategy that reinforced Francoism's core messages regarding race. In the words of Woods Peiró, "Gypsy hypervisibility maintained the imaginary boundary between white European Spain and its internal and external others, just as it reassured spectators that there were no 'racial problems in Spain,' meaning that Gypsies were appropriately placed at the margin or safely assimilated."[36] In focusing on Romani identity as a form of difference that could potentially be assimilated into the project of the Francoist state, Spanish cinema erased other forms of regional difference as well as the historical complexities of the wider Iberian cultural landscape.

The Davis-Evans album *Sketches of Spain* nonetheless engages in a similarly superficial appropriation of flamenco. Its success is owed in part to the way it mobilized signifiers of Spanishness; that is, to the fact that its musical contents approximated Adorno's description of popular jazz tunes that were designed to be "just like" previous music and yet "original." If one follows critics such as Peter Manuel and Juan Zagalaz in their appropriate skepticism regarding the authenticity of the purportedly flamenco elements of the album, there is little to differentiate it from, for example, *Porgy and Bess* (1959). The latter is, of course, another iconic Davis-Evans collaboration, with similar emphasis on symphonic arrangements, and where the specific link with the urban geography of Charleston, South Carolina, is established through George Gershwin's operatic text. It becomes tempting to regard the Andalusian and flamenco tropes of *Sketches of Spain* as mere ornamental overlays or "aromas." Tacked on to an established method of orchestrated composition that can be traced back through *Porgy and Bess* and *Miles Ahead*, these tropes promised viability in a jazz market that had already validated this mode of composition in previous releases by Davis and Evans.[37] While this reduction may not be entirely fair with regard to the quality of the music itself, it is in fact useful if we are to understand how the trope of Spanishness was becoming a marketable trait of the mid-century transnational jazz commodity.

The visual composition of the album's iconic original cover also contributed to the way that consumers received *Sketches of Spain* through somewhat superficial tropes of Spanishness. A broad swatch of yellow sky and a red earth divide the cover in two vertical halves, using the two colors of the Spanish flag (see figure 1.1). (Note that the colors of the flag of Republican Spain, which was defeated by Franco's church-and-military

Figure 1.1 Miles Davis and Gil Evans, *Sketches of Spain* (1960, Columbia CK-65142), cover, scan by the author.

conservative coalition in 1939, included not only yellow and red but also purple, which is absent here.) At left stands the lonely figure of a trumpet player, his shadow stretching out to the right to meet the large capital letters M-I-L-E-S at the center of the image. At right, charging, its horns almost embedded in the "S" of the trumpeter's first name, is a black bull. The image features irregular blotches that convey a sense that sections of the cover have been worn away by time. This is an original conceit, yet it adds another unfortunate connotation. The overall effect is that the cover offers a visual equivalent of the narratives that had painted Spain as a backward and primitive social landscape—narratives that, as Richard Wright's 1957 travelogue had demonstrated, may have been all too easily accepted by Americans who took an interest in Spain's seemingly exotic cultural landscapes. In the end, the album's cover art only strengthens the release's connection to tropes that had long reduced Spain to flamenco and bullfighting.

Both musically and visually, then, *Sketches of Spain* remains an ambivalent signifier that recapitulates the ambivalent positioning of Spain within a discourse of European nationalisms. Lou Charnon-Deutsch has explained this ambivalence by writing that "Spanish culture has had a dual relation with the master narrative of orientalism, both as a culture that has repressed a constitutive element of its historical identity, projecting it onto the figure of the exoticized gypsy . . . , and one that has represented, from the 1700s onward, an exoticized Other to its northern counterparts."[38] The Davis-Evans album testifies to the way this dual relation, over time, acquired a third, transnational dimension. The ambivalent positioning and potential co-optation of the Romani identity thus feeds narratives of authenticity not merely within Spain, and within Europe, but also within the United States. The transnational reach of jazz music became fertile ground for newly exoticized appropriations of Spanishness. Whether one considers the music itself, the liner notes, or the cover art, it is evident that *Sketches of Spain* is not truly Andalusian flamenco, nor can it be considered Spanish jazz. Instead, it is closer than fans may want to admit to being a musical object designed for easy international consumption. In this context, Tete's aforementioned distaste for combinations of flamenco and jazz can be understood as a reaction to the burgeoning transnational market that was taking root just as he was making his first strides into the wider world of jazz.

Vibing with Lionel Hampton on *Jazz Flamenco* (1956)

Lionel Hampton's *Jazz Flamenco*, which predated *Sketches of Spain* by four years, invoked a similarly simplistic understanding of flamenco for international listeners. Juan Zagalaz concludes that "[l]a aproximación del vibrafonista se antoja un tanto superficial, dada la presencia de clichés no del todo logrados como el uso superficial de las castañuelas" (the vibraphonist's approach seems somewhat superficial, given the presence of ineffective clichés like the superficial use of the castanets).[39] Yet due to the fact that Tete Montoliu performed on the album, it is of great interest for tracing the pianist's progressively expansive involvement in international jazz circuits. Moreover, because *Jazz Flamenco* was itself recorded in Spain by a traveling American bandleader, it simultaneously provides the opportunity to assess the transnational spread of jazz from the United States to Europe.

In the first half of the twentieth century, Europe had a reputation for being an inviting place for those jazz artists who could cross the Atlantic. The Continent could be successfully cast as a welcoming place for American musicians due to two key factors. First, there was the inhospitable social climate in the United States. It has been noted that in the "strange world of Jim Crow, blues and jazz could only be accepted when its black originators' fingerprints were removed," and thus it was "no wonder that the real originators and practitioners of jazz sought greener pastures to ply their trade, the Old World of Europe, eager for change after the debacle of World War I."[40] Representative of the increased American presence in Europe were the visits of jazz artists like Sidney Bechet and Duke Ellington, who both became associated with France. Bechet performed in Europe in 1919, and "lived and performed in France during the latter 1920s," while Ellington's association with France—not only Paris but also twenty-six other French cities—endured for forty years.[41] American artists not only toured broadly in Europe but also recorded while there. By one account, the first Black jazz band to record in Europe was led by American drummer Louis Mitchell in Paris in 1922.[42] The Ellington orchestra was influential in expanding the scope of this transnational connection during the 1930s, as evidenced by their fifty-five-day tour through not only France but also Great Britain and Holland in 1933.[43] While Spain may not have enjoyed the same reputation for "jazz" that France did at the time, scholar Iván Iglesias notes that newspapers used the word to describe performances in Madrid and Barcelona during 1919 and 1920.[44] "The term was soon linked to dances such as the one-step, the ragtime, and the foxtrot, which had appeared in Spain before jazz proper reached the country. The spread of jazz in Spain was initially modest, especially in terms of its social base: its first listeners were mainly aristocrats and intellectuals. However, from the mid-1920s, jazz was leaking extensively into musical theatre and cinema, helped by the enthusiastic reception of the Charleston."[45]

In many respects it is difficult to make a hard distinction between the history of American jazz in Spain and the history of American jazz in Europe. Popular music forms spread with ease through the transnational spaces of Europe, accounting of course for the political and social differences that shaped their reception and contributed to their changing forms. Individual artists linked disparate places through their musical pathways. Here the case of Harlem-born multi-instrumentalist Benny Carter can serve as an example. The US musician's stint in Britain from 1936 to 1937 was "formative for both Carter and for British jazz."[46] Prior to this stint, his big band and the Quintette du Hot Club de France had played at the Barcelona Hot Club in January 1936, not too long after the club's opening.[47] Carter's path—first to France, in fact, then to Spain and Britain, among other European destinations—is suggestive of the necessity that American jazz performance and reception itself be approached within a transnational framework.

Second, there was the fact that jazz tended to follow, or even precede, US economic and military interests. This was certainly the case in Latin America and the Caribbean,[48] where musical languages placed in contact with one another through imperial and colonial legacies produced the music's "Spanish tinges." US interests in Spain were markedly subdued during the first half of the twentieth century—particularly when compared to the pursuit of American military and economic interests in Latin America. While the United States did not officially intervene in the Spanish Civil War, the case of the American volunteer soldiers who made up the Lincoln Brigade and fought in many major battles is well known—recall the "box full of swing music" that Langston Hughes brought out during the Francoist bombings of Madrid. Next, while the dictatorship of Francisco Franco began with a period of strict autarky during the 1940s, its gradual opening to the exterior involved strengthened relationships with the United States. In 1951 the United States ceremoniously embraced Spain as an ally, and the 1953 Pact of Madrid committed economic and military aid that resulted in the creation of American air and naval bases on the peninsula.

The case of Lionel Hampton—or just Hamp, as he was known—is testament both to the opportunities jazz artists found in Europe and the way that US-Spain relations may have benefitted from even unofficial cultural exchange.[49] As a bandleader, Hampton "carried American jazz to more countries of the world than any other musician," in the words of record producer Irving Townsend.[50] There is quite a bit of evidence to back this up. To wit, one of Hamp's trips to Europe was "a seven-month gasser, [that] rocked thirteen countries: Austria, Belgium, Denmark, France, Germany, Holland, Israel, Italy, Luxembourg, Norway, Spain, Sweden and Switzerland."[51] During the 1950s, prominent American jazz musicians were recruited by the US Department of State for travel that was sanctioned by the government due to its potential gains for international diplomacy. Jazz pioneer and trumpet virtuoso Dizzy Gillespie's 1956 tour of the Middle East is one such example.[52] Yet while Gillespie's tour was scheduled to begin in April 1956, Hampton's band played two dates in Madrid in mid-March of the same year, and, moreover, apparently did so without any state sponsorship.[53] While it has been said that Hamp's was "the first band to tour Spain," his group was far from being the first American jazz act to perform in the country.[54] Though perhaps they did not travel on extended tours, a number of leading US jazz musicians had been invited to perform at the Hot Clubs in Barcelona and in the nearby city of Granollers. Beyond the case of Benny Carter, mentioned above, visits to Spain by noted US musicians included the likes of Willie "The Lion" Smith (1950), Dizzy Gillespie himself (1953), and Louis Armstrong (1955).[55]

As the story goes, Tete had been in attendance when Lionel Hampton played at the Windsor cinema of Barcelona in January 1955, presented by that city's Hot Club. He was quite impressed by what he heard. When the vibraphonist returned to Barcelona the next year, he organized a jam session after his second performance of the night and invited local musicians to join in—on March 13, 1956, as the Catalan pianist remembered it.[56] In Tete Montoliu's own words:

Era el 13 de març de 1956, me'n recordo perfectament: un dimarts tretze. Quan va acabar el concert, com que Hampton no estava cansat i tenia ganes de tocar, la gent del Hot Club . . . li van organitzar una *jam* en petit comitè i, a contracor, m'hi van convidar. Des del primer moment jo em vaig asseure al piano perquè no hi havia cap altre pianista i ja no em van moure al llarg de tota la nit. Vam a tocar fins a les quatre o les cinc de la matinada. Lionel Hampton es va desfer en elogis i jo vaig pensar que ho havia fet per mer compliment, era una persona extremadament educada, però l'endemà va quedar clar que ho deia de cor. Hampton tenia dues actuacions més al Windsor i, com que no sabia el meu telèfon, va trucar a Alfredo Papo i li va ordenar (Hampton era així: mai no demanava res) que m'anés a buscar ja que em volia presentar al concert. Jo estava treballant a l'Atelier, però els amos em van donar permís tota la nit i, a més, orgullosíssims.[57]

(It was March 13, 1956, I remember perfectly: a Tuesday the thirteenth. When the concert ended, because Hampton was not tired and was still eager to play, those at the Hot Club . . . organized a jam by small committee and promptly invited me. The first thing I did was sit down at the piano because there was no other pianist there and I did not move all night long. We played until four or five in the morning. Lionel Hampton lavished on the praise and I thought he was merely being polite, he was an extremely proper person, but the next day it became clear he had meant it. Hampton had two more performances at the Windsor and, since he did not know my telephone number, he called Alfredo Papo and ordered him [Hampton was like this: he never asked for anything] to look for me since he wanted to present me at the concert. I was working at the Atelier, but the owners gave me permission to leave for the night, and were very proud to do so.)

Performing at Hampton's side in the subsequent Windsor concert, Tete remembered a version of the song "Tenderly" that lasted half an hour, and the fact that the bandleader repeatedly announced to the audience that he, Montoliu, was "the best pianist in Europe."[58] This superlative found its way into print in a column of the Barcelona newspaper *La Vanguardia Española* on March 24, 1956, and would be associated with Tete Montoliu throughout his career.[59]

This meeting between Tete and Hamp is a transnational jazz encounter that can be used to support two divergent, national narratives. The pianist's own description of the event clearly emphasizes the formative thrill, during his early years as a performing musician, of playing with a bandleader from the United States. Yet, curiously, in the gatefold liner notes for the re-release of Montoliu's first LP recording with his trio, *A tot jazz* (1965, with Billy Brooks and Erich Peter), the event does not even appear. In the remarks included there, which seem intended to be an origin narrative of how Tete came to fame as a musician, critic Albert Mallofré does mention an important performance with Rahsaan Roland Kirk, but does not even mention Lionel Hampton in passing. It is as if this encounter simply did not exist. By the same token, those who are acquainted with Hamp's reputation may be tempted to overstate the importance of this moment for Tete. By suggesting that this moment was a definitive musical discovery, such a narrative plays into the fact that, as Leonard Feather pointed out, Hampton was an extremely wealthy and well-connected musician, so much so that he was "sometimes known as the Vibes President of the United States."[60] The bandleader may have indeed been as close to jazz royalty as was possible at the time. Yet this musical encounter—if we focus on its practical elements and consequences—has a transnational importance that transcends its mere connection with the divergent threads of US or Iberian jazz hagiographies.

While some may gravitate toward the idea that Hamp anointed or even discovered the pianist, the other story here is about the notoriety Tete had already amassed within Barcelona's jazz circuits. The fact that the owners of the Atelier were all too pleased to release Tete for a performance with the American vibraphonist suggests they were well aware of the transnational appeal of his talents. Also speaking to Tete's reputation is the fact that Pere Casadevall and Alfredo Papo of the Hot Club felt obligated to invite Tete to the jam session with Hamp—despite their ongoing difficulties with the young pianist, among them aesthetic disagreements linked to the nature of the jazz world.[61] Lionel Hampton's praise for the Catalan pianist aside, this particular transnational jazz encounter reveals much about Tete's own well-deserved trajectory toward the international spotlight.

Hamp and Tete may have been kindred musical spirits. They are often described in the same way by critics and scholars. Characterized as Tatumesque purveyors of high quantities of notes, they strive to reach the limits of what their instruments can produce. All three musicians—Hamp, Tete, and Art Tatum—are somewhat unfairly held to be less attentive to stylistic or formal matters as a consequence of their sheer virtuosity with regard to speed.[62] In this respect, the messages sent by some jazz critics can often be dismissive. They seem to say, "You can't swing if you play that fast."[63] If such a categorical statement can ever be taken seriously, Montoliu's record of musical production provides a compelling counter-argument.

Tete agreed to join Hampton's band for the part of the tour heading through Spain and into the south of France,[64] and while passing through Madrid, the album *Jazz Flamenco* was recorded.[65] Tete plays on three of the album's tracks, though he and the other local musicians remain uncredited on the album to which they contributed. Beyond "Tenderly"—a callback to the lengthy unrecorded jam session in Barcelona—two other songs are credited to "Hampton and the Flamenco Five" on the album—"Toledo Blade" and "Spain."[66]

The omission of the names of the local musicians who played on the record's three tracks can be explained—though, not justified, of course—by the nature of the album's engagement with flamenco. That is, the release plays up what is a rather superficial and reductive engagement with flamenco, more as a testament to Hamp's virtuosity and range than as a musical influence in its own right. Miquel Jurado put it this way:

> L'única relació entre el disc de Hampton i el flamenc era el títol del plàstic, ja que la música que contenia no tenia res a veure amb cap pal flamenc i s'apropava més a la visió de Hollywood de la música llatina que a un possible acostament espanyol. Tot quedava justificat amb la incursió d'unes castanyoles, títols tan suggerents com *Flamenco de Bop City, El torero de Madrid* o *Alma flamenca* i la presència (a l'edició espanyola) de Hampton amb un barret cordovès i una jaqueta curta torera.[67]

> (The only relationship between the Hampton album and flamenco was the title of the record, since the music that it contained had nothing to do with anything flamenco per se and was closer to Hollywood's vision of Latin music than to a possible Spanish approach. Everything was justified with the inclusion of some castanets, suggestive titles such as "Flamenco de Bop City," "El torero de Madrid" and "Alma flamenca," and the presence [in the Spanish edition] of Hampton with a Cordovan hat and a short bullfighter-esque jacket).

Tete Montoliu himself concurred with Jurado regarding the album's lack of engagement with flamenco.[68]

The liner notes on the English release of *Jazz Flamenco* prove to be just as problematic as those on *Sketches of Spain*. For Hamp's album, David Drew Zingg of *Look* magazine wrote notes suited for American consumers eager to read of an exotic and authentic Spanish landscape full of flamenco and bullfighting. Little care is taken to present the context for the recordings. Rather than mention the March 1956 performances at the Windsor cinema or the all-night jam sessions cultivated by the self-styled Hot Club glitterati, Zingg wrote on the back of the album cover that "[i]n Barcelona, the band performed in a bull ring to a roaring, rocking audience of 19,000."[69] There is evidence suggesting this bull ring show happened in July 1956, after the album was recorded, in fact, and not before. Yet the album cover's misleading tale continues nonetheless—and does so in a way that neither Jurado nor Tete would find convincing given their aforementioned remarks. The liner notes highlight that "Señorita Angelica and Hampton worked hard to capture the color and emotion of each other's musical approach. The band picked up a certain tinge of Castilian flavor, and Miss Angelica's castanets can, on occasion, be heard to swing just a bit." Zingg not only omits Tete's name, he also subsumes the uncredited pianist's Catalan identity under the banner of Spanishness. He writes, "Unhappily, little specific data on the local performers who worked with Hampton's band is available here. Spanish musicians did blow on some of the sides, while Hamp's rhythm section played on all cuts."[70] One wonders if Tete's international reputation would have developed differently if he had been credited for these performances.

The album's cover art presents another set of curiosities. Neither the Spanish nor the English version of the cover includes Tete or any other local performers, beyond the figure of the castanet player. Miquel Jurado reports that Hampton's wife and manager purposely kept Tete's image off the album cover because she didn't want a white musician to be pictured with Hamp's Black orchestra.[71] The cover for the English release of the album features instruments with no actual performers (see figure 1.2). Only the blurred movement of hands over a vibraphone suggests Hamp's presence. Interestingly, on the cover of the Spanish release, one sees Señorita Angélica playing castanets at Lionel Hampton's side. The vibraphonist's face appears to have been intentionally darkened in accordance with racist invocations of Blackness prevalent at the time.[72] Contemporary American consumers of vinyl should have little difficulty identifying the problematic visual representation of Hamp on the Spanish cover, while the appearance of the seemingly exotic and authentic Señorita Angélica might require a bit more context to critique. In both cases, however, these images—taking into account both what they foreground visually and the social contexts they hide—reveal the tendency of transnational cultural exchanges toward simplification, especially when seeking a broad audience of consumers.

If a review in the jazz periodical *DownBeat* is any indication, the album's historical significance seems to have often been emphasized at the expense of any evaluation of the music itself.[73] The idea that these tracks are in any way flamenco fades quickly when one begins attending to the composition and structure of the three tracks on which Tete plays. The theme titled "Spain" is in fact a 1924 composition by Isham Jones and his frequent writing partner Gus Kahn.[74] The castanets that feature decoratively at the beginning and

Figure 1.2 Lionel Hampton and His Orchestra, *Jazz Flamenco* (1956, Madrid, Spain, RCA-Victor, LPM-1422), cover, scan by the author.

end of the track do not change the fact that this is a jazz song with a solid blues structure. On the recording, Hamp takes the lead by introducing the thirty-two-bar AABA form and melody, and playing the tune straight. Next comes Tete's solo over the same AABA form. The pianist is relatively sub-dued at first, but when he reaches the midpoint of the second A section he releases an extended flurry of notes over four entire bars, ending only on the first note of the B section, otherwise known as the "middle-eight." This is an early indicator of the Tatum-esque style that, here or there, must have found its way into Tete's more conventional gig life in Barcelona playing, not jazz proper, but rather what he would refer to as "música de ball" (dance music). Hampton and electric guitar player William Mackel then each take turns at their respective solo AABA runs, with Tete adding punctuating rhythm chords in the background. The last thirty-two-bar sequence of the song features Hamp and Tete trading off with one another in what is a rather entertaining musical duel.

"Toledo Blade"—a Hampton original—is an up-tempo romp. Here the effect of the castanets is pronounced, as they are elevated to the same level as the other jazz instruments. That is, not merely does María Angélica begin the song with her castanets, but she is also given the opportunity to perform her own percussive castanet "jazz solo," which can be heard between the solos of the Vibes President himself and Mackel on guitar.[75] Tete oscillates nicely between providing accompaniment and then taking the spotlight with his own up-tempo solo. In the latter he manages both to settle into the song's grooves and—in line with his own style—hover above them.

Of the tracks on which Tete plays, the most deserving of attention is the recording of "Tenderly," a composition by Walter Gross and Jack Lawrence. This song was already a jazz standard by 1956, and had been recorded by Art Tatum in 1953,[76] as well as vocalists Sarah Vaughan in 1946 and Rosemary Clooney in 1951. For this track, Hampton gives the Catalan pianist the space to introduce the melody and structure solo, and Tete makes the most of the opportunity. Playing for a full five minutes unaccompanied—before any of the other instruments can be heard (including the castanets)—he seems to be both showing off his skills and also losing himself in the musical moment. His characteristic modern jazz phrasing overflows measures that cannot contain it, but he also returns to the beat dramatically when needed. Listeners will hear a continually varied delivery of the melody: a quick flourish here, a momentary classical riff there, and a few ornamental key changes throughout. Despite these frequent variations, there is a sense that he is at ease. His chords are warm, his key attack is gentle, and there is a lilt in his pace. But above this calm and patient presence there hover a few sheets of quick fingering that leave no doubt that this is not the album's credited pianist, Oscar Dennard, but rather the one and only Tete Montoliu.

The five-minute solo piano opening segment from "Tenderly" is an early example of the dynamics that come to shape Tete's eclectic playing style throughout his career. The characterization of the pianist's style given by Miquel Jurado can help readers to reflect on his extensive and fluctuating range. In 1998, Jurado provided his own reflection on how he felt Montoliu's style had changed over time:

[L]es imparables cascades de notes que havien caracteritzar la seva música, especialment durant els anys setanta i vuitanta, els seus constants devessalls de tècnica i virtuosisme (sovint no buscats, totalment inconscients però presents) es van anar diluint a favor d'una música més reflexiva, sentida i elaborada interiorment. El *toc Montoliu* que, durant tants anys, havia influït en centenars de pianistes (la llista seria llarga i, probablement, sorprendria més d'un) persistia i era reconeixible ja des del primer acord (que pocs pianistes que hi ha als quals passi això mateix!), però ja no hi havia pressa per a exterioritzar les idees, les notes ja no fluïen mai atropelladament, la música havia trobat una dimensió molt més real i reconfortant.[77]

(The unstoppable cascades of notes that had characterized his music, especially during the seventies and eighties, his constant avalanches of technique and virtuosity [often unsolicited, totally unconscious but present] were to become diluted in favor of a music that was more reflective, felt, and elaborated inwardly. The Montoliu touch that, for so many years, had influenced hundreds of pianists [the list would be long and would probably surprise a few] persisted and was still recognizable from the first moment [there are few pianists of whom one can say the same!], but there was no longer a rush to exteriorize the ideas, the notes no longer flowed at a fever's pitch, the music had found a much more real and comforting dimension).

Jurado's intention in this passage may be to pay homage to a friend and a brilliant musician by praising where he ended up, at what was in truth the end of his career. Perhaps he is reflecting on Tete's loss of energy as he began to suffer from lung cancer. Either way, however, what Jurado conveys as a contrast between one decade of the pianist's legacy and another should be understood as a tonal contrast continually present within the musician himself—that is, throughout his career. After listening to his later musical creations—repetitively and extensively—readers may be more willing to agree that this early "Tenderly" recording offers listeners the opportunity to hear Tete at his best, which is to say at his most contradictory. His virtuosity comes from his inimitable style, which threads together elements that few other pianists are able to combine. In this 1956 recording, he is both relaxed and intense; calculated and playful; patient and driven; hurried, imbalanced, and at rest—all at one and the same time.[78] This is to say that Tete's virtuosic technique and his reflective interiority each acquire significance from their interrelation.

Montoliu's recordings and performances with Lionel Hampton are simultaneously of interest from different musical perspectives. From a cultural studies standpoint, they are testament to the transnational allure and embrace of American jazz in Spain during the twentieth century. Stylistically, they represent a generational musical fusion of sorts—this album brings to listeners both Hamp's extension of the big band sound into the late 1950s, and twenty-three-year-old Tete's emerging modern jazz sensibility. This was not the first time that Tete played with an American jazz musician, of course, but it was a high-water mark of sorts given Hampton's reputation. More important still, it started a transnational dialogue that would push Tete further and further into both the European and American spotlights of modern jazz fame.

To *The European All Stars 1961* and Beyond

One of the early signs that Tete was being recognized as one of the Continent's most talented jazz pianists was his appearance on *The European All Stars 1961*. As its vinyl sleeve notes, this album was produced by Joachim-Ernst Berendt and recorded on May 21, 1961 in front of a live audience at Berlin's Kongresshalle. The album attributes tunes to both American and European composers: "Charlie" Mingus, Magidson and Wrubel, Sadi, Thelonious Monk, Martial Solal, Akst and Clarke, K. A. Roberts, and Francis Borland. Chosen by a group of well-known jazz critics, thirteen musicians from twelve countries played on the tracks. Two of those musicians were pianists. The album's liner notes dare to give Montoliu second billing, stating, "The second pianist of the All Stars was the blind Spaniard Tete Montoliu, the first to introduce Spanish jazz into the European jazz scene." Yet this suggestion of secondary status is contradicted by the content of the album itself. Tete Montoliu plays on two more tracks than the other pianist, France's Martial Solal. One of these additional songs is the Thelonious Monk composition "Blue Monk," which is notable for being the only track on the album showcasing merely a trio and not a full glut of performers. Based on these considerations, it is Tete, and not Solal, who seems to merit top billing.

On "Blue Monk"—one of the pianist's favorites—Tete joins Norway's Erik Amundsen on bass and Denmark's William Schiöpffe on drums. The trio gets into synch as Montoliu begins the tune's initial double finger-crawl up the keys. Throughout the track, the pace is leisurely—almost too slow in fact. Tete is clearly restraining himself to match the timing of the rhythm section. But in the middle section of the song, which is essentially a blues, the pianist nonetheless settles into a masterful groove. The drums and bass fade into the background and merely accompany his mood. Tete's quick right-hand fingerwork entrances, detaching from and rising above the steady beats of the blues progression, then falling back into place within the steady rhythm as if it had never been far from home. The left hand marks the time sparely, sparsely, and is mostly imperceptible despite a few carefully chosen assertive moments. When the pianist returns to the tune's character-istic double-finger crawl and the band wraps up, the audience applauds with verve. So closes the first side of the record—not with thirteen musicians blaring, but with a quiet piece performed by Montoliu's makeshift European trio. The fact that Tete got this much space on an album meant to be a broad international showcase is testament to the reputation he had earned among Europe's most select critics. The mere fact that he was Spain's representative on the album at all, of course, perhaps says all that needs to be said regarding this point in his career: Tete was moving on toward greater things, and in the process he was putting Spain—and Catalonia—on the international map of modern jazz.

His most iconic performances and collaborations were yet to come—a list that includes further appearances on vinyl recordings with American jazz artists. From *Ben Webster Meets Don Byas* (1968), to *Gentle Ben* (1972)— once again with Webster—and on to *Steps Up* (1981) with the Eddie Harris Quartet, Tete developed a career as a sought-after accompanist and a fea-tured soloist. His recordings with Lucky Thompson in Barcelona from 1970, released as *Soul's Nite Out*, showcase well his ability to match the saxophonist's cool and relaxed sound. In the words written by Carlos Sampayo for the album's re-release by Ensayo, "En esta sesión la sintonía con Tete Montoliu . . . es absoluta" (In this session, there is total empathy with Tete Montoliu).[79] As particularly evident in Tete's solo on that album's "I Got It Bad" (Ellington), the pianist is markedly and comfortably re-strained, refraining from the up-tempo runs featured in his solo on the very next track—Lucky's own composition "Soul Carnaval"—but no less en-gaged, intimate, and reflective. Montoliu also performed with a range of fe-male vocalists, from early recordings with Pilar Morales, to albums featuring Catalan singers, among which *Núria Feliu with Booker Ervin* (1965) and *Elia Fleta / Tete Montoliu Trio* (1967) stand out (see figure 1.3). As a top-billed duo performer, with Catalan pianist Jordi Sabatés on *Vampyria* (1974) and

Figure 1.3 *Ella Fleta / Tete Montoliu Trio* (1967, Barcelona, Spain, Concèntric 6043-ZC), cover and 45 rpm disc, scan by the author.

with American saxophonist George Coleman on *Meditation* (1977), he created two unconventional and even provocative records.

An album that Tete Montoliu recorded with sax player Buddy Tate in 1975 is a good indication of how far his star had risen during the 1960s. While Tete had not received recognition on the cover of his albums with Ben Webster and Don Byas, here the appearance of his name is quite marked. Moreover, it is emphasized with a pun of sorts. First billing goes to the "Buddy Tate Quartet," but the large print underneath reads "and Quintet featuring Tete Montoliu—Tate a Tete at La Fontaine, Copenhagen." It may warrant explanation that the phrase "Tate a Tete" evokes the French *tête a tête* (face-to-face), a pun that was repeated in the 1976 release of the Tete Montoliu Trio's album *Tête à Tete*. It appears yet again with the duo *Face to Face* (1982) that he later recorded with longtime collaborator bassist Niels-Henning Ørsted Pedersen. The pun can be traced back to Buddy Tate's own album titled *Tate-a-Tate* (1960), and its adoption for Tete's recordings itself speaks to the pianist's strong positioning within a transnational US-European jazz culture.

Since performing on *The European All Stars 1961*, Montoliu's style had undoubtedly continued to evolve as he performed with some of the most notable jazz musicians from the United States and Europe in the interim and established his own trio. *Tate a Tete* is a great reminder of how stilted the playing was on *The European All Stars 1961*. While the latter was a somewhat artificial formation of a group of nonetheless stellar European performers, by contrast, Tete's performances with Buddy Tate's group in 1975 cohere seamlessly. Listeners can hear the players' collective enjoyment as they work through a number of standards. As the liner notes by Alun Morgan make clear, Tete relishes in "Monkish phrasings" on "Stompin' at the Savoy," and he achieves an "Earl Hines-like tremolo" in the last chorus of "Buddy's Blues." On "Body and Soul," he intercuts long runs up and down the keys with pleasingly dissonant chords, and ends his solo with a quotation from the Rogers and Hart standard "Bewitched." On the group's rendition of Monk's "I Surrender Dear," Tete plays the first chorus "alone and completely out of tempo . . . using rich multi-noted runs in the treble."

The group's mammoth performance of Ellington's "In a Mellow Tone" extends into the eighteenth minute with lengthy jams by Buddy Tate, violinist Finn Ziegler, and an intense solo by Montoliu. Relatively early, beginning in the fourth minute of the track, Tete solos for two full minutes before the other instruments drop out. He then continues for another two and a half minutes without accompaniment in a dynamic tour-de-force. Immediately launching into a brief double-time whirl, Montoliu then slows down to syncopate against the continuing rhythm—which by this time he is hardly marking on the keys. Subsequently he reintroduces the left-hand baseline while building up his right-hand runs, flourishes, and rhythmic overlays, eventually finishing to the crowd's applause as Bo Stief begins his solo on the bass. And when Buddy wraps up his lengthy sax solo in the sixteenth minute, Tete takes yet another piano solo, after which the band segues into the song's finale.

This performance with Buddy Tate was far from his first in Copenhagen. Montoliu had built up a storied past in Denmark, having performed and recorded there mostly at the Montmartre Jazzhus with both European and American luminaries. During 1963–64 alone he performed at the Jazzhus with Bent Jaedig, Archie Shepp, Kenny Dorham, and Dexter Gordon, adding Yusef Lateef and Don Cherry to the list in 1967.[80] Perhaps the most important of his performances there, however, was one with Rahsaan Roland Kirk, released as *Kirk in Copenhagen* (1963), to which the next chapter returns in the urban context of Tete's European music circuits.

2

The Urban Soundscapes of Modern Jazz

To delve into Tete Montoliu's musical legacy is at once to answer the call to urbanize the study of jazz. Although the interdisciplinary jazz-urban intersection is one that may threaten to take scholars too far from their home disciplines—whether they are specialists in musicology, the history of jazz, or even urban geography—there are potential gains for many fields in charting out this interdisciplinary terrain. In doing so we come to recognize certain commonalities between the collaborative nature of jazz music and an understanding of the urban phenomenon as an ongoing and collective social process, rather than a thing already given. Such an exploration of the relationship between cities and jazz music also promises to push scholarship beyond the national frameworks that have limited our understanding of the jazz form.[1]

For such an approach to jazz, the discourses of disciplinary specialization and national specificity prove to be more of a hindrance than an aid. They do nothing to help listeners appreciate the inter-urban flows that constitute the music's transnational circuits. Such circuits are forged through the movements of multiple actors—musicians, bandleaders, promotors, and the like—who crisscross a network of urban jazz sites. As demonstrated by the international tours of Dizzy Gillespie and Lionel Hampton mentioned in chapter 1, these urban jazz networks are not independent from larger sociocultural forces or matters of state. Likewise, adherence to disciplinary specialization or to national frameworks also works against a deep understanding of the nature of the modern city. Urban life is not itself something to be broken up piecemeal, with each part inviting analysis by a specialized science working in isolation from the others. It is instead a complex composition, made up by the interconnection of a vast number of seemingly disparate elements. Hallmark sociological accounts of the urban, by Jane Jacobs and others, have defined it precisely as a meeting place for difference.[2] The case can certainly be made that cities, at their best—as it is, too, with Fumi Okiji's notion of jazz—can serve as models of an alternative sociality or a gathering in difference.

This chapter advances just such an argument by relying on key insights from urban theory. Beyond the mere presence of urban life in the titles and themes of jazz standards, there are deeper aesthetic connections that can be made between jazz music and the experience of urban modernity. The urban jazz circuits of Europe sustained many artists and led to intriguing transnational encounters in jazz-rich cities such as Copenhagen, Denmark, in particular. In the end, Tete Montoliu's musical production not only elucidates the urban locations of jazz, but also prompts us to actually hear the phenomenon of urban modernity through modern jazz music.[3]

Jazz and the City

Scholarship has tended to take the connection between jazz and the city for granted, rather than investigate the topic thoroughly.[4] E. Taylor Atkins (2003) asserts that jazz developed out of urbanization, but leaves this comment unexplored.[5] Burton W. Peretti's book *The Creation of Jazz: Music, Race, and Culture in Urban America* (1994) states that "jazz was essentially an urban music that grew out of stimuli and fulfilled uniquely urban social functions."[6] The comments of Robert Witkin in his book *Adorno on Music* (1998) are more textured, but similarly concise. He writes that "[j]azz was a music that seemed to be part and parcel of the modern city and its leisure spaces, a music that was accessible, in its various forms, to city people everywhere; a genuinely popular modern music, sounding the dreamscape of the metropolis and reflecting the colour and pulse of life and relations in the city."[7] In the existing scholarship on jazz, references to cities are not too hard to find, even if extended considerations of the form's links to urban culture have proven to be elusive.

Perhaps the most obvious way of reading the presence of the urban in jazz is to look at song titles, or, for those songs originally developed for vocalists and appropriated by instrumental jazz, at song lyrics. Urban toponyms are not hard to find in the titles of modern jazz tunes, and Tete Montoliu's repertoire is no exception. One such prominent jazz standard linked to the urban imagination is Vernon Duke's "Autumn in New York," which Tete recorded on *Songs for Love* (1971), *Live at the Keystone Corner* (1979), and *Catalonian Nights, Vol. 1* (1980). Recordings and performances by the Catalan pianist provide ample evidence of urban referencing, for example in renditions of Manning Sherwin's "A Nightingale Sang in Berkeley Square," Vernon Duke and E. Y. Harburg's "April in Paris," and Joan Manuel Serrat's "El meu carrer" (My Street). The titles of Montoliu's original compositions equally feature a number of evocative urban references: "Muntaner 83A" refers to his home address in Barcelona; "Gentofte 4349," which features on both *Songs for Love* and *Music for Perla*, highlights the name of an urban area northeast of central Copenhagen; and "Apartment 512" refers to a time and place when Tete and his first wife, Pilar, were no longer in love, and his affections turned to a Danish woman.[8] Steve Elman's liner notes to Tete's *Boston Concert* characterize the latter composition's inclusion there, saying: "It suggests an escape from the sadness and pressure of city life." And "Yellow Dolphin Street"—also the title of a Montoliu trio album on which it appears—showcases the pianist riffing on the jazz standard "Green Dolphin Street," debuted in the eponymous 1947 film and famously recorded by the Miles Davis sextet in 1958.[9]

One urban-titled composition that deserves special mention is perhaps "Barcelona Shout," a Ben Webster composition that the saxophonist recorded with the Tete Montoliu Trio for the album *Gentle Ben* (1972). The title evokes the classic early jazz tune "Carolina Shout," which was composed by James P. Johnson. Johnson was himself an important New York pianist who influenced Fats Waller and Art Tatum, among other luminaries. The use of the word "Shout" in Webster's title serves as reference to a style of dance associated with the blues in the early twentieth century. Interestingly, blues singers would later become known as "shouters." The fact that there is no vocal accompaniment on this song serves to highlight the vocal role of the saxophone, which effectively becomes the song's titular "shouter." The substitution of Barcelona for Carolina in such a title is a significant displacement of an American toponym by a European one. All this considered, "Barcelona Shout" speaks to Webster's enjoyment while performing with Tete in the Catalan pianist's home city, and the song's title underscores the transnational European variant of modern jazz.[10]

"Lush Life" is undoubtedly one of the most storied songs in the modern jazz tradition that deals with what Robert Witkin called the "colour and pulse of life and relations in the city." Composed by Duke Ellington's writing partner Billy Strayhorn in the 1930s, and debuted in the late 1940s, the song derives its punch from urban imagery. The lyrical voice of the tune, depressed by a recent breakup, narrates a return to the lonely bars, the "jazz and cocktails," that prior to a now failed romance seemed to provide such sustenance. The song's melodic shifts and striking key changes similarly evoke not merely the rising and falling moods of romance, but also the shifting character of an urban life filled with unpredictable encounters. Here, the references to a failed relationship are defined by their urban context. It is thus the modern metropolis that makes human connection both possible and so fleeting. The lyrical content and form of the song work together to convey the rush of spontaneity and the feelings of isolation that together make up urban modernity.

Tete recorded "Lush Life" early in his career with the release *Elia Fleta / Tete Montoliu Trio* (1967), where the Catalan vocalist sings in English. He also recorded it as a solo piano piece on an album bearing the name of Strayhorn's famed song title itself, *Lush Life* (1971). On the latter recording, Tete modulates his playing speed from the beginning of the track. During the first run-through, his playing can seem as if he is merely rehearsing the tune—he is overly cool, collected, and perhaps even a tad indifferent. He punctuates the verse by ending it with a single forced note, struck again at a high octave, seemingly as an echo. The repetition can be taken as an arch reflection that intentionally takes listeners out of the tune—perhaps an announcement of the avalanche of notes to come, given the pianist's characteristic style. On a second listen, that single forced note continues to echo in the ears of listeners as his technical virtuosity overflows the rest of the performance.

The relationship between jazz music and the city goes far beyond the titles and themes of individual compositions. An important starting point for this consideration is a single essay published in the *Routledge Companion to Jazz Studies* (2019), which promises to delve even more deeply into the links between urbanization and jazz. Andrew Berish's contribution, titled "Space and Place in Jazz," situates jazz music within the spatial turn in the humanities. He does well in asserting that "jazz has been more than the soundtrack to twentieth- and twenty-first-century modern life," noting too that "it has been a spatial force on par with other social forces, shaping our fundamental ideas and experiences of modern life."[11] Berish's argument notably employs insights from the work of spatial humanist Henri Lefebvre, who is a crucial point of reference in this chapter's urban take on Tete's legacy. From a brief exploration of Lefebvre's key ideas—as well as their resonance with the work of other urban thinkers, including Louis Wirth, Lewis Mumford, Jane Jacobs, Georg Simmel, and Manuel Delgado Ruiz—four main points can be distilled that will help to establish the connection between Tete Montoliu's jazz aesthetics and the speed, spontaneity, and shifting conditions of the modern urban experience.

Henri Lefebvre—who was a taxi driver in Paris for two years, was considered the intellectual godfather of 1968, and who developed reputations as a spatial theorist, Marxist thinker, existentialist philosopher, scholar of everyday life, cultural critic, and committed pedagogue—deserves recognition first and foremost as an urban theorist.[12] All of the various strains of his thinking can be seen as coming together in the production of an urban theory that blends concerns of the humanities and the social sciences. Lefebvre's hallmark approach was to distinguish the "urban" from the "city," and "urban culture" from the "culture of urbanism."[13] While the city could be understood as a thing—as a set of roads, buildings, districts, parks, and so on—the urban, by contrast, was an ongoing social process, a continual reproduction of sorts. While the "culture of urbanism" was led by planners who understood the city to be a conceived space or a static blueprint for social activity, "urban culture," by contrast, was actually lived, irreducible to a plan, unpredictable, and always changing. Those who would mistake urban culture for the culture of urbanism thus ignore all of the interconnected social relationships that produce the city as a complex social space.[14]

Intriguingly, as Lefebvre pursued a theoretical model that would be adequate for understanding a shifting and changing urban phenomenon, he turned more and more toward musical language and metaphor. This is perhaps most evident in the posthumously published volume *Rhythmanalysis*, which was conceived as an additional fourth volume to his *Critique of Everyday Life* trilogy.[15] Therein, the urban theorist advocates a form of thinking whereby "[the rhythmanalyst] thinks with his body, not in the abstract, but in lived temporality." He notes that those willing to think in this way "will come to 'listen' to a house, a street, a town, as an audience listens to a symphony."[16] Listening for musicality in the city and hearing the urban phenomenon through music may be two sides of the same coin. This aspect of Lefebvre's project may prove to be indispensable for the interdisciplinary extension of urban jazz studies.

From such volumes as *The Right to the City* (1968) and *The Urban Revolution* (1970) onward, Lefebvre's calls to acknowledge the urban as an ongoing social process were built on long-standing traditions of anti-urbanism. In the twentieth century, one can look to the writings of Louis Wirth, Lewis Mumford, and Jane Jacobs for critiques of urbanism that re-emerge, transformed, in the French philosopher's oeuvre. Lefebvre's understanding that the urban overflows the concept of the city and its physical limits is anticipated by Louis Wirth's essay "Urbanism as a Way of Life"

(1938). Therein, Wirth had characterized the city not only as the "dwelling-place and workshop" of modern humankind, but also as the "controlling center . . . that has drawn the most remote parts of the world into its orbit and woven diverse areas, people, and activities into a cosmos."[17] Lewis Mumford disdained the way in which city design tended to privilege bureaucratic aims, and he criticized the dehumanizing effects of unmanaged industrialization and mechanization. His critique finds a complement in Lefebvre's rejection of the bourgeois science of urbanism, and Mumford also examines and underscores the symphonic qualities of urban life in a way that anticipates the French philosopher's later rhythmanalytical project.[18] Lefebvre's notion of rhythmanalysis is itself also indebted to the reappropriation of the organic and artistic metaphors of the city put forth in *The Death and Life of Great American Cities* by Jane Jacobs. Chief among these are Jacobs's notions that the city should be understood as a living organism, and that the constantly unfolding movements of urban life can be characterized as what she referred to as a "sidewalk ballet."[19]

More important than this brief genealogy of anti-urbanism, however, are its consequences for urbanizing the study of jazz music, and specifically for analyzing the piano style of Tete Montoliu. First, one of the key lessons to be extracted from Wirth's fundamental essay and Lefebvre's subsequent distillation of urban theory is that the effects of urbanization cannot be limited to the spatial confines of the individual city. In this sense, for example, the tropes of rural experience, agriculture and the natural world, or the countryside that are found in Catalonian folk music, and that later present themselves in Tete's modern jazz, pose no conflict whatsoever with an urban approach to his modern jazz. In addition, one may find continuity, rather than disconnection, in the jazz musician's repeated movements through European cities (e.g., Barcelona, Berlin, Copenhagen, Lisbon, London, Madrid, Weesp), as well as his recurring pathways through urban performance venues (e.g., La Fontaine, the Jazzhus Montmartre, the Palau de la Música, Whisky Jazz, the Jamboree), and the recording or engineering of his music at a range of locations (e.g. Bavaria Studio, Dureco Studios, Estudios Celada, Fendal Sound Studio, Rosenberg Studie, Tonstudio).

A second lesson put forth by Lewis Mumford and carried on by Henri Lefebvre is that urban life is not constrained by the rational and regularized character of urbanism. Here it is worth mentioning that Tete himself grew up in Barcelona's storied Eixample district, and that he continued living there, off-and-on, in the family residence located at 83A Muntaner. This central area of the contemporary city was one of the foremost examples of the regularization and rationalization implicit in the modern urban planning legacy. During the nineteenth century, a specialized planning class had emerged in Europe, along with corresponding shifts that greatly impacted the social division of labor. As a consequence, the planner's static birds-eye vision of the urban fabric was privileged, as the modern city itself became a commodity subject to exchange value.[20] In this historical context, the work of Catalan urban planner Ildefons Cerdà to redesign Barcelona can be compared to the work carried out in Paris in the name of planner Baron von Haussmann. According to Lefebvrian geographer David Harvey, Haussmann had "bludgeoned the city [of Paris] into modernity" during the nineteenth century, and Cerdà had followed a similar path, conceiving of Barcelona in an expansive way that went beyond the medieval walls of the city that were demolished in 1859.[21] The creation of the Eixample district was carried out via the imposition of a rectilinear grid and the construction of broad tree-lined avenues whose openness contrasted sharply with the enclosure and meandering trajectories of the streets of the old city. As the examples of both Paris and Barcelona show, modern urban planning prized conceived space over lived space.[22] This planning vision led to a geometrical product that would facilitate trade and transportation over the use value that the city held for its inhabitants.[23]

The regularization brought by the industrialization of the city form and the overly rational character of modern urban planning share a certain aesthetic parallel with what occurred in the development of popular music during the early twentieth century.[24] Here one must keep in mind Theodor W. Adorno's critique of modern music. For the German theorist, the regularized structure and invariable beat of popular hits are tied to the regularized character of contemporary life. In this sense, both the city itself and popular music played within it are increasingly subjugated to the mechanistic and rectilinear logic of industry. Despite the ubiquity and power of this machine logic, however—despite the threat it poses to reduce all cultural production to the pattern of easy exchange and regressive consumption—neither the modern city nor modern music can be evacuated entirely of their use value. Everyday urban life and musical composition alike still retain, in principle, the potential for enjoyment and the possibility to function as critique. From this perspective, it is possible to approach jazz music, along with its varied entanglements with urban space, within the framework of this struggle between use and exchange. It is this struggle that comes to be synonymous with urban modernity, and it is the urban environment's use value for the human senses that suggests a bridge between the listener's enjoyment of the jazz form and the urbanite's enjoyment of the city as a lived space.

Third, recuperating arguments from Jane Jacobs and Henri Lefebvre regarding the complexity of the city, the urban space, is not a strictly geographic but rather a more broadly social matter. This insight is in line with Lefebvre's theorizations in *The Production of Space* (1974), one of the books whose translation to English by Donald Nicholson-Smith in 1991 galvanized widespread interest in the spatial turn in the humanities. A perspective grounded in the notion of social space understands the city as not merely the container for musical activity but as in fact a complex organism produced in tandem with cultural understandings inextricable from notions of art, sound, and music. Thus, Tete's musical production cannot be considered in isolation from Barcelona's place in the transnational urban imaginary.

Fourth, there is the matter of urbanized consciousness—that is, the idea that as society has become urbanized, human consciousness has also been urbanized along with it.[25] Georg Simmel's foundational essay "The Metropolis and Mental Life" (1903) had famously characterized urban life in terms of movement, excess, and the "intensification of emotional life." Thus, the adaptive urbanite, he argued, developed the ability to cultivate a state of "indifference" in response to the rapidly changing conditions of modern city life.[26] This ability to detach from the visual and aural excesses of the city and yet remain present and mobile within urban life can be understood as a productive urban adaptation. The figure of the flâneur—the seemingly aimless modern urban wanderer—best exemplifies such semi-detachment. As captured in the fleeting scenes of urban life delivered through Charles Baudelaire's nineteenth-century prose poems, for example, the flâneur is an insouciant figure who witnesses drastic shifts in urban sociability while remaining immersed within the city's fabric and not fully detached from it.[27]

Urban theorist Manuel Delgado Ruiz continues this line of thinking within the specific context of Barcelona, calling attention to the transient movements of the pedestrian.[28] In truth, he argues, pedestrians can be taken as urban wanderers who, for however brief a time, become uncodified, stateless beings. In their liminal positionality they become merged with the ongoing shifts that define the urban as a process. This characterization is important, as by implication the act of walking in the city contains within itself a potential resistance to a totalizing modern culture of urbanism. It is this urbanistic culture, Delgado Ruiz argues, that has subordinated the human being to the large-scale design and exchange value of the city as a commodity.[29] Here it might be ventured that the ephemeral act of urban wandering expresses a central tension of urban modernity that is also relevant to understanding the appeal of jazz music. For urban wanderers, city space has a value that is tied to its use, to its enjoyment, rather than to any notion of exchange. In their undirected walking, they deviate from the established urbanistic plan to follow a whim. Likewise, for musicians of the modern jazz tradition, even the performance of so-called standards has a value similarly tied to use and enjoyment. In playing their own versions of a standard, modern jazz musicians deviate from codified expectations—melodies, harmonies, rhythms—to play whatever notes they desire. In both cases, musicians and urbanites recuperate modernity's hallmark spontaneity as a use value. The ability of jazz musicians to detach from the music they are playing—evidenced in complex rhythmic layers, uncommon time signatures, or polyphony, for instance—can be understood as the manifestation, in musical practice, of the state of indifference that characterizes an urbanized form of consciousness.

Other connections between the city and jazz should be acknowledged. In the urban environment, tropes of speed and displacement become a sort of shorthand for acknowledging the deeper social shifts brought about by urban modernity. While these shifts are evident enough in European literature from the nineteenth century—coming to be theorized extensively by Simmel and others in the early twentieth—with the arrival of bebop to the continent they markedly accelerate. Rehearsing the argument from a key article by Eric Lott titled "Double V, Double-Time: Bebop's Politics of Style" (1998), Andrew Berish characterizes "the emergent bebop style as an aesthetic of speed and displacement that modeled itself on the black urban experience."[30] While this assessment is useful in explaining bebop as a whole, it is also instructive for those seeking to understand how Tete Montoliu positioned himself stylistically and aesthetically within the transnational urban soundscapes of modern jazz.

Tete and the Speed, Spontaneity, and Shifting Conditions of Urban Modernity

Beyond the matter of titles and themes, Tete Montoliu's jazz work approximates the aesthetic qualities that are most associated with modern urban life in a number of ways: his characteristically quick fingering, his penchant for rapid changes, his carefully calibrated and somewhat jarring rhythmic displacements, his embrace of dissonance, the disruptive structure of his original compositions, his fondness for discordant crashes, and his full acceptance of the hallmark spontaneity of jazz. All these musical elements simultaneously serve as aesthetic tropes of the modern urban experience.

The speed of Tete's movement across the piano keys is a performative echo of the fast pace of the modern urban environment. This aspect of his musical style is quite often referred to as a technical skill, particularly in descriptions that group him with the likes of Art Tatum. On the liner notes to *Catalonian Fire* (1974), where Tatum is explicitly referenced as if an unavoidable reference, Ib Skovgaard writes of Tete that "he can stand out on his own, with a total command of the keyboard, and a dazzling technique that goes hand in hand with his fast responding ear and ideas" (Skovgaard 1974). His defiant speed can be heard as early as his uncredited performance on the "Spain" track of Hampton's *Jazz Flamenco* (1956), discussed in chapter 1, but it is a hallmark quality of his piano style that is consistent throughout his career. It is not surprising that when critics comment on the speed of his playing they tend to invoke language that could apply equally to the modern urban experience. One example can be found in Chris Sheridan's liner notes to the album *Tête à Tete* (1976). These notes begin by highlighting New York's role as an urban site holding great influence over the development of jazz piano, and lead into a characterization of the Catalan pianist that could equally describe urban life: "He sees each piece he approaches as a continuous state of flux, its outlines melting in a luminous haze, its horizons swept by flurries of notes. It is a stream of consciousness, borne along by a tremendous internal urgency and propulsion." Like the gathering of difference that is jazz performance, the city is also a meeting place for different temporalities, for varying flows and streams of consciousness and movement.

Yet playing at speed is far from being Montoliu's only contribution. Beyond his technical mastery of the keyboard, his lyricism is frequently on full display in tracks like "I Guess I'll Hang My Tears Out to Dry" from *Boston Concert* (1980), where he starts out at his most deliberate and relaxed pace. On the mid-tempo rendition of "Satin Doll" from the early album *King Neptune* (1964), Tete matches Dexter Gordon's laid-back sax playing, saving carefully calculated chord crashes for the tail end of his piano solo and employing only a modicum of dissonance. Other performances that are particularly charming examples of his ability to exude tranquility include versions of "You Go To My Head" and "When I Fall In Love"—the two soothing tracks that open *That's*

All (1971)—the recordings of "Old Folks" and "Lament" on *Body and Soul* (1971), and "Ballad for Carmen" from *Words of Love* (1976). On this latter piece, Tete begins with warm chords in the lower register in a lulling pattern reminiscent of Keith Jarrett's improvisations. From the outset he already seems less concerned than usual in covering the full range of the keyboard. As he embraces a form of stillness in these early chords, a wistful and melodic song emerges, driven by a gentle rocking lilt and featuring an ending that dissipates slowly. At other times, Montoliu can manage to produce a hybrid performance style, bridging both rapid intensity and affective interiority. Consider his version of Ellington's "Come Sunday" on *Tete Montoliu al Palau* (1979).[31] On this track, the dynamism produced between the distinct styles of the pianist's left and right hands delivers a unique fusion of two moods or voices. While the right hand grows increasingly intense, the left hand is ever more reserved, demure, patient, calm, and steady. This disconnect allows for a sort of dual-vocalism to emerge from the jazz work of a single instrumentalist. The more that Tete's right hand flows over the piano with tremendous urgency—with flurries of fingers attacking the keys—the more his gentle left-hand accompaniment catches the listener's attention precisely because it recedes into the background, remaining calm and reserved. Here is a compelling aural metaphor for the very model of the adaptive urbanite who observes striking urban changes with some measure of detachment. It is in this internal contradiction between a breakneck pace and a comforting lull that Tete's jazz work approximates the unevenness of urban modernity.

It is not difficult to find other examples of this unevenness in his musical production. The album *Piano for Nuria* (1968) features a standout recording of Benny Golson's tune "Stable Mates," where Tete demonstrates his ability to replicate not just the speed but also the shifting conditions of urban life. Here two distinct rhythms are starkly and expertly juxtaposed. The pianist and his trio unexpectedly switch back and forth from Al "Tootie" Heath's relaxed bossa nova beat to an up-tempo swing propelled by Peter Trunk's walking baseline. Intermittently, the piano strikes the melodic line of the song over Tootie's languishing beat, evoking a bent note through a quick flourish, only to transition seamlessly to a faster-paced modern jazz sensibility. This iteration of the Tete Montoliu Trio comes back to the bossa rhythm no fewer than four times throughout the brief four-minute track, insistently repeating the melodic line three times to close the number.[32] This recording's use of two distinguishable rhythms in the same track is a defiant challenge to Adorno's criticism of the plodding and predictable monotony of the regularized beat of modern music.

The musicians' collective ability to adapt back and forth between these two rhythms repeatedly echoes the variable rhythms of modern metropolitan life.

Those who become familiar with Tete's repertoire must continually grapple with his fondness for unevenness. This word can be applied equally to many aspects of his jazz work, including abrupt shifts between melody and cacophony, the dissolution of a tune or a piano run into chaos, and even what might be described as a penchant for nonsense chords. Certainly, the pianist frequently channels Thelonious Monk's inclination for dissonance through half notes, uncommon intervals, and even what sounds like ham-fisted note clusters. Montoliu's respect for Monk is evident in a great number of recordings and performances of his compositions, such as "'Round Midnight," "Blue Monk," "Ask Me Now," "Bemsha Swing," "Blues Five Shot," "Eronel," "In Walked Bud," "Jackie-ing," "Let's Call This," "Misterioso," "Monk Medley," "Monk's Dream," "Monk's Mood," "Reflections," "Rhythm-a-ning," "Straight No Chaser," and "Well You Needn't."[33] For his part, Thelonious Monk seems to have also enjoyed Tete Montoliu's music. Hearing Tete perform at the Village Gate in New York once, Monk was said to have told the Catalan pianist: "I dig you, I dig you."[34] But Monk-like dissonance is one thing, and disruption another. The second side of the album *Music for Perla*, which features five original compositions, boasts what is perhaps the highest concentration of songs contributing to Montoliu's aesthetics of disruption. Descriptions of Tete's musical performances tend to affirm that he never played a wrong note.[35] On tracks like these, however, that is clearly because he is playing the wrong note quite intentionally, much as Monk would tend to do in his recordings. While the effect of Monk's dissonance is to inject a certain humor into his music, Tete's penchant for speed and intensity turns humor into disorientation. Tete leans so far into dissonance, one might even say he creates it needlessly, gratuitously. "What Is It?" is a 1'11" composition that approximates the sound of nonsense. "Circe" is a dreamlike cacophony that ends in an echoing drone. "Apartment 512" might be taken as an exercise in giving oneself over entirely to chaos.

Perhaps no song demonstrates Tete's enjoyment of unevenness better than his original composition "Blues for Nuria," which was written to honor his daughter. This song, its title in English, kicks off the Tete Montoliu Trio's early album *Piano for Nuria*, on which "Stable Mates" also appeared.[36] Rhythmically, the track's beginning harnesses the rhythm and state-of-mind of someone embarking upon an urban stroll. The piano leads the melody of the jaunty introduction with a punctuating series of five groups of marked two-note pairs. The second note of each pair is higher than the first, and each pair is complemented by another played higher up on the keyboard, such that a call-and-response structure is created through the pairings. After five pairs of notes and their corresponding five echoes, Tete then plays a distinct dissonant nonsense phrasing, abruptly bringing the entire exercise to a complete halt. Peter Trunk's baseline reinforces the steady momentum of the jaunty pace, but drops out in anticipation of the nonsense phrasing, coming back in to repeat a single note with a repeating drumbeat. Once the verse begins, Trunk sustains a walking baseline while Heath keeps the forward momentum going with a relatively steady cymbal.[37] Tete alternates between notes played to sound intentionally "off" and his more traditional extended melodic flourishes. During Trunk's bass solo, the piano is largely quiet, with only a few occasional accompaniments that oscillate between discord and melody. Tete's piano continues to focus on "off" notes and discordant passages that threaten to devolve completely away from melodic expectation. In the discord summoned on this track by the pianist, there are traces of the dissonance and repetition one hears in phrasings from Thelonious Monk's tune "Four in One," from the *Genius of Modern Music, Vol. 2* recording.

What is so interesting in the example of "Blues for Nuria" is the disjunction between Tete's style of playing and the subject matter of the piece. Because this song was composed in honor of his beloved daughter, it is unlikely that he intended it as a meditation on sadness, pain, or other complex negative emotions. Instead, it is easier to conclude that Tete's use of dissonance and disruptive composition on this track is intended as an affirmation of a certain belief about modern jazz form—about how divergent aesthetic forms of beauty come to be coded in modern music.[38] The disjunction between style and subject in this composition can perhaps only be explained as a musical tribute to a certain unevenness, a jazz evocation of the disconnect and detachment synonymous with the modern experience. This unevenness can even be heard as a sonic form of joy or beauty.

Those readers familiar with European artistic movements from the first half of the twentieth century will certainly know of the "dehumanization of art" carried out by the moderns (cubists and surrealists) in the realm of painting.[39] In this category one can find famed Barcelonan artist Joan Miró's flourishes of bright color and complex exercises in geometrical organicism. Despite the popular acceptance of his work today, some who experience Miró's painting and sculpture may not be aware of his declaration, in 1927, that he wished to "assassinate" painting. Joan Miró's aesthetics were driven by the jarring sociocultural shifts that came with the turn-of-the-century modernity. These were larger-scale changes that similarly influenced the work of his European contemporaries. In *The Production of Space*, Henri Lefebvre describes a break-point in the development of modernity wherein long-standing aesthetic, sociopolitical, moral, and urban norms and values were all called into question:

> Around 1910 a certain space was shattered. It was the space of common sense, of knowledge, of social practice, of political power, a space hitherto enshrined in everyday discourse, just as in abstract thought, as the environment of and channel for communications. . . . Euclidean and perspectivist space have disappeared as systems of reference, along with other former "commonplaces" such as the town, history, paternity, the tonal system in music, traditional morality, and so forth. This was truly a critical moment.[40]

Here, as throughout Lefebvre's work, the urban theorist threads together what are seemingly discrete areas of modern experience. Art and music, for example, can be severed from neither sociopolitical nor urbanistic discourse. The impact of the "shattering" of social space analyzed by Lefebvre has had enduring consequences for the trajectory of contemporary artistic practice in general. As evident in the quotation above, the adjustments to the tonal system of music that continued to play out in the realm of jazz are an important part of this picture. Robert Davidson uses the example of Barcelonan cultural commentator Sebastià Gasch's writings during the late 1920s to explore how critics of the time were drawn to making aesthetic comparisons across poetry, prose, painting, and jazz music.[41] Just such an interdisciplinary perspective on the implications of urban modernity's aesthetic ruptures is necessary for understanding not merely the early twentieth-century avant-garde, but also the emergence of mid-century cultural and musical forms such as bebop.[42]

When approached within this broader context of modernity's avant-garde aesthetics, Tete Montoliu's modern jazz work suggests that urban modernity's unevenness can be represented stylistically in the sonorous symbolism of jazz cacophony, through an aural chiaroscuro effect trading on the juxtaposition of melody/harmony, on the one hand, and what might be taken as spontaneous or haphazard noise, on the other.

Here Tete's fondness for recording "Margareta," a composition by Perry Robinson, is a case in point. The song is named after Robinson's Swedish girlfriend, whom the US clarinetist met while in Barcelona.[43] In November

1959, Robinson had received a telegram from Spain, sent by Chuck Israels and Jon Mayer, which read "We're in Spain, come over."[44] Robinson was a fan of freer jazz sounds, a trait that can be traced to his contact with two notably experimental jazz musicians—free jazz pioneer Ornette Coleman and Don Cherry—at the Lenox School of Jazz in Massachusetts.[45] Once in Spain, Perry performed with Israels and Mayer at the Whisky Jazz club in Madrid. He was fired the first night, reportedly due to reactions that his playing was "out there" and thus induced a panic among listeners expecting more traditional musical fare.[46] This was saying something, particular given the club's reputation for playing modern jazz.[47] Jordi Pujol Baulenas describes the scene: "[T]anto sus compañeros como la audiencia quedaron completamente atónitos al escucharles improvisar en un lenguaje puramente *free*. Nadie entendía nada. . . . Los músicos profesionales le tomaron por loco, e incluso hubo quien se atrevió a decir que no tenía ni idea de armonía" (His companions and the audience alike were completely stunned hearing him improvise in a language that was truly *free*. Nobody understood a thing. . . . The professional musicians took him to be crazy, and some dared to say that he had no idea of harmony).[48] In a passing tribute to Montoliu's fame and impact, Robinson's memoir describes meeting and playing with Tete for the first time, as well as his experiences over the course of period of a year and a half that he spent "playing all over Spain and also touring Portugal" in a quintet that included the Catalan pianist.[49] Perry remembered that "the way [Tete] anticipated what I was about to play was psychic."[50] Certainly, if the musical connection was reciprocal, this would explain Montoliu's attachment to the song "Margareta." Yet it is just as likely that the unusual structure of the song caught the pianist's attention.

Two different versions of the song appear on *Lush Life* (1971), and *Music for Perla* (1974) includes yet another. While "Margareta" does include a truly warm melody, Tete restricts this melody's presence to very brief sections of the composition. He begins the song driven by a pensive, dissonant mood whose sense of anxiety is increased through the marked silence between notes. The first sounds one hears in Tete's versions are two discordant piano chords followed by a dissonant interval echoed in the instrument's upper range. This gives way to a swift melodic section that comes as a relief, but whose effect is all too fleeting. As with the version on *Music for Perla*, Tete's two takes of the song on *Lush Life* are discordant and full of sonorous splatter. He consistently leans into the pace of the melodic section, accentuating its rushed nature and thus minimizing the relief of musical tension it might otherwise achieve. Robinson himself had played the tune at a much slower pace, for example with a quartet on the album *Funk Dumpling* (1962). In contrast with Tete's versions, Perry Robinson's recording is much more relaxed, a difference that can be explained in part as an effect produced by the way he harnesses the clarinet's sound. Yet the matter of pacing is also crucial here, as a more relaxed approach allows the dissonant notes of "Margareta" more time to mellow and blend in to the flow of the overall composition, and more time to resolve at the end of certain phrasings. The faster pacing that Tete pursues exaggerates the un-evenness of the composition, thus creating a much more jarring effect. In point of fact, all three of these recorded versions of "Margareta" showcase Montoliu's preference for the destabilizing effects and the imbalance that both speed and discord bring to modern jazz.

Overall, Tete's jazz work serves as a fitting example of the inextricable re-lationship between the spontaneity of jazz music and the spontaneity of the urban experience. His musical approach is full of surprises. In fact, in the liner notes for *Carmina* (1984), producer Jim Brown describes Montoliu as "a jazz artist who epitomizes Whitney Baillet's fundamental jazz dictum, 'the sound of surprise.'" Tete's unusual approach to composition, his predilection for dissonant notes and jarring piano crashes, the superb technical skill on dis-play in his flurries of spontaneous improvisation—these attributes surprise because they refuse to be confined within the existing expectations of what jazz was in Francoist Spain. His transnational embrace of an American bebop aesthetic—at a time in which it had yet to fully take hold in Europe, let alone Spain—is similarly defiant. Yet in seeking to make sense of his musical pro-duction, it is imperative to link it with a cultural understanding of the modern city. If jazz is a form of critique, then it is possible for this critique to function not merely in sociopolitical terms, and in musical terms, but also in urban terms. If modern jazz is a counternarrative of sorts, then it is possible to see this counternarrative as defying nationalist dictatorial culture, subverting the regularized beat of modern music, and also pushing back against the predict-ability and rigidity of the staid urban form. In each of these dimensions of modern life, then, it is possible to seek a human expression unconstrained by the mechanistic logic that emerges with industrialization. It is in this sense that processes of urbanization also imbue jazz performance with meaning. The jazz improvisation functions to amplify and extend the expressive power of the human voice, elevating creative musical practice to the status of a cri-tique against the stultifying logic of the machine age and the planned city.

Europe's Urban Jazz Circuits, *Kirk in Copenhagen* (1963), and *Lliure Jazz* (1969)

Tete Montoliu was not merely important as a virtuoso performer. Another worthy aspect of his jazz work to consider is the way in which he helped to revitalize connections between Barcelona and the transnational urban jazz circuits of Europe through his musical practice. There are two complementary ways in which one might think about this revitalization.

On one hand, this is a sociopolitical matter. With the devastation and death wrought by the Spanish Civil War and the violence for which Francisco Franco's dictatorial regime was known, Spain was much more isolated than it had been in the early twentieth century. As discussed further in the next chapter, Barcelona's reputation for being a cosmopolitan European urban center and a welcoming site for musical performance had been quite strong in the 1920s. Yet the wartime destruction of the city of Barcelona and the Spanish state's subsequent isolation during the 1940s changed all this. The fascists in control of postwar Barcelona actively persecuted those who, like the pianist's father, Vicenç Montoliu Sr., were suspected of being critical of the regime. For quite some time, then, few foreigners visited Spain, and not many musicians from Spain traveled outside of the country. Tete's travels to perform outside of Spain in the 1950s thus meant that he was one of the first musicians to be engaged in rebuilding those transnational connections between Barcelona and other European cities. Commenting on why he left Spain to pursue his career elsewhere, Montoliu once said, "Vivo en Holanda. . . . Sí, allí estoy en el centro, los desplazamientos a Alemania, a Francia, a Bélgica . . . no son tan costosos como si tuviera que trasladarme de Barcelona. Además aquí el 'jazz' se murió un buen día, y yo tengo que comer" (I'm living in Holland. . . . Yes, there I'm in the center, so heading out to Germany, to France, to Belgium . . . it isn't as expensive as if I had to depart from Barcelona. What's more, here "jazz" died one fine day, and I have to eat).[51] In this sense, the fascist hold over Barcelona during the dictatorship is partly responsible for the transnational scope of his urban jazz performances.

Tete's role in the revitalization of transnational urban jazz circuits was also significant in aesthetic and cultural terms. While, for a time, the only paid work he could get in Spain was to perform popular dance music, he nonetheless yearned to play bebop and ultimately to become a figurehead for what would become known as modern jazz. Early on, this stylistic divergence brought him into conflict with the conservative perspective of many in Barcelona's relatively small and traditionally minded jazz scene. Even well into the 1950s, clubs in Barcelona continued to be oriented exclusively toward classic jazz, a fact which meant that "els aficionats al jazz més modern s'havien de reunir en cases particulars per intercanviar discos i sentir les novetats que acabaven d'arribar dels Estats Units or França" (fans of more modern jazz had to get together in private residences to exchange records and listen to new releases just arriving in from the United States or France).[52] Tete's aesthetic connection with the new directions of jazz, which he understood to be rooted in Black US expression, set him apart. Beyond the Fats Waller and Duke Ellington records in his mother's collection, and beyond those few performers such as Don Byas and George Johnson who visited Barcelona in the 1940s, for instance, it is essential to recognize that Barcelona's postwar reintegration into the urban jazz circuits of Europe followed, rather than preceded, Tete Montoliu's transnational movements. These two perspectives—sociopolitical and aesthetic-cultural—are thus necessarily entwined in any understanding of how jazz developed during the dictatorship.

The story of jazz in Spain is necessarily transnational in both its historical roots and in terms of musical practice. Directly inspired by urban jazz culture in the United States, the so-called *hot* clubs had been crucial anchors for the spread of jazz music in Europe in the second half of the 1930s. As Iván Iglesias explains, the usage in Spain of the term *hot*—left in the original English rather than translated—paid homage to the improvisational American jazz style and the urban centers from which it had spread to Europe: New Orleans, Chicago, and New York, for example. In the US context, the intention was to differentiate *hot* music from the symphonic, commercial, classical-influenced style that was performed from sheet music. In Europe, the term also functioned as a marketing strategy. In Madrid and Barcelona, the proliferation of clubs and music branded as *hot* promised exotic authenticity while in truth delivering music that was easy to consume and had very little in common with American jazz.[53]

The Hot Club of Barcelona, Alfredo Papo recounts in *El jazz a Catalunya* (1985), was founded in 1935. This was the third such club in Europe, after the first two were established in Belgium and France in the early years of the decade.[54] Additional clubs were later opened, in Madrid and Valencia, for instance, but there was not much evidence of early activity in the rest of Spain.[55] Barcelona's Hot Club began in a location at Passeig de Gràcia, 35, which was squarely in the Eixample district. The venue changed location a few times, introducing a pattern that would continue throughout Tete's lifetime as jazz clubs in Barcelona struggled to stay in business over the long term. The first challenge the club would face was that its activity would be interrupted by the Spanish Civil War.[56] This was not before achieving some renown, however. At the start of the civil war, there were 472 members of the Hot Club, "la qual cosa indica que la nostra música començava realment a tenir bastants adeptes a la Ciutat Comtal" (which indicates that our music was truly beginning to gain plenty of followers in Barcelona).[57] The third Hot Club festival was held in 1936 and included US bandleader and saxophonist Benny Carter, accompanied by the Hot Club de Barcelona Orchestra and the Quintet of the Hot Club of France, with Django Reinhardt on guitar and Stéphane Grappelli on violin.[58] Even at the start of the Spanish Civil War, Barcelona was hoping to regain its prewar prestige as a cosmopolitan European jazz city. The compilation of lectures delivered in Barcelona by the composer and musicologist Baltasar Samper in 1935, edited by Antoni Pizà and Francesc Vicens, show that "entre l'any 1935 i la primavera de 1936, els mesos abans de la Guerra Civil, Barcelona encara gaudeix d'un període d'intensitat màxima en el jazz" (between the year 1935 and the spring of 1936, the months before the Civil War, Barcelona is still enjoying a period of maximum jazz intensity).[59] Indications are that the musical form was on a fast track to surge in popularity in Catalonia—and across Spain, for that matter.

The Spanish Civil War and World War II, however, did set the development of jazz back considerably.[60] As Papo writes, instead of exponential or even steady growth, the consequence of continued war in Europe was that jazz in Barcelona was eschewed by those across the political spectrum. "Un cop acabada la guerra civil, el règim franquista va imposar una rígida censura a totes les activitats culturals. El mot 'jazz' no era ben vist, ja que si el jazz era una música 'capitalista' per als extremistes d'esquerra, per als de dreta era una música *negroide* i 'estrangeritzant' que no s'havia d'afavorir de cap manera" (Once the civil war was over, the Francoist regime imposed a strict censorship on all cultural activities. The word "jazz" was not well seen, given that if jazz was a "capitalist" music for those on the extreme left, for those on the right it was a black and estranged music to be avoided at any cost).[61] Miquel Jurado reports that across Spain it was almost as if interest in jazz had ceased to evolve in the 1940s: "El nou jazz encara no havia irromput als escenaris hispans i, sense discos i sense concerts, ni el públic ni els músics mateixos sabien de què es tractava" (The new jazz had still not appeared on the Spanish stage and, without records and without concerts, neither the public nor the musicians themselves knew what it even was).[62] In the late 1940s, Tete—who in his teenage years was already playing gigs and leading groups bearing his name—navigated this challenging situation as best he could.

In the 1950s, too, Tete frequently had to set aside his avant-garde aspirations in order to make a living. He was often hired to play popular tunes, rather than jazz, for example at the American Stars piano bar in Madrid.[63] In 1952, given the regime's official support of Catholicism and the ambiguous but nonetheless threatening political connotations of jazz, one of Tete's planned gigs in Mallorca was called off because it was too close to a church.[64] In the context of a Francoist Spain whose twentieth-century violence echoed a much longer history of the persecution of Jews and Muslims, this interesting anecdote shows how systematically jazz music was effectively stigmatized under the Spanish state. At other times, Tete was even specifically instructed not to play jazz—due, one suspects, to its social stigma—for instance during a one-month stint at Club Embassy in 1953.[65]

At the same time, however, there was an uptick in the visits of foreign artists to Spain. Along with the example of Lionel Hampton (1956), there were a number of other significant concerts. Invited performances by Bill Coleman (1952), Dizzy Gillespie (1953), and Big Bill Broonzy (1953) helped to grow the domestic audience for jazz and blues from the United States.[66] Iván Iglesias notes that the performances of US jazz musicians in Spain during this decade were generally covered by the press using language approaching the "collective hysteria" that figured in descriptions of the spread of rock and roll.[67] This enthusiasm even began to spread from international to domestic acts. As in the example of Tete's own participation in what has been recognized as the first bebop concert performed by musicians from Spain—at the Casal del Metge de Barcelona in 1952—there was some evidence, among the music's consumers at least, that the stigma attached to modern jazz under the early dictatorship was beginning to weaken.[68] This gradual weakening notwithstanding, the Spanish state prohibited Tete Montoliu's band from traveling to play in France that same year. They had been invited by the organizers of the prestigious Salón del Jazz de Paris, but in the end the group had to cancel their plans due to the dictatorship's continuing restrictions on travel. Tete later reflected on their disappointment:

> Entonces pasó algo: nosotros estábamos para irnos y de repente nos dijeron que no íbamos porque la Policía había prohibido el viaje. Imagínate nuestra frustración. Se trataba del mejor festival de jazz que se hacía entonces en

Europa, en el que se presentaron por vez primera Miles Davis y Dizzy
Gillespie. Aparte de este, no tuve demasiados tropiezos con la Dictadura si
no se cuentan las prohibiciones que entonces eran normales, Franco era tan
ignorante que ni siquiera prohibió el jazz.[69]

(Then something happened: we were ready to leave and suddenly they told us
we weren't going because the Police had prohibited the trip. Imagine our frustration. At the time it was the best jazz festival that had been held in Europe,
in which Miles Davis and Dizzy Gillespie were first introduced. Aside from
this, I didn't have too many run-ins with the Dictatorship if one doesn't count
the prohibitions that were normal back then, Franco was so ignorant that he
didn't even prohibit jazz.)

Due to this politically motivated cancellation, the pianist's first travel outside
of Spain would have to come two years later, in 1954. That successful trip
was a three-month stint in The Hague, from June through August.[70] Latin
music was quite popular in Holland at the time, and Tete joined Jordi Pérez
(guitar, percussion and voice), Enrique Cifuentes (bass), and vocalist Pia
Beck to form El Latin Quartet. He later commented that, "[c]om que érem
espanyols, podíem passar per llatins i triumfàvem de valent" (as we were
Spanish, we could pass for Latin and we triumphed bravely).[71] The pianist reported that the money was better in Holland than it was in Spain, and that he
was enthused to encounter 33-rpm LPs, which at the time had not yet made
it to Barcelona.[72] This experience making money through Latin-inflected
jazz was in a sense formative—in point of fact, Tete would record a number
of Latin albums, including *Temas latinoamericanos* (1974, also released as
Vereda tropical) and *Brasil* (1975) (see figure 2.1).

Returning to Spain after the trip to Holland in 1954, however, meant the pianist
had to once again resign himself to accept whatever steady work was available.
Unfortunately, this meant pandering to the expectations of regressive audiences
who continued to find jazz's new directions unpalatable. He particularly disliked
having to perform popular tunes the same way from one night to the next. Tete
fully embraced values that were in truth common to both the modern urban experience and bebop music itself—spontaneity, wandering—in short, the constantly shifting conditions of metropolitan jazz. As he later reflected:

Tocar dues vegades una cosa de la mateixa manera és l'antimúsica. Si
m'hagués agradat fer-ho d'aquella manera, m'hauria dedicat a la música

Figure 2.1 *Tete Montoliu* (1975, Barcelona, Spain, Belter 00-104), cover and 45 rpm disc, scan by the author.

clàssica. Doncs bé, a l'Atelier, com a l'American Bar, jo vaig sortir cada nit a l'escenari amb el ferm propòsit de no tocar jazz, de limitar-me a interpretar cançons franceses o americanes sense cap canvi, però a poc a poc m'anava encenent i, al final, acabava arrencant amb un blues o una improvisació *be bop.*[73]

(To play something the same way twice is anti-musical. If it had made me happy to do things that way, I would have dedicated myself to classical music. So at venues like the Atelier and American Bar, I would come out onto the stage every night having resolved not to play jazz, to limit myself to playing French or American songs with no modifications, but as things went on I found my resolve weakening and by the end I would finish up with a blues tune or a bebop improvisation.)

This sort of deviation from the expectations of regressive listening, of course, proved threatening to club managers and audiences alike. In at least one instance, the pianist gave in to his frustration with being limited to popular tunes, played jazz, and was promptly thrown out.

Opportunities were still quite limited in a postwar landscape where the aesthetics of bebop were not being accepted as quickly as Tete would have liked. He later remembered that, in 1959, he took part in a tour that sought to bring selected Barcelonan jazz musicians to audiences that might appreciate their music in Valencia, Granada, Bilbao, Seville, and Madrid. Rather than perform at clubs, however, the tour brought the musicians to "biblioteques universitàries, col·legis majors o locals del Sindicat" (university libraries, upper schools or union chapters).[74] According to Pujol Baulenas, the attendees at those shows were young—between eighteen and twenty-three years old—and had never been to a live jazz concert before.[75] As this anecdote conveys, Spanish cities lacked both the urban audience and infrastructure necessary to sustain a strong jazz music scene through the late 1950s.

Despite such conditions, however, the decade nevertheless saw a host of improvements for Tete's career ambitions, both at home and abroad. Toward the end of the 1950s, he was able to record and release two albums with vibraphonist Francesc Burrull under the titles *Tete Montoliu y su cuarteto* (1958) and *Tete Montoliu y su conjunto* (1958).[76] Also in 1958—perhaps making up for his cancelled trip to France just a few years earlier—Tete played in his first great festival of jazz in Cannes. This was an extremely significant moment, as performers the likes of Dizzy Gillespie, Ella Fitzgerald, Stan Getz, and Coleman Hawkins were also on the bill. A few months later, in February 1959, he played in the Festival de Jazz de San Remo, in Italy.[77] Due to the success he was experiencing in Spain, and now also across Europe, Pujol Baulenas writes that the pianist was becoming a significant propulsive force for the Barcelona jazz scene as a whole: "El ambiente jazzístico de la ciudad iba en aumento gracias a la figura de Tete Montoliu, que representaba el centro neurálgico en torno al cual se movían las actividades locales. Su paso por Cannes le había consolidado artísticamente en España, y su nombre empezaba también a ser conocido en el ámbito del jazz europeo" (The jazz environment of the city was improving thanks to the figure of Tete Montoliu, who represented the central point around which local activities circulated. His trip to Cannes had consolidated his artistic reputation in Spain, and his name also was beginning to be known in the European jazz circuit).[78] There is additional support for the idea that his European notoriety was leading to an increased reputation for Montoliu in Spain. For instance, Sandra Milena Moreno Sabogal discusses the appearance of Tete's group in Valencia in 1959 as a sign that the city had entered "una época que encuentra en el jazz una identidad" [an era that found an identity in jazz].[79] It seemed that through his transnational urban performances, Tete was becoming a true ambassador of modern jazz form.

This last year of the 1950s marked a further significant change in the possibilities for forward-minded jazz musicians like Tete in Barcelona, if not yet in Spain as a whole. While the Hot Clubs had been revived in the mid-1940s, and a host of other music clubs had followed suit, a true jazz club had been lacking until the creation of the Jamboree, in Barcelona, which opened its doors at the beginning of 1959. To make this happen, a club named the Brindis had changed its name as well as its artistic direction. In the process, this single club marked a new phase in the creation of the urban infrastructure needed to support jazz in the Catalonian capital. As Tete described it, the venue relatively quickly went from being a place for marines and prostitutes to a place for the "intel·lectualitat catalana" (Catalan intellectual elite).[80] The pianist played regularly at the Jamboree, and he is said to have marked the official opening of the club with a concert, a fact that invites speculation about whether the Jamboree cemented Tete's reputation, or whether Tete's reputation brought notoriety to the club.[81] Iván Iglesias goes so far as to attribute the acceptance of modern jazz in Spain in the late 1950s and early 1960s precisely to Tete's jazz work.[82] Either way, however, it is crucial that the Jamboree's significance went beyond the Spanish borders to impact all of Europe. Tete puts it this way: "El Jamboree el coneixia tot Europa. Als seus primers anys va ser un dels clubs més importants del continent" (All of Europe knew of the Jamboree. During its first few years, it was one of the most important clubs on the continent).[83] While other clubs opened, changed locations, and closed in Barcelona—all due to the city's ascendant reputation within the urban circuits of Europe—Montoliu nonetheless continued to be frustrated by having to play for Spanish audiences who tended to remain relatively unfamiliar with modern jazz.

While some may want to explain Tete's travels to other urban centers of European jazz as being solely a direct consequence of the dictatorship, this is far too convenient. For example, Manfred Straka's chapter in *Eurojazzland* states that "[d]uring the Fascist dictatorship in Spain, which lasted from 1939 to 1975, jazz was condemned as a symbol of capitalism and Western decadence and was practically forbidden. As a result Spanish jazz musicians, such as Tete Montoliu, were forced to emigrate."[84] This conclusion is misleading. Here the sociopolitical explanation cannot be accepted in isolation from the aesthetic-cultural one. That is, one must recognize that Tete's jazz aesthetics were still very much ahead of his time. Montoliu's regular travels—not just to the Whisky Jazz in Madrid, but more importantly beyond the borders of the Spanish state—provided him with truly significant opportunities to grow as a musician. Through 1959 the situation in Spain was still quite bleak, as Pujol Baulenas notes: "El jazz seguía siendo una música sólo apta para ser practicada en ocasiones puntuales, no para ganarse el sustento diario. En Barcelona faltaba un local con un dueño decidido a programar jazz de verdad" (Jazz continued to be a music only suitable for specific occasions, not for earning a living. Barcelona lacked a venue whose owner was committed to scheduling real jazz).[85] Tete's response to the lack of possibilities on the Iberian Peninsula was to seek a cultural climate more favorable to modern jazz. In his own words, "De haberme quedado en España, no hubiera podido avanzar" (If I had stayed in Spain, I wouldn't have been able to advance).[86]

Across Europe's cities, a circuit of urban jazz environments was taking off in the 1960s. The best jazz artists of the time were drawn to those cities where they could jam together, push the boundaries of the form, and learn from one another. The introduction to *Eurojazzland* includes Madrid and Barcelona in the list of "single cities, [that] were relevant as well in terms of a 'cultural environment'. . . . Paris, Brussels, London, Berlin, Moscow, and then Copenhagen, Oslo, Amsterdam, The Hague, Munich, Barcelona, Madrid, Rome, Milan, Perugia, Montreux, all became perennial or seasonal-specific jazz environments."[87] The single club that provided the most significant opportunities for Tete early in his career was perhaps the Jazzhus Montmartre in Copenhagen, Denmark.

Tete Montoliu first arrived in Copenhagen from Berlin in 1963. He had been invited to Germany by Peter Trunk to inaugurate the famous Blue Note club, where Tete's trio had been selected as the house band. Musicians such as Benny Beiley, Herb Geller, Lucky Thompson, Sahib Shihab, and Ark van Rooyen all passed through while he was the resident pianist there.[88] But the Jazzhus in Copenhagen was on another level entirely. "Al principi dels anys seixanta el Montmartre Jazzhus era un dels clubs més prestigiosos d'Europa i en Tete ni tan sols va preguntar amb qui tocaria: va fer les maletes i es va plantar a Copenhaguen amb la Pilar" (At the beginning of the 1960s the Montmartre Jazzhus was one of the most prestigious clubs in Europe and Tete didn't even bother to ask who he would be playing with: he packed his bags and moved to Copenhagen with Pilar).[89] Hired for a one-month contract, he was over the moon when he was asked to replace the Danish pianist in Dexter Gordon's band at the American bandleader's request. After the contract ended, he returned to the Blue Note in Berlin, but with the desire to return to Denmark once again as soon as it was feasible.

By October 1 of the same year, he was once again playing at the Jazzhus Montmartre. Fortuitously, on October 22, 1963, he began playing as the

fourth member of a quartet with Rahsaan Roland Kirk (sax), Alex Riel
(drums), and Niels-Henning Ørsted Pedersen (bass). Niels-Henning ended
up becoming a lifelong friend of Tete's, and served as the Tete Montoliu Trio's
bassist for quite some time. In truth, the 1963 quartet had been put together
entirely by the Jazzhus and none of the members even knew each other. What
is more, neither Tete nor Kirk knew they would be playing with another musician who had a visual impairment. In Montoliu's own words:

> Ens van presentar el dia abans de començar a tocar en una espècie de roda
> de premsa que va muntar l'amo del local per fer una mica de promoció. Van
> ser les nostres respectives dones les que ens ho can dir. Kirk es va encendre
> d'ira i va dir a l'amo del Montmartre que no volia actuar amb un cec perquè
> els cecs no sabien res de música. El patró, que també tenia bastant mal
> caràcter, li va contestar que aleshores li rescindia el contracte [amb Kirk]
> per ser cec i no saber res de música. Kirk es va haver de conformar encara
> que amb un emprenyament important. El primer dia l'únic que em va dir
> va ser: 'Coneixes la meva música?' Jo li vaig respondre que, els últims dies,
> havia estat sentint el seu disc. Va dir: 'OK' i se'n va anar.[90]

(We met each other the day before beginning to play together at a kind of
press conference that was set up by the place's owner to do a bit of promotion. Our respective women were the ones that informed us. Kirk suddenly
got angry and told the Montmartre's owner that he wouldn't perform with
a blind person because blind people did not know anything about music.
His employer, who was also quick to anger, replied that he would then have
to rescind the contract [with Kirk] on account of his being blind and not
knowing anything about music. Kirk had to give in, though not without
some irritation. That first day the only thing he said to me was: "Do you
know my music?" I responded that I had been listening to his album the
past few days. He said: "OK" and took off.)

The vinyl release of *Kirk in Copenhagen* (1963) was a sign that things paid
off after this initial challenge. The album contained six tracks, four of which
were Kirk originals: "Narrow Bolero" (R. Roland Kirk), "Mingus-Griff Song"
(R. Roland Kirk), "The Monkey Thing" (R. Roland Kirk), "Mood Indigo"
(Ellington-Mills-Bigard), "Cabin in the Sky" (Duke-Latouche), and "On the
Corner of King and Scott Streets" (R. Roland Kirk). Beyond the contributions
of Kirk, Tete, and Niels-Henning Ørsted Pedersen, the album featured Don

Moore (bass), J. C. Moses (drums), and a performer going by the name Big Skol on harmonica.

Despite the rough beginning to the friendship between Kirk and Tete, there is no sign on the recording that their musical collaboration was anything but amicable. In fact, during the year following the album's release, jazz magnate George Wein put together an international tour of the Newport Jazz Festival, and Tete once again played in Rahsaan Roland Kirk's quartet. The traveling concert was conceived as a series of twenty concerts performed in twenty days. It is remarkable that none of the dates were in Spain. The bill for the festival, which began on September 10, 1964, featured the Coleman Hawkins Quartet, the Miles Davis Quintet (with Herbie Hancock, Wayne Shorter, Ron Carter, and Tony Williams), the Dave Brubeck Quartet, and an homage to Charlie Parker that included J. J. Johnson and Sonny Stitt, among others.[91]

Beyond meeting Kirk, Tete had a number of other fortunate encounters while playing at the Montmartre, including trumpeters Chet Baker and Kenny Dorham. The overlap of Montoliu and Dorham in Copenhagen was particularly fruitful, in that the trumpet player's "Skandia Skies" ended up becoming one of Tete's most frequently recorded songs.[92] Having met Dexter Gordon there during his first visit to the Danish capital in 1963, he went on to perform with Dex, Niels-Henning, and Alex Riel from October 1963 through June 1964,[93] leading to a number of albums released under Dexter Gordon's name, such as Billie's Bounce (1964) and later Bouncin' with Dex (1975). Montoliu also played on the two-album release by Anthony Braxton titled In the Tradition (1974). All things considered, however, Tete's enjoyment of the city was not limited to musical considerations. He preferred the Montmartre and Copenhagen to the Blue Note and Berlin, because "la gent era més simpàtica, tenia més ganes de riure que a Berlín" (people were nicer, they had a better sense of humor than in Berlin), and quite simply it was easier for him get around: "Copenhagen és l'única ciutat del món on en Tete es va atrevir a desplaçar-se sense companyia, utilitzant els taxis i l'amabilitat de la gent" (Copenhagen is the only city in the world in which Tete dared to go out unaccompanied, relying on taxis and the friendliness of the people).[94] Tete continued living in Copenhagen for some time, with sporadic trips to Barcelona, where his daughter Núria was living, and to Madrid to play a few days at the Whisky Jazz.[95]

The Jazzhus Montmartre was also important because it exposed Tete to the transnational currents of free jazz. When he had returned to play in Copenhagen again in October 1963—before he even met Kirk, that is—his first assignment was to play with the New York Contemporary Five, made up of Archie Shepp, John Tchicai, Don Cherry, Don Moore, and J. C. Moses.[96] This was an experience he found challenging, musically speaking, and also somewhat less than enjoyable.[97] Previously he had, of course, played in Spain with Perry Robinson, who had notably been a student of Don Cherry and Ornette Coleman.[98] Yet keeping up with the New York Contemporary Five was a different experience entirely. As Tete described it:

> Musicalment ens trobàvem en extrems oposats. La primera nit Archie Shepp va dir que comencéssim amb un blues. Doncs bé, vam marcar el temps i tots cinc van començar a fer coses estranyíssimes: allò no era un blues ni era res. Jo estava totalment deconcertat, sense saber què havia de fer. En Cherry que estava completament boig però era molt bona persona, em va socórrer dient-me que toqués el que em sortís del cor sense preocupar-me de res més. Jo, que continuava sense saber què havia de fer, em vaig posar a fer escales i arpeigs com si estigués practicant a casa. En acabar en Cherry em va dir molt seriós: "Has comprès el missatge, ara ja entens aquesta música." Jo vaig continuar igual la resta de les vint-i-una nits que vam tocar junts i ells van quedar molt contents de mi.[99]

> (Musically we were extreme opposites. The first night Archie Shepp told us to start with a blues. Well we marked the time and all five began to do the strangest things: that wasn't a blues nor was it anything. I was totally bewildered, not knowing what I should do. Cherry, who was completely crazy but a great person, came to my aid, saying I should play what came from my heart without worrying about anything else. Still not knowing what I should do, I started to play scales and arpeggios as if I was practicing at home. After finishing Cherry said to me quite seriously: "You've understood the message, now you get this music." I kept doing the same thing the rest of the twenty-one nights we played together and they were very happy with me).

Tete's later experience recording with Anthony Braxton proved to be similarly bewildering, and he professed to dislike free jazz.[100]

The problem for critics comes from having to reconcile such statements with his jazz legacy. The fact is that the notion of free jazz became fashionable enough in European circles so as to influence the title of *Free boleros* (1996), one of his most popular albums. It was recorded with the singer Mayte Martín, who was a star in her own right, and released solely on compact disc. Its release came at a moment in Tete's career when his reputation had long been cemented among jazz listeners. Yet more interesting still, in this regard, is the Tete Montoliu Trio's recording *Lliure jazz* (Free Jazz) (1969). The recording date of the album places it at the middle of the decade spanning the pianist's first exposure to free jazz with the New York Contemporary Five in 1963 and the recording of *In the Tradition* with Braxton in 1974.

Lliure jazz (1969) itself seems to follow in the footsteps of the landmark Ornette Coleman album *Free Jazz* (1961). Coleman's album was recorded in December 1960 from a single, uninterrupted session lasting 36′23″, and the featured musicians were selected in order to best express a form of sonic immediacy, the direct expression of the artists' "minds and emotions" rather than a collective project whose direction would be decided in advance.[101] Martin Williams's liner notes for the Atlantic records release of *Free Jazz* make two pertinent points. First is the comparison Williams makes between the free jazz sound and the visual aesthetics on display in "non-objective painting." In illustration of the shared nature of this aesthetic across visual and aural modalities of art, the gatefold vinyl release includes a large (approximately 8″ x 10″) color reproduction of Jackson Pollack's *White Light* (1954). Second is the key invocation of the concept of "difference" in the final two paragraphs of the liner notes. While the uninitiated may hear only cacophony at the root of free jazz style, the music instead aspires to convey a sense of the unexceptional, the quotidian. In this sense, the music is remarkable precisely because of the ways in which it reflects the everyday and creates an open collaborative space for diverse musical voices. Williams puts it this way: "It is surely a most telling tribute to the importance of this music that all of these young men of different experience in jazz, were able to contribute spontaneously and sustain a performance like this one. On the other hand, the man who isn't bothered about 'newness' or 'difference,' but says only that, '*He sounds like someone crying, talking, laughing,*' is having the soundest sort of response to Ornette Coleman's music."[102] In this description there are echoes of both Fumi Okiji and Georg Simmel, reaffirming the notion that free jazz is a musical distillation of everyday attributes of the modern urban experience.

Attempts to classify and distinguish European free jazz from American free jazz, such as the one put forward by Arrigo Cappelletti,[103] have yet to grapple with the transnational commonalities of the form. It is significant that US musicians in fact brought the free jazz style to Europe, and moreover that these transpositions not only involved European musicians in landmark performances and recordings, but also left an imprint upon the subsequent directions of European jazz. For Black American artists performing in Europe, free jazz was no less of a radical political project, a form of resistance. The French jazz critics who published the book *Free Jazz/Black Power* in 1971 were intent on exploring the encounters between radical politics in both America and Europe. They reflected on the way in which politics were built in to the creation of a style that "rejects the musical and extra-musical values of dominant ideology. . . . It endeavors to regain and *build* a specifically Afro-American culture."[104] Archie Shepp once said that "jazz is a music itself born out of oppression, born out of the enslavement of my people."[105] This cultural significance was transposed onto the urban geography of the continent and into the transnational Black imaginary through performances in Europe. The transnational jazz work of musicians in Spain—such as that of Shepp, Coleman, Cherry, Kirk, and Braxton— thus continued to "testify to the oppression of black Americans, to express their revolt, and even to play a role in their revolutionary struggle."[106] Tete Montoliu's engagement with a politically meaningful American jazz form is not synonymous with this expression of revolt, but it nonetheless occurred in an adjacent musical space.

On *Lliure jazz* (1969), the Tete Montoliu Trio is made up of Erich Peter (bass) and Peer Wyboris (drums). Of course, the sound of a mere trio attempting free jazz is necessarily going to sound quite different from what a double quartet can produce. Ornette Coleman's *Free Jazz* (1961) had featured eight musicians playing at the same time, and none of them were pianists: Ornette Coleman himself (alto sax), Eric Dolphy (bass clarinet), Don Cherry (pocket trumpet), Freddie Hubbard (trumpet), Scott LaFaro (bass), Charlie Haden (bass), Billy Higgins (drums), and Ed Blackwell (drums). Thus, listeners comparing Tete's release with Ornette Coleman's earlier album will note right away there are crucial differences. The introduction of the piano to Coleman's concept of free improvisation places more emphasis on structured but variable rhythms, given that it is in truth an additional percussive instrument. Tete and the group take advantage of this to play, as a group, with frequent changes of pacing.

Strangely enough, *Lliure jazz* represents some of Tete's least cacophonous jazz work. The beginning of sides one and two of the LP present a marked contrast with the crash of sound that launches Coleman's *Free Jazz*. There were quiet moments on that 1961 release as well, but there seem to be many more of them on this 1969 recording. Here Tete's trio entertains extended and repeated moments where the instruments are not overlapping at all. The languishing pace of some moments on side two of *Lliure Jazz*—along with the sparse accompaniment of bass and drums, which avoid any hint of competition with Tete's flourishes—evokes a lyricism absent from many of the pianist's more heady recordings, and also a sort of conventional feel. On side one, a moment comes when the pianist seems to be revisiting patches of his solo work, or quoting from it, rather than forging new sounds, and here Peter and Wyboris drop out completely as if to confirm this is the case. Afterwards, Peter undertakes a meditative bass solo that relaxes into a propulsive riff centered around an insistent single note as Wyboris and Montoliu come back in. In fact, this riff sounds curiously like the one the bassist strikes in the trio's performance of "La dama d'Aragó" on the album *Tete Montoliu interpreta a Serrat* (1969)—for reasons that will be explained in the next chapter. The bass solo and insistent riff promises to lay the groundwork, if not for some chaotic free jazz improvisation, then at least for a crescendo. But this crescendo never comes, and as the pace quickens, this propulsive energy is lost to what might be considered to be, on the whole, a comparatively lackluster performance.

Despite a certain conventionality and the relatively uninspired result produced by this approach, *Lliure jazz* throughout demonstrates that willingness to wander and experiment that was key to avant-garde visual art and music. In its many shifts from slow to fast rhythms and its pursuit of undirected collaboration, this album is no less a musical expression of the essence of the urban. It is the sum total of distinguishable actors, whose individual actions become fused together into a gathering of difference. While the Tete Montoliu Trio's recording clearly diverges both aesthetically and politically from the free jazz work of artists like Ornette Coleman and Archie Shepp, the aesthetic style and political engagement pioneered by those artists had an impact on Tete's legacy. In his subsequent jazz work, the pianist internalizes and borrows from free jazz its model of the interconnection between music and politics. Billy Higgins, who played with Coleman's landmark *Free Jazz* double quartet, even become one of Tete's favored drummers—perhaps precisely for his ability to create a freer space for the pianist's own preference for rapid changes. The next chapter continues with a consideration of the political dimensions of the Catalan "new song" movement and its impact on the political context in which Tete's musical production was increasingly immersed.

3

Performing Catalanism

Catalan language, culture, and literature—as it was with the cases of Galician and Basque—were threatening to the Franco dictatorship's constructed idea of Spain's undifferentiated unity. This idea was, of course, a convenient fiction imposed violently on a rather heterogeneous grouping of peoples, cultures, and languages. Use of the Castilian (Spanish) language was enforced by the state, Catholicism was the official religion, and certain carefully selected cultural forms—no matter how unrelated to the project of modern nation-building, as in chapter 1's example of flamenco—were appropriated and held up as paradigmatic expressions of Spain's constructed national soul. Jazz was certainly not one of those national expressions, and thus the conditions were in place for jazz music to function as a form of resistance. During the dictatorship's later years, Tete Montoliu's jazz work became intertwined with Catalan popular music's socially critical role in contesting Francoism.

In "Becoming Normal: Cultural Production and Cultural Policy in Catalonia" (1995), Josep-Anton Fernández documents the suppression of a Catalan cultural market during the dictatorship, as well as the gradual re-surgence of Catalan-language arts, theater, and publishing through its later years. As he explains, the Catalan language was banned and, for a signifi-cant period of time, was virtually absent in the press. Systematic censorship allowed the regime to keep a relatively tight grip on which cultural products made it to market and which did not. Publications written in Catalan were suppressed, readership patterns dissipated, and the spoken language itself was largely limited to clandestine use in the home. As Fernández describes in detail, it was not possible to point to tangible gains for Catalan cultural markets until much later in the dictatorship: "[W]ith the regime's modest lib-eralization in the early 1960s some expansion was possible: new publishing houses were founded, as well as associations for the promotion of culture and the teaching of the language, and the songwriters' movement of the *nova cançó* achieved important popular success."[1] These efforts and their contin-uation throughout the 1970s were strategic and politically motivated. Their goals were "to maintain the prestige of Catalan as a language of high culture, to prepare the ground for expansion in the post-Franco period, to maintain a minimum level of cultural production and consumption, and to guarantee the visibility of Catalan culture."[2]

While the market for Catalan jazz on vinyl was virtually nonexistent when the Tete Montoliu Trio released the two vinyl LPs *A tot jazz* and *A tot jazz 2* (1965)—particularly when compared with its status in the twenty-first century—its development was encouraged by certain affinities with the popular song movement of the time.[3] Known as the *nova cançó*, this movement coalesced in the 1960s, and was as much a political statement as it was a musical one. With its strong emphasis on Catalan lyrics and identity, the *nova cançó* was perceived by many as a cultural arm of the Catalanism that had been forced underground by the Franco regime. As Spain took further steps toward rejoining the international community during the late 1960s and early 1970s, this subterranean Catalanism was once again raising its head. It is of note that Tete somewhat frequently performed songs composed by Joan Manuel Serrat (1943–), who was strongly identified with the *nova cançó*.[4] In Tete's own words, "[L]a nova cançó no em feia el pes, però el catalanisme sí i protegir els de la nova cançó, tant si m'agradaven com si no, era signe de catalanisme" (The new song did not itself move me, but Catalanism, yes, and protecting those involved with the new song, whether I liked it or not, was a sign of Catalanism).[5] The pianist was drawn to the politics of the movement, but—if his jazz legacy is any guide—also to the potential that both popular and traditional Catalan songs held for innovative directions in jazz composition. Overall, Tete Montoliu's modern performances and recordings certainly have received far less popular and critical interest than the *nova cançó* tradition.[6] Yet he nonetheless contributed to the same resurgence of musical expressions of Catalan identity in the 1960s and 1970s via the modern jazz form.

This chapter situates the pianist's jazz work within a tradition of Catalanism that has ebbed and flowed over the decades. It begins by acknowledging 1920s Barcelona as a key moment in Catalan musical culture, before emphasizing the 1960s as a decade of cultural rebirth, and finally asserting Tete's role in projecting Catalan musical culture into the transnational consumption patterns of the post-dictatorship years. Spanning these decades also allows readers to get a sense of how the re-emerging Catalan cultural markets of the 1960s can be understood not merely as a challenge to the Francoist dictatorship, but also as a response to long-standing debates over Catalanism that can be traced to the 1920s dictatorship of Miguel Primo de Rivera, and of course even further back in time. Tete's jazz work is unique in the way that he speaks, through his music, not merely to Barcelona's cosmopolitan reputation, but also to the wider rural traditions of Catalonian identity.

Jazz Age Barcelona and the First International Jazz Festival

Tete Montoliu's felt connections with the city of his birth cannot be underestimated. Barcelona was a crucible that at once catalyzed the international reputation he earned as a musician and imbued his jazz work with a defiant streak of Catalanism. As Robert A. Davidson explores at length in his study *Jazz Age Barcelona* (2009), prior to the Spanish Civil War the city's urban environment was crucial in forging a culture that supported a reinvigorated Catalan nationalism. By the time that Tete was born in 1933, the city was already bustling with "international Jazz Age codes and styles" and an urban cultural aesthetic cemented by the city's "connection to European cultural currents."[7] In the 1920s and early 1930s, matters of urbanism, mass spectacle, and a specifically Catalan modernity were instrumental in defining Barcelona as what Davidson calls a "Jazz-Age city."[8] Jazz music became one of the ways in which twentieth-century Catalanists melded a re-emergent European cosmopolitanism with a long-standing discourse of cultural specificity that differentiated Catalonia from the hegemonic culture of the modern Spanish state.[9]

Part of the energy that sustained this re-emergent cosmopolitanism in Barcelona came from the post-1914 influx of European immigrants who were encouraged by Spain's neutrality in World War I.[10] There is reason to believe that, on account of the devastation brought by the war to France, for a time Barcelona even came to displace Paris as the pan-European city *par excellence*.[11] As Jordi Pujol Baulenas notes, the migration pattern that WWI brought into being helped to cultivate two locations of urban musical culture in the Catalonian capital. Those consumers seeking more elegant forms of entertainment went to El Conde del Asalto (Nou de la Rambla) and Las Ramblas, whereas the more popular classes went to the Avenida del Paral·lel.[12] These two areas together sustained a vibrant urban nightlife that lived up to and arguably even surpassed the reputation of the French capital. The two cities were very much subject to the same fads, the same differing levels of clientele, and even the same types of musical acts:

Siguiendo la moda que imperaba en la capital francesa, empezaron a inaugurarse en Barcelona los primeros cabarets decorados al estilo parisino y sugerentemente ambientados con atractivas y sofisticadas chicas de alterne, a las que se conocía con el nombre de "tanguistas." . . . Muy pronto aquella renovación en el mundo del espectáculo impuso su ley en el Paralelo, donde salieron relucir una considerable colección de nombres parisienses: Moulin Rouge, Folies Bergère, Ba-Ta-Clan, Odeon, Royal Concert, Paris Concert. . . . En sus variopintos programas cabía todo: cupletistas, *divettes*, rumberas, acróbatas, ventrílocuos, bailarinas, funámbulos, típicas parejas de baile español, prestidigitadores, cómicos, ilusionistas, frívolas y osadas hembras del genero picaresco o "sicalíptico," y un sin fin de atracciones más. La fulgurante vida nocturna que Barcelona ofrecía a sus visitantes no tenía parangón con ninguna otra capital de España.[13]

(Following the fashion that reigned in the French capital, Barcelona saw the inauguration of the first cabarets decorated in the Parisian style and suggestively staffed with attractive and sophisticated hostess girls, who were known by the name "tanguistas." . . . Very soon that renovation of the world of spectacle imposed its law in the Paral·lel, where a considerable collection of Parisian names could be seen: Moulin Rouge, Folies Bergère, Ba-Ta-Clan, Odeon, Royal Concert, Paris Concert. . . . Anything could be found among its varied programs: cuplé singers, divas, rumba dancers, acrobats, ventriloquists, ballet dancers, funambulists, typical Spanish dance pairs, magicians, comedians, illusionists, frivolous and daring women of the picaresque or "sicaliptic" genre, and an endless list of other attractions. The shimmering nightlight that Barcelona offered its visitors was unparalleled by that of any other Spanish city.)

After World War I ended, jazz bands in Barcelona could also be counted among the city's many borrowings from Parisian musical culture.[14]

By the early 1920s, the Catalonian capital was one of the most important sites for music and dance developments in Europe.[15] Musical traffic between the two cities was frequent. In January 1921, as Pujol Baulenas reports, a jazz band composed of American musicians came to the Principal Palace in Barcelona after having performed at the Ba-Ta-Clan in Paris.[16] Barcelona and Paris often fought over the same musicians. The case of Lorenzo Torres Nin is a prime example. Torres Nin was a Barcelonan pianist who directed an orchestra known as the Jazz-Band Demons. He was quite famous in the

Catalonian capital for playing waltzes, ragtimes, and *chotisses* in the venue known as the Cabaret Catalán. His notoriety earned him the nickname of "Rey del Jazz-Band" (King of the Jazz-Band). Torres Nin was offered a lot of money to move to Paris, and in fall of 1922 the management of the Barcelona club at which he performed was forced to double his salary in order to retain him.[17] The Rey del Jazz-Band accepted the new salary and went on to perform with many of the top international acts that would visit Barcelona prior to the irruption of the Spanish Civil War.

Among the obstacles slowing the development of jazz historiography, there are biases that privilege certain times and places over others. Even at the dawn of the twenty-first century, to discuss jazz in the widest popular imagination is often to sanctify the decade of the 1930s at the expense of others. Evidence of such a bias can be seen, for example, in the documentary *Jazz* (2001) by Ken Burns. As E. Taylor Atkins points out, that documentary's "gushing hagiographies of Louis Armstrong and Duke Ellington . . . deprived other worthy artists of screen time."[18] Similarly, this tendency to focus excessively on this golden era of US jazz also keeps the critical spotlight from delving more deeply into jazz geographies outside the United States.[19] For its part, Spanish historiography has long been fascinated by the 1930s, given the upheavals constituted by the brief formation of the Republic, its dissolution into the violence of war, and the consequences of this war for the impending Francoist dictatorship. Interest in the large-scale chaos of the 1930s has often overshadowed those cultural histories deemed to be less closely tied to this sociopolitical turmoil. Nevertheless, the 1920s are a crucial decade, not merely for appreciating Barcelona's Jazz Age reputation, but also for understanding how the dictatorship strengthened the ties between musical expression and political opposition in Catalonia.

The Spanish dictatorship of Miguel Primo de Rivera (1923–30) may certainly be less well known than the regime of Francisco Franco that followed and lasted close to forty years. Still, in cultural terms, it was similarly retrograde, and had quite a negative effect on musical culture. As Davidson explains, the state censorship of the 1920s under Primo de Rivera was systemic and prolonged, and the effects this had on the Catalan press were not only brutal in themselves but also a sign of things to come.[20] Carlos Losada, the dictator's "designated man in Catalonia," carried out the regime's crackdown on perceived cultures of immorality in Barcelona, as did his successor Milans del Bosch.[21] Both Primo de Rivera and Franco sought to enshrine conservative tradition under the guise of protecting "las buenas costumbres" (the good customs). His dictatorship quite predictably brought about a cultural and economic downturn.[22] As part of this effort, Primo de Rivera's regime spurned cabarets and music halls, which were seen as threats to the order of the day. Barcelona's reputation for bustling night life that had been built up, using Paris as a model, at the start of the 1920s suffered accordingly. Interestingly enough, however, those clubs with jazz bands were able to get by.[23]

Musical culture was threatening for Primo de Rivera's regime, and perhaps no song was more threatening than "Els Segadors" on account of its strong connection to Catalan identity. The regime's approach to establishing control in Barcelona "did not begin with illegal substances or closing times but rather with the performance of one spectacle in particular: the singing of the Catalan national anthem, 'Els Segadors,' which was banned outright."[24] This detail will help explain the significance of Tete Montoliu's solo piano performance of the song for his album *Catalonian Folksongs* (1977), to which the end of this chapter returns. Part of the reason that the pianist's modern jazz innovations of the post-dictatorship years were so powerful was because they contributed to the recovery of a broader Catalan musical culture whose repression by the Spanish state, starting in the decade of the 1920s and continuing through Francoism, had not been forgotten either in urban or rural geographies.

One of the most important musical performances of the 1920s unfolded near the Avenida del Paral·lel at Barcelona's Teatro Olympia from January 15 to January 20, 1926. The racialized landscape of musical culture in early twentieth-century Spain bore a resemblance to that of France, Germany, and the United States. It was thus common for concert advertisements to utilize recognizably racist imagery to exoticize musicians and their music alike. Posters for one event in the January 1926 series featured drawings of dark-skinned monkey-like men dressed up in glasses and tuxedos, accompanied by the written announcement that US bandleader Sam Wooding's "Chocolate Kiddies" would perform music by Duke Ellington. Another such poster for the same group promised that the performance it advertised would be the "[e]spectáculo más exótico y original y de más éxito que se ha presentado en Barcelona" (most exotic, unique and successful spectacle that has been presented in Barcelona).[25] Necessarily dealing in the racist tropes that white Europeans were eager to consume, Wooding's orchestra was successful throughout Europe and even contributed to the widespread acceptance of the Charleston there. The bandleader later returned to record in Barcelona, for example in 1929, the year of the Exposición Universal in the Catalonian capital. Wooding was only one of many US musicians who sought to make a living in Europe, of course. Barcelona had continued to be a hub for musical culture following the cultural reputation the city had developed at the expense of Paris due to the mass migrations during World War I. At the time, the city was thus a natural draw not merely for Wooding but for many other notable acts as well. Not least of these was Josephine Baker, who famously performed in the city's Principal Palace on March 3, 1930.[26] As her accompaniment in entertainment, Baker enjoyed none other than the famed Barcelonan bandleader of the Demon-Jazz orchestra himself, the aforementioned Lorenzo Torres Nin.[27]

With the ability to attract international acts such as Josephine Baker and to retain jazz bandleaders such as Torres Nin, Barcelona's fame as an international jazz city only grew. Pujol Baulenas writes of the effects of this increasing fame on the Conde del Asalto and the lower part of Las Ramblas, the area that attracted bourgeois consumers of elegant entertainment. After 1932, he writes,

> En esta zona de la ciudad se respiraba una atmósfera muy *hot* y excitante. Un frenesí propiciado, sobre todo, por la numerosa colonia de músicos y boxeadores negros (procedentes en su mayoría de Cuba, Puerto Rico y Santo Domingo, pero también de Estados Unidos, e incluso de Senegal), que se instalaron en el barrio, convirtiéndolo en nuestro pequeño Harlem.[28]

> (In this zone of the city one breathed in an air that was very *hot* and titillating. A frenzy prompted, above all, by the numerous colony of black musicians and boxers [hailing in the majority from Cuba, Puerto Rico, and Santo Domingo, but also from the United States, and even from Senegal], who established themselves in the neighborhood, converting it into our little Harlem.)

Anticipating the pull that Barcelona would exercise on musicians like Don Byas—the young Montoliu's houseguest and mentor during the mid-to-late 1940s—the early 1930s saw many American musicians take root in the city. Another prominent example was violinist Robert Edward "Juice" Wilson.[29]

Jazz was a burgeoning consumer culture in Barcelona, as confirmed by the installation of a vinyl jukebox at the Bar Edén that contained the music of numerous contemporary US musicians. For a small sum—merely ten *céntimos*—customers could play recordings by Louis Armstrong, Duke Ellington, Fletcher Henderson, Coleman Hawkins, or Fats Waller.[30] In this context, Tete's mother would have been merely one of many music fans who owned 78s recorded by Fats and the Duke. Indeed, Tete Montoliu was thus born into a thriving 1930s jazz city where transnational connections with the music of US jazz artists were an everyday experience.

By the time that Tete was old enough to play his foot-pedal harmonium, however, all of this thriving jazz culture would become muted by Francoist Spain's ideologically driven culture war. Any musical practice that threatened its normative concept of conservative morality was suspect. The dictatorship was intent on eradicating the remaining traces of the cosmopolitan political and aesthetic cultures that had thrived in Jazz Age Barcelona. Nonetheless, despite such efforts, something from those earlier years lingered in the city's fabric even under the dictatorship. As time progressed and everyday life acquired whatever degree of functional normalcy was possible for residents in postwar Barcelona, Montoliu became the central figure around whom the city's residual jazz energies began to coalesce. This was true to some degree even as early as the late 1940s—as the pianist played in bands boasting his name, like El Conjunto Montoliu Jr. in the fall of 1947[31]— yet it was particularly true as the strength of the dictatorship waned. During the 1950s and 1960s, the pianist's fame in Barcelona and across Europe grew considerably.

It should come as no surprise that when Barcelona finally became the first city in Spain to host a jazz festival, in 1966, the Tete Montoliu Trio was the first act to perform. During this same time, Joan Rosselló, who ran the Jamboree club in Barcelona, had invited the trio to play at his club. The group's tenure at the Jamboree coincided with a brief period between 1965 and 1967 that some recognize as being the club's greatest years. The 1966 incarnation of the Tete Montoliu Trio included Erich Peter on bass and Billy Brooks on drums, and Tete would later remark that "[a]quest va ser un altre dels grans trios de la meva vida, dels que guardo els millors records" (this was another of the great trios of my life, of which I have the best memories).[32]

The I Festival Internacional de Jazz de Barcelona (Barcelona's First International Festival of Jazz), which took place from October 25 through November 6, 1966, even predated similar festivals in Paris and Montreux.[33] It was a culminating event, celebrating jazz's rise throughout the entirety of Catalonia during the period of 1951–65. Alfredo Papo sees these years as another golden age for jazz in Barcelona.[34] Tete's trio was given a privileged position in the 1966 festival's stunning lineup, which included the Dave Brubeck Quartet, the Max Roach Quintet with Sonny Rollins, Bud Freeman with the Alex Welsh Orchestra, the Uptown Swing All Stars, and the Stan Getz Quartet with Astrud Gilberto.[35] This festival brought welcome attention to existing jazz acts and encouraged further efforts to develop the cultural market for Catalan jazz. It also made a name in international jazz for both Tete Montoliu and the city of Barcelona. Tete's success in this re-emerging market owed much to both his strong Catalan identity and the connections he sustained with members of the popular song movement in Catalonia that was developing alongside his prominence in modern jazz in Europe.

Tete's Catalanism, *A tot jazz* (1965), and the *Nova Cançó*

Tete Montoliu's strong identification with the Catalan language, the urban culture of Barcelona, and Catalonia as a whole were important aspects of his ever-expanding international reputation. It is surely due to these identifications, combined with his prolific musical production and dedication to jazz, of course, that in his later years he received many public honors. These included the highest forms of recognition awarded by the municipal government of Barcelona and the regional government of Catalonia.[36] He was awarded the Medalla al Mérito del Ayuntamiento de Barcelona on March 18, 1983, and the Creu de Sant Jordi de la Generalitat on November 11, 1983. These honors came to him only in the post-dictatorship, however, after the death of Franco. Under Francoism, given the prohibitions against using the language or acknowledging the diversity of Spain's cultural geographies, it was more difficult to assert Catalan identity, let alone celebrate it.

Throughout his life, Tete was consistently proud to be from Barcelona, Catalonia. He sustained an oppositional attitude toward the excesses of Spanish nationalism both under the Franco dictatorship and following Spain's transition to democratic governance. The Barcelonan pianist loved spending time in his native city, not just because of the opportunities it offered him to play music, but also for how it allowed him to reconnect with his Catalan identity.[37] Speaking with Miquel Jurado in 1992, he had the opportunity to reflect on the feelings of belonging he experienced upon returning to his home city once again, after a stint performing elsewhere. It seems that, in this respect, Madrid was just as far away as Berlin or Copenhagen. He commented on his connection to Barcelona by referring to the sports team and the traditional food that have become highly symbolic for Catalans:

Jo no puc estar sense ser a Barcelona. M'agrada la pudor que té aquesta ciutat, sense poder escoltar els partits del Barça, sense poder menjar pa amb tomàquet. Se'n pot menjar a tot arreu, però el pa no fa gust de pa ni el tomàquet de tomàquet i em ve una tristesa horrible. La prova és que quan jo vivia a Madrid, cada setmana em portaven a l'aeroport i m'agafaven un bitllet per venir a Barcelona, perquè si no m'agafava una depressió que no podia suportar-ho.[38]

(I can't go without being in Barcelona. I like the vibe this city has, [and I can't go] without being able to listen to the football matches Barça plays, without being able to eat tomato bread. You can eat it anywhere, but the bread doesn't taste like bread, nor the tomato like tomato and it makes me horribly sad. The proof is that when I was living in Madrid, every week they'd drive me to the airport and give me a ticket to come to Barcelona, because if I didn't I would suffer from an unbearable depression.)

Barcelona never lost that feeling of being a home for him, no matter how far and wide Tete traveled, and despite his lengthy stays in Copenhagen, for example, a city that he enjoyed tremendously.

One anecdote in particular drives home just how important it was for Tete to maintain his connection to sport. Certainly the pianist's passion for the Barcelona football club (Barça) was quite well known, and he often made references to the sport itself in many interviews, stating, for instance "Jo vaig aprendre de molt petit que Catalunya era un país i el Barça simbolitza aquest país" (I learned very young that Catalonia was a country and that Barça was its symbol).[39] Once, when the pianist was set to accompany Joan Manuel Serrat in a musical performance that had been scheduled at the same time as a Barça match, he felt obligated to devise an appropriate solution. Using a hidden earphone, Tete was able to listen to the match even as he ran his fingers over the piano keys. Journalist Frederic Porta has confirmed that this was not merely an urban legend by discussing it with Montoliu himself during an interview. In the Catalan-language newspaper *Avui*, Porta later described the strange performance that resulted from Tete's emotional responses as he followed the action of the match: "Segons anava el Barça, la *jam session* variava de sentiment. El piano entristia o generava alegria en cada nota, les peces se succeïen segons el joc de l'equip" (The feeling of the performance varied in accordance with how Barça played. The piano generated sadness or happiness in each note, the pieces followed one another depending on how the team was playing).[40] While it is hard to imagine that such an intensely professional musician would prioritize anything over a performance, the symbolic association between Barça and Catalan identity, for Tete, seems to have been of a higher order even than jazz.

Regarding the question of Tete's Catalanism, one easily finds supporting evidence. The pianist's uncompromising affirmation of his Catalan identity can be seen in his perennial refusal to be introduced as a Spanish musician during his gigs. Miquel Jurado notes of Tete that "[n]o deixava, per exemple, que ningú el presentés com un pianista espanyol i sempre puntualitzava: pianista català" (he wouldn't let, for example, anyone introduce him as a Spanish pianist and would always [take the opportunity to] punctuate: Catalan pianist).[41] This refusal is instructive in that it encourages scholars to expand beyond the construction of Spanishness to embrace the true heterogeneity of jazz production in the Iberian Peninsula.

Early in the post-dictatorship years, Tete Montoliu became a member of the Catalanist party Convergència i Unió. Speaking in an interview on the question of his Catalan identity, he once said: "Jo no sóc espanyol. En tot cas, ho podem agregar dient que Catalunya és un país dintre d'un estat. És la solució més fàcil però jo no puc fer res per canviar-ho. A mi m'agradaria molt tenir un passaport per anar a Madrid" (I am not Spanish. In any case, we can add that Catalonia is a country within a state. It's the easiest solution but I cannot do anything to change it. I would very much like to have a passport to go to Madrid).[42] For him, as for many Catalanists, there was a hard line separating Catalan culture from any construction of Spanishness. From this perspective, the hegemony of the dictatorial Spanish state functioned to obscure the brute fact of the rich linguistic and cultural diversity that can be found across its many territories.

The liner notes on some of Tete's vinyl albums offer the opportunity to assess popular conceptions of Spain's linguistic, cultural, and political geographies. Such notes do not always differentiate Catalonia from Spain as emphatically as Montoliu himself might have preferred. On Ib Skogaard's virtually identical liner notes for the SteepleChase releases of both *Tete!* (1974) and *Catalonian Fire* (1974), the pianist is introduced with this unambiguous, even thoroughly educational, declaration: "Tete Montoliu is Spanish, but he would like you to know that first of all he is a Catalan!" Elsewhere, comments on the backs of album covers can be more ambiguous. On liner notes for a collaboration with Buddy Tate, released by Storyville Records in the United States as *Tate a Tete at La Fontaine* (1975), Alun Morgan first writes that

"Tete is from the north-east province of Catalonia," but later refers to him as "the young Spanish pianist." If Spain/Spanish and Catalonia/Catalan are diametrically opposed references—as Tete's own politics would suggest—then it seems that at best Morgan's description is insensitive to the jazz artist's preferences. Chris Sheridan perhaps adopts a practical attitude of sorts when, on *Tête à Tete* (1976), he affirms for readers that "Catalonia, in Spain, has given us Tete Montoliu."

Over time, the liner notes for his albums show a certain change in transnational perceptions of his identity. Consider the following two US album releases, separated from each other by twenty years: on the back of *Kirk in Copenhagen* (Mercury Records, 1963), the US saxophonist's wife, Edith Kirk, describes Tete solely as "an outstanding Spanish jazz musician," while on *Carmina* (Jazzizz Records, 1984), Jim Brown refers to him as a "proud and intense Catalonian." By the time that Jørgen Frigård pens the notes for the 1986 release of *Lush Life* (1971), there is seemingly no need to make geographical references to either Spain or Catalonia. Yet the slippages in commentators' identifications of the pianist that occur along the way—that is, the tendency to refer to Tete as a Spanish artist—are quite curious, given that they appear precisely as part of a musical object designed to be sold as an authentic product of the artist's jazz work. These slippages reflect the distance between the artist's musical production itself and the way this musical production is packaged and sold to consumers. While liner notes are a genre steeped in or adjacent to professional music criticism, they nonetheless reveal popular attitudes. This is undoubtedly the case of liner note authors trying to grapple with Tete's transnational positioning. The pianist was, after all, a Catalan, from Spain, largely recording in Denmark, Germany, and Holland, and playing in a modern jazz idiom with strong ties to the American consumer market.

As he rose to international renown, Tete progressively became one of the most sought-after collaborators and bandleaders of his domestic Catalan musical market. The way he balanced both of these roles in his career as a professional musician was key to his success. On *Kirk in Copenhagen* (1963) his performances were somewhat restrained in order to help foreground the work of the lead saxophonist. As intensely as he could play, Tete seems to have always known when to play the mannered accompanist. In his role as a bandleader, too, he was becoming equally sought-after, as evident in his trio's selection to headline the 1966 Barcelona Festival of Jazz. Montoliu's reputation in European circuits was a powerful draw—his trio's visibility could be leveraged to propel the careers of female jazz vocalists, for example. Since his early years he had collaborated with vocalists Pilar Morales and Pia Beck. Vocalist-jazz collaborations of this sort became more plentiful in the 1960s in the transnational Catalan-European market. The vinyl release of *Núria Feliu with Booker Ervin* (1965) by the Edigsa label brought the Tete Montoliu Trio together with the Catalan vocalist and the US tenor saxophonist. At the Festival d'Antibes-Juan Les Pins in France in 1966, his trio also featured singer Anita O'Day, while substituting Billy Brooks for John Poole on drums. The Concèntric label released the 7″ vinyl EPs *Tete Montoliu Presenta Elia Fleta* in 1966 and *Elia Fleta con Tete Montoliu Trio* in 1967.[43] This collaboration is in truth a testament to not only the pianist's reputation but also that of the singer, who was designated as "la millor cantant espanyola de 1966" (the best singer of 1966) by Radio Peninsular in Spain.[44] And when the Spanish Chamber of Commerce organized a series of events dedicated to Barcelona in 1967, they invited Tete Montoliu and Núria Feliu to be part of it, a sign that the rest of Spain was slowly—very slowly, perhaps—catching on to what all the buzz was about.[45]

While the modern jazz pianist recorded more frequently with Danish, Dutch, and German labels, the Tete Montoliu Trio's two vinyl LPs released on the Barcelona-based label Concèntric in 1965 deserve greater recognition as milestones for Catalan jazz. *A tot jazz* and *A tot jazz 2* were not Tete's first domestic recordings, but they nonetheless had the potential to truly cement his reputation as a bandleader for both Spanish and European audiences. He had a slim catalogue of previous recordings dating from the late 1940s, which had been released under a series of shifting group names and had thus been unlikely to reach a wide or consistent audience. As documented in chapter 1, Tete Montoliu was never credited for his contributions on three tracks of Lionel Hampton's *Jazz Flamenco* (1956). A decade later, however, these two *A tot jazz* albums presented audiences in Catalonia, Spain, and Europe as a whole with an undeniable truth: Tete was not just an accompanist, but also an accomplished bandleader who, moreover, was well-versed in the contemporary currents, styles, and controversies of modern jazz.[46]

A tot jazz and *A tot jazz 2* were released during a time when the Catalan cultural market had still not yet regained its vibrancy. It can help readers to situate these albums within the context of Spain's dictatorial history. Official forms of censorship were bolstered by the creation of the Ministry of Information and Tourism in 1951, loosened with a law passed on March 18, 1966, and finally ended on April 1, 1977, almost two years after the dictator's death in 1975.[47] In 1969, Prince Juan Carlos was named as Franco's appointed successor, an event that in practice would encourage more overt discussions of the futures of minoritized cultural markets. But at the time that Tete talked about the two jazz LPs with Josep Maria Espinàs, artistic director of Concèntric, the idea was "una cosa inaudita en aquella época en un mercat tan pobre com el català per al qual el jazz ni tan sols existia" (unheard of in that era in a market that was as impoverished as the Catalan one was and in which jazz hardly existed).[48] Moreover, the fact that Concèntric was based in Barcelona also poses a real challenge to accounts of European jazz labels that tend to validate only established centers such as Timeless (Holland) and SteepleChase (Denmark).[49]

Tete has explained that the tracks selected for the first *A tot jazz* LP were a way of paying tribute to the jazz artists who had inspired him or with whom he had shared the stage.[50] "Scandia Sky" was a tribute to Kenny Dorham; "I Guess I'll Hang My Tears Out to Dry" was a tribute to Dexter Gordon; "Au Privave," of course, honored the song's composer, Charlie Parker; "Fly Me to the Moon" was a version of the tune that Tete thought Donald Byrd would appreciate; "Lament" was a tribute to its recording by Miles Davis and Gil Evans on *Miles Ahead*; and "Stella by Starlight," which launched the LP, was motivated by Montoliu's memory of hearing the tune interpreted by Davis. There is more of a relaxed feel to this album, such that it is tempting to classify it as adjacent to the cool West Coast jazz that developed in California in the 1950s with notable musicians such as the pianist Dave Brubeck.

The tracks on *A tot jazz 2* continue with the cool jazz sound—for example on "Polka Dots and Moonbeams" (Johnny Burke and Jimmy Van Heusen), one of the most frequently recorded standards; "Secret Love," a composition by Samuel Fain and Paul Francis Webster written for the motion picture *Calamity Jane* (1953); and "Come Rain or Come Shine," by Harold Arlen and Johnny Mercer. On such low-tempo tracks, Erich Peter and Billy Brooks are just as relaxed as Tete, and they provide effective musical ground using textures that heighten the emotive qualities of the pianist's approach. Nevertheless, "Chim Chim Cheree" (R. M. Sherman, R. B. Sherman), which opens the album, strikes a somewhat different tone. Tete begins with a meandering and discordant piano intro, before launching into the song's melody. Just before a brief solo interlude by Peter, the pianist deconstructs the melodic line, by both presenting and eroding a possible harmony. Following each delivery of the melody, Tete serves up thick chord improvisations in the form of crashes that sustain tension throughout the tune and contrast with the sparse sound on the album's low-tempo tracks. These dense chord structures are never stabilized; instead, they are continually subjected to modifications by Montoliu. This 1965 performance may remind listeners of the style of

US pianist McCoy Tyner, who was known for his collaborations with John Coltrane on *A Love Supreme* (1964) and *Live at the Village Vanguard, Again!* (1966). The track "Israel" (John Carisi) highlights Brooks during recurring extended drum fills that function as concise solos, and Peter indulges in a splendid bass solo himself on "Sometime Ago," a composition by Argentine pianist Sergio Mihánovich. Both sides of *A tot jazz 2* end with up-tempo standards. Ever a fan of Dizzy Gillespie, Montoliu here records "Salt Peanuts" (Gillespie and Kenny Clarke) to close side one, and "Have You Met Miss Jones?" (Rodgers and Hart) is then the side-two closer.[51]

One way to gauge the projected impact of the *A tot jazz* LPs is to examine Albert Mallofré's liner notes on the gatefold re-release from 1989.[52] His comments are a clear attempt to provide context for listeners unfamiliar with Tete's career to that point and establish him as a Catalan artist with an international reputation. The description approaches the excessive praise demanded of hagiography when Mallofré concludes that Tete is not "el millor d'Espanya, ni el millor d'Europa, ni el millor de res, sinó justament un dels creadors més sòlids, més fèrtils, més madurs, saborosos y substancials que es poden trobar en tot el panorama mundial del jazz d'avui" (the best in Spain, nor the best in Europe, nor the best of anywhere else, but instead one of the most solid, most productive, most established, appealing and substantial [musicians] that can be found in the wider global panorama of today's jazz). Mallofré also extends this excessive praise to the reputation of the Concèntric label itself, which he takes to be contributing to the circuits of civilized communication that distinguish neither between "races ni de credos" (races nor credos). This rhetoric, of course, is representative of a much broader theme of the transnational extension of jazz music. Jazz in global contexts is often imbued—in its marketing and reception—with the power to connect, to bring both musicians and listeners of varying languages, cultures, and geographies together in a gathering of difference. The point is, however, that these two albums are a concerted attempt to inject the notion of Catalan jazz into a transnational market. This was a growing global market that for too long had ignored the heterogeneity of musical culture under the Spanish state in favor of a tidy notion of Spanishness.

Josep Maria Espinàs was quite aware of the social factors that impeded the development of Catalan culture and music under the dictatorship. He was not merely the artistic director of Concèntric during the production and release of both volumes of the Tete Montoliu Trio's *A tot jazz* (1965), but also an accomplished singer in his own right. As a vocal artist, his musical production was aligned with social forces that underscored the persistence, presence, and value of Catalan identity in a dictatorial context that sought its eradication. In her article on the legacy of the *nova cançó* published in the *Journal of Spanish Cultural Studies*, Pepa Novell reminds readers that Espinàs was one of a small group of singers who defiantly performed their songs in Catalan in a prominent concert delivered in 1961.[53] For many critics, the Catalan new song is born with that concert, after which sixteen performers form a group called Els Setze Jutges. This name comes from a Catalan tongue-twister full of fricative sounds thought to be difficult for Castilian speakers to pronounce—"setze jutges d'un jutjat menjen fetge d'un penjat" (sixteen judges on a tribunal eat the liver of a hanged man). Historian Robert Hughes contextualizes the movement within Catalan history in his sprawling epic *Barcelona*, wherein he writes that "[p]op singers who wrote and performed in Catalan saw themselves as the heir of Carles Aribau i Farriols, the romantic poet whose 'Oda a la Pàtria,' written in Catalan in 1833, was the emblematic starting point of the nineteenth-century cultural separatist movement in Barcelona known as the Renaixença."[54] Els Setze Jutges included five women singers—including Guillermina Motta and Maria del Mar Bonet—and the group's legacy would have a collective impact not merely in Catalonia, but also on Iberian and Latin American music broadly considered.

The transnational dimension of Tete Montoliu's modern jazz project should be approached in parallel to the transnational dimensions of the *nova cançó*. As Catherine Boyle recounts in "The Politics of Popular Music: On the Dynamics of New Song," protest songs by members of the *nova cançó* movement—such as "La estaca" (The Stake) by Lluís Llach and "Al vent" (To the wind) by Raimon—would become touchstones for international audiences.[55] The New Song impacted artists whose musical communities spanned Argentina, Brazil, Cuba, and Chile, as well as Spain. In due course, Llach's iconic contribution "La estaca" even became a song of choice among political movements in Poland, Afghanistan, and Tunisia.[56] Of course, as Jaume Ayats and Maria Salicrú-Maltas underscore, the *nova cançó* itself draws from American singer-songwriters such as Pete Seeger, Woody Guthrie, Bob Dylan, and Joan Baez, whose music also had great resonance in Latin America.[57] The original Catalan auteurs associated with the movement had themselves been inspired by French singers.[58] Here, too, as in the case of modern jazz music, transnational influences are the norm rather than the exception. Within Spain, the way that Catalan popular music influenced Basque and Galician communities, not to mention movements in Andalusia,

Aragon, and Extremadura, for example, also suggests its privileged role in galvanizing critique of the dictatorship.

Among members of Els Setze Jutges, the case of Joan Manuel Serrat, with whom Tete had a long-standing friendship, is most notable. As Boyle relates, the singer Raimon had entered and won a Mediterranean Song Festival in 1963, with a contribution in Catalan. In subsequent years, however, European contests began disallowing entries with Catalan lyrics. The stage was thus set for controversy when, in 1968, Serrat was chosen to represent Spain in the European Song Contest. He set out to perform in Catalan, but refused to continue when he was informed that he would have to sing in Castilian. Boyle alludes to the complex international attitudes in play when she notes that the contest "was won that year by the singer Massiel, singing in Castilian the song Serrat had refused to sing."[59] Elsewhere, it has been alleged that the contest was rigged.[60] In truth, Serrat had already been singing on tour in both Spanish and Catalan, a decision that had unfortunately raised the hackles of divergent sets of fans. Here is a figure who could speak out against the dictatorship—as when he condemned the regime's 1975 execution of Basque ETA and anti-fascist revolutionaries, and was banned from entering Spain for one year as a consequence—and yet would still be subjected to judgment by Catalan fans who saw his singing in Castilian as a crossover-market betrayal.[61]

Given the ongoing controversies surrounding Serrat,[62] it is important to underscore that Tete Montoliu's support for the New Song was not limited to a single figure, even if he performed most frequently with Joan Manuel. Instead, he extended this support to a number of others in the movement, among them Guillermina Motta, Quico Pi de la Serra, and Enric Barbat.[63] The pianist once accompanied Maria del Mar Bonet in a televised performance of the song "Jim," and Marina Rossell in a performance of "Les feuilles mortes" at Barcelona's Hivernacle.[64] Despite these and other forms of support for members of the new song, Tete remained intent on defining himself apart from the movement: "Mai no vaig tenir res a veure directament amb la nova cançó, però era una mica com el pare de tots ells" (I never had anything to do directly with the new song, but I was a bit like the father of them all).[65]

His collaborations with Joan Manuel Serrat were certainly more extensive. Interestingly, as they discovered when first meeting each other, their connection went beyond the realm of music. Serrat's father was in fact the electrician who did work on Tete's family home.[66] In 1967 the pair of musicians performed together in a festival put on by the prestigious Palau de la Música in Barcelona, and they went on tour together in 1968. The recording of *Tete*

Montoliu interpreta a Serrat (1969) is another milestone in Tete's career (see figure 3.1), and it is a testament to the enduring impact of that recording that it was later followed up with the CD-only release of *Tete Montoliu interpreta a Serrat Hoy* (1996). The former album, however, is additionally important because it provides the most concentrated early evidence of Tete's intention to record Catalonian folk songs. With his confidence undoubtedly increased through this experience, the pianist would later invest even further in the connections between this folk tradition and innovative approaches to jazz composition in preparation for the freer environment of the post-dictatorship.

Figure 3.1 *Tete Montoliu interpreta a Serrat* (1969, Madrid, Spain, Discophon SC 2050), cover, scan by the author.

Catalan Jazz Composition and *Catalonian Folksongs* (1977)

Whether due to the release of the *A tot jazz* LPs in 1965, the Tete Montoliu Trio's headlining of the Barcelona jazz festival in 1966, or simply because the pianist's hard-earned reputation had finally reached a saturation point in the transnational market for modern jazz in Europe, opportunities for the Catalan pianist expanded considerably in the late 1960s. The pianist's collaborations with singer and composer Joan Manuel Serrat are among the most significant of these opportunities in the sense that they bolstered his reputation, connecting him with the cultural undercurrents of the protest song in Catalonia. The result was that Tete became the progenitor of what one might call Catalan modern jazz.

The Discophon release of *Tete Montoliu interpreta a Serrat* (1969), which was recorded on the heels of the pair's tour together, certainly testifies to his increasing domestic fame. In truth, only Side A of the album features songs composed by Serrat, and it closes with Montoliu's own original composition titled "Sintonía." Side B opens with a song composed by Guillermina Motta, "Qui em diria on van," which is followed by four traditional and popular Catalan songs. The first track on the album is a medley of songs that begins with "Marta," and runs through "Una guitarra," "Cançó de matinada," and "Me'n vaig a peu." One thing many fans may not know is that Serrat's song "Marta" was actually written by both Serrat and Montoliu.[67] "Una guitarra" is significant, too, as it was one of the first songs Serrat recorded as an artist. Here it is necessary to acknowledge that Tete's recordings of Serrat's songs are not limited to a single album release, but are also scattered throughout his discography. Some examples are "Camí avall" (*Songs for Love*, 1971), "De mica en mica" (*Songs for Love*, 1971), "Paraules d'amor" (*Words of Love*, 1976), and "El meu carrer" (*Catalonian Nights, Vol. 2*, 1980).[68] Tete's *Catalonian Folksongs* (1977) also contained a number of Serrat compositions, a fact to which this section will return, and "Cançó de matinada," which was one of Serrat's most emotive and popular songs, appears both there and on the Serrat-inspired 1969 album. The song was particularly significant due to the fact that "it became a number one best-seller throughout Spain and helped to popularize the New Song movement."[69] Similarly, "Paraules d'amor" is a composition that "remains an enduring symbol of the New Song"[70] and has exerted a proportionally similar impact on the jazz work of Tete Montoliu.[71]

Precisely because this version of "Paraules d'amor" is so concise, the second track on *Tete Montoliu interpreta a Serrat* invites repeated listenings. The lyricism of Tete's phrasings conveys his emotional response. This response is, of course, not just to the song—not just to the fact that it was composed by a friend and musical collaborator—but moreover to its association with the *nova cançó* and thus with the pianist's emotional connection to his Catalan identity. In the track's immediate beginning, Montoliu's pacing can sound rote. This may very well be just a conceit, however, since as this recording of "Words of Love" moves on, Tete quickly adjusts to allow the silences between notes and passages of the song to become more and more pronounced. Toward the end of the track, he produces a certain wistfulness through a controlled, two-handed curtain of descending notes and finishes with a few flourishes that one might be excused for hearing as musical teardrops. Comparing this track to the up-tempo version of "Paraules d'amor," from the later solo piano album *Words of Love* (1976), the earlier performance of the song seems to be stripped-down, reduced to its emotional core. The very short duration of the song (2'39") on *Tete Montoliu interpreta a Serrat* supports the idea that this version represents a distillation of emotion. Quite simply, the pianist is searching for purity rather than extravagance. Tete avoids here many of the playful tendencies that are endemic to his inimitable style. He does not abruptly change speed, nor does he display the technical virtuosity or fast runs for which he is known. By contrast, the 1976 recording comes in at a much longer duration (5'42"), which creates space for his characteristic improvisational playfulness and heady exploration of the song rather than the concentrated emotional depth he delivers in the concise 1969 version.

Perhaps most surprising for those expecting a full album of solo piano performances from Tete is the fact that the final two tracks on Side B of the album are delivered in tandem with the members of his trio. On both "La dama d'Aragó" and "El cant dels ocells," Erich Peter (bass) and Peer Wyboris (drums) join the pianist, which brings an up-tempo swing to an otherwise quiet release. Listeners should note that this album was actually performed and recorded on April 23, 1969, and that on this same date the trio played and recorded the collective improvisation that would later be released as *Lliure jazz* (1969).[72] As a consequence, certain similarities can be heard that stem from the energy of a single recording session. The most notable of these may well be that one of the standout moments of Erich Peter's bass line on *Lliure jazz*—mentioned earlier in chapter 2, the propulsive riff centered around an insistent single-note that emerges toward the end of that vinyl record's Side

A—is virtually the same as he performs it here in "La dama d'Aragó." While the energy built-up in the trio's free jazz attempt dissipates there with little payoff, however, here the bassline coheres as an organic part of the piece and provides continuity from the beginning through the end of the track. That said, the similarities between these separate vinyl releases cut both ways. There are certain digressions within "La dama d'Aragó" where Tete seems to wander off into a noticeably freer realm and the bass and drums drop out. One of these wandering moments occurs, for example, just before the group comes together for the final performance of the song's theme.

Tete Montoliu's connection with Serrat and the *nova cançó* in general seems to have encouraged him to intensify the connections between his jazz practice and his Catalan identity. Even though the dictatorship continued until 1975 and the Spanish Constitution was not promulgated until 1978, the late 1960s and early 1970s were defined by Spain's continued opening to the exterior. At this point in Spanish history, cultural markets and institutions were hoping to recover some of vibrancy lost to Francoism's legacy of brutal repression.[73] Beginning with 1974's release of *Catalonian Fire* on the SteepleChase label, one sees a clear uptick in album and song titles that prominently asserted his connection with Catalonia. A few representative examples should suffice to chart Tete's more intentional pursuit of a Catalan-inflected strain of modern jazz.

Tete's original and lengthy composition "Catalan Suite" (20′01″) was recorded during a session that spanned February 15–16, 1976, and was released on *Tête a Tete* the same year. In composing the piece, the pianist stitched together five traditional Catalonian songs, much as he had done with the "Marta"-driven medley on *Tete Montoliu interpreta a Serrat* (1969). There are two key differences, however. The first involves personnel. While Tete had played solo on that earlier medley, here Niels-Henning Ørsted Pedersen (bass) and Al "Tootie" Heath (drums) provide some stunning accompaniment as well as extended solos that function as bridges between the movements that make up the extended piece. Tete's reflections on the trio's process for those February 1976 sessions attribute a spontaneity to the musicians' collective performance that can be heard on the album's three lengthy recorded tracks:

Ens reuníem per dinar en un restaurant xinès o per prendre una copa, parlàvem de tot, de a vida, de política, de dones, de qualsevol cosa menys de música, explicàvem acudits i després tocàvem. Tan fàcil com això. Per no assajar no havíem ni assajat la *Catalan Suite*, formada per fragments de cançons tradicionals catalanes que ells no coneixien. No feia falta: la química entre tots tres era enorme. Un cop a l'estudi, jo els vaig explicar l'estructura de les cançons que volia incloure en aquella suite i ho vam enregistrar directament en una sola presa.[74]

(We would meet for lunch at a Chinese restaurant or for a drink, we would talk about everything, from life to politics to women to anything but music, we would tell jokes and afterward we would play. It was as easy as that. Because we hadn't rehearsed at all, we hadn't rehearsed the *Catalan Suite*, which was made up of fragments of traditional Catalan songs they didn't know. And there was no need: the chemistry between the three of us was magnificent. Once we were in the studio, I explained the structure of the songs I wanted to include in that suite and we recorded it directly in a single take.

Just as important as the chemistry among the trio's personnel—not to mention the musical stitching involved in the piece, which speaks to a certain compositional intentionality—is the title "Catalan Suite" itself. The composition's title goes beyond the idea that traditional Catalonian folk songs could serve as the source material for jazz music to suggest that they might also constitute the building blocks for a potentially career-defining oeuvre. It is not necessary for listeners to be familiar with those building blocks to appreciate the track. The composition moves through meditative piano, bass, and drum solos while returning regularly to the trio's rollicking groove in a way that seems natural. It is not surprising that, when pressed by his friend and interviewer Miquel Jurado, Montoliu would later list this album as the clear favorite among his own recordings.[75]

Other examples are not hard to find in Montoliu's body of work. On March 20, 1976, Tete recorded "Iru Damachu" and "Pietsie." Both were based on traditional Catalan songs, as Bob Porter discussed in the liner notes to the *Words of Love* release in 1978. A few years later, with John Heard (bass) and Al "Tootie" Heath (drums) on May 29–31, 1980, he recorded the tracks that would subsequently be released as *Catalonian Nights, Vol. 1* (1980), *Catalonian Nights, Vol. 2* (1980, released in 1989), and *Catalonian Nights, Vol. 3* (1980, released in 1998, following Tete's death in 1997).[76]

Then there is *Vampyria* (1974) to consider. Recorded as a duo with Jordi Sabatés, this album is an estranging and entrancing musical experience, and yet one that is no less connected with Tete's intent to chart a trajectory of Catalan-inflected modern jazz. Sabatés was himself an accomplished pianist—known for original compositions, for providing soundtracks to films, and for an avant-garde aesthetics he demonstrated also on this inimitable and mesmerizing album. *Vampyria* has also proven to be quite popular in certain circles. It was recognized as the Best Catalan Jazz Recording by *Jaç* magazine and as the Best Catalan Jazz Record since 1920 by Spanish music critics. The strangest aspect of the album for fans familiar with Montoliu's discography may be that here he plays the electric piano, layered over the acoustic piano played by Sabatés. Even if Montoliu's playing seems a bit hesitant, perhaps due to a personal distaste for the electronic sound, his performance remains compelling and his style varied. Neither is his ability to channel the style of other performers hindered by the electronic medium. For example, at one point during "Invitation au voyage," he vamps back and forth on two warm chords in a way that recalls the rhythmic two-chord oscillation on "What Game Shall We Play Today," the final track from Gary Burton and Chick Corea's classic electronic-acoustic duo collaboration *Crystal Silence*. On that album from 1973, it was Corea who played the similar two-chord oscillation, and it is likely, given Tete's interest in Chick's piano work, that he might have acquired the popular album during his travels. Interestingly, too, the Barcelona fusion band Jarka, which had been formed by Jordi Sabatés himself in the early 1970s, was heavily influenced by Gary Burton's electric sound in particular.

If there was a sign that at long last Tete was finally receiving the recognition he was due within Catalonia, it was his invitation to perform at the Palau de la Música in Barcelona. This performance was possibly the culminating moment of his career, as the prestige accompanying an artist's performance at such a venerated venue might be compared to a performance at New York's Carnegie Hall. For Montoliu it was doubtless just as thrilling, keeping in mind that he would also perform at Carnegie Hall itself in the 1980s. *Tete Montoliu al Palau* (1979) was released as a double LP commemorating that evening's event. This was the same year in which *Billboard* magazine in the United States was calling for its readers to "See Spain as Emerging Jazz Site," the latter being the title of an article that mentioned the Tete Montoliu Trio alongside notes of the performances of modern jazz pianists such as Dave Brubeck, Herbie Hancock, and Chick Corea in various Spanish cities.[77] The Palau release's liner notes, written by Albert Mallofré, bemoan the reality that Tete's fame around the world still outweighed his acceptance at home: "Arreu del món, en TETE és un èxit i, a casa seva, 'no es ven'!" (Around the world, TETE is a success and, in his own home they say, "he doesn't sell!"). The comments on this subject—printed in both Catalan and Spanish, presumably as a nod to an expanding potential audience—are actually quite extensive and thread the entirety of the notes. Nevertheless, the brief and lucid quotation included here is quite to the point. That is, why did it take so long for Barcelona, Catalonia, and Spain to recognize the incredible home-grown talent in their own backyard? The Palau performance was orchestrated to rectify that lamentable situation, and at the end of his notes, Mallofré sternly cautions his readers not to let this opportunity pass them by.

The compositions selected by the pianist for the Palau performance are highly representative of the influences he embraced in his forging of a career in modern jazz.[78] It is the integration of the totality of these influences into a musical production linked with Catalan identity that cements his reputation as a modern jazz performer. The pianist was frequently eager to display the interconnection of these influences and the personal meaning they held for him, as a brief consideration of the structure of his Palau concert will demonstrate.

Tete understood and appreciated, as well as any jazz performer, that the roots of the US jazz style were to be found in African American blues traditions, and thus he accordingly begins with the original composition "Blues del Palau." He once stated unequivocally in a televised interview that "[e]l blues es la esencia de la música del jazz" (the blues is the essence of jazz music).[79] The pianist was known for performing and recording a great number of original tunes labeled as blues, and those that stand out are usually dedicated to a beloved person or place in his life. Not only did he play "Blues for Nuria," "Blues for Anna," "Blues for Line," "Blues for Perla," "Blues for Myself," "Blues for Wim and Maxine," and "Blues for Coltrane," but also "New England Blues" at a concert in Boston, "Blues at Steeple Chase" when recording with Eddie Harris, "Blues before Lunch" and "Blues after Lunch" when recording with Chick Corea for Contemporary in Los Angeles, and "Blues del San Juan Evangelista" when performing at the eponymous school in Madrid. This is not even to mention his interest in blues titles composed by modern jazz composers such as John Coltrane, Miles Davis, Charlie Parker, and Chuck Israels, for example. One is compelled to imagine that for Tete, as perhaps for other jazz artists as well, honoring someone or some place with a "Blues" was the highest form of compliment. Thus when he begins the Palau de la Música concert with a "Blues del Palau," it must be taken as a doubled acknowledgment. It is a way of honoring the venue, and also by extension a way of honoring Barcelona as a whole—a sort of humble musical genuflection to the city whose admiration he had sought since he was a child. Simultaneously, of course, it is a nod to the transnational history of modern jazz and, moreover, a stark demonstration of the fact that jazz in Europe cannot refuse to acknowledge its connection to the Black American experience.[80]

The grounding of jazz in the Black American experience is also on display in Tete's selection of compositions like Duke Ellington's "Come Sunday," and the Sonny Rollins original "Airegin." As mentioned earlier, the Ellington piece was first performed at Carnegie Hall as part of the *Black, Brown and Beige* (1943) suite, and was a song deeply steeped in the social and spiritual lives of members of Black American communities. For its part, "Airegin," by the saxophonist Rollins, was a song that the pianist had recorded before, on *Secret Love* (1977) and *Lush Life* (1971), for example. The latter album in fact opens with "Airegin," where Tete doubles down on the song's already strong energy and complex rhythmic thrust. In the Palau performance, the pianist opens by alternating between playing the theme in a disfigured modernist mode and an almost classical mode before repeating it straight. During an improvised middle section, his fast runs, flirtation with recursive note sequences, perpetual rhythmic changes, and predilection for hitting clumps of keys together as if splashing paint on a canvas add a characteristic Montoliu texture to the song. It is of note that "Airegin" is "Nigeria" spelled backward, and that Rollins reportedly had been inspired by a magazine photograph of Nigerian dancers to compose a song that in practice speaks to the notion of a transnational Black diaspora.[81] In addition, the performance of two songs composed by Thelonious Monk—"Round Midnight" and "Blue Monk"—showcase one of Tete's hallmark influences while also recognizing a pioneering figure of the shift toward 1940s bebop in the American jazz form.[82]

On the last side of the Palau concert's double LP, Montoliu reserves a space for a medley of traditional Catalan songs—"Cançó del lladre," "La dama d'Aragó," and "El cant dels ocells," the latter adapted also by cellist Pau Casals as a favorite tune[83]—as well as his own original composition "Jo vull que m'acariciis." At 10'01", the latter piece is one of the longest on the release, along with "Round Midnight" (17'45") and also, quite understandably, the traditional three-song medley (11'57"). Through these selections, the pianist folds his love of Catalan language and culture and his identity as a Catalan composer into the transnational legacy of modern jazz. The personal, the professional, and the political are thus all subsumed in this iconic performance.

Beyond its historical importance for investigations of the development of Catalan modern jazz, close listeners will find a treasure trove of remarkable details in the tracks on *Tete Montoliu al Palau*. One such example occurs on the performance of Slide Hampton's tune "The End of Love." In the midst of an improvisation, Tete's right hand throws in a quick quotation of the punctuating nonsense phrasing he originally composed as the end of the abrupt initial theme from "Blues for Nuria" (*Piano for Nuria*, 1968). This self-referential flourish works musically and also meta-musically. It serves as a way of introducing discord over a hastily advancing, one might say speed-walking, left-hand bassline—thus producing the aesthetics of unevenness that for Tete was synonymous with modern jazz. Yet in referring to and even quoting from the artist's own previous jazz work, it reveals how Montoliu allowed himself the pleasure of reflecting on his own career and transposing that reflection into his Palau performance for others to hear.

While Tete's performance at the Palau and its subsequent vinyl release by Edigsa provided crucial recognition of the value he had amassed through his jazz work in both domestic and European markets, it was arguably the release of *Catalonian Folksongs* (1977) that brought him to the attention of jazz fans in the United States.[84] This album is important for critics on a few interrelated levels of analysis: economic, cultural, and sociopolitical.

The Catalan cultural market had grown substantially in the later years of the Franco dictatorship, and this improvement surely resulted in no small measure from the *nova cançó*'s popularity. An instructive parallel here would be with the Catalan literary market's resurgence: in 1976, finally, "the number of books published in Catalan per year reached the same figures as in 1936 (around 800 titles)."[85] In 1965 an album of Catalonian folk songs released by a jazz artist who spent most of his time outside of Barcelona in other European cities may not have been viable, economically speaking. It is worth remembering that *A tot jazz* (1965)—in its formulation and inclusion of standards and recognizable jazz fare—sought merely to legitimize Tete as a modern jazz artist who was still relatively unknown within Spain. Thus, many of the recordings released there were modern jazz selections rather than the Catalan-inflected themes one can hear in his jazz work of the 1970s. Yet in 1960—five years prior to *A tot jazz*, before the significant 1961 concert by singers who would become part of Els Setze Jutges, and in the same jazz landscapes dominated by *Sketches of Spain*—a Catalonian folk-song jazz album would have been much less viable. This is not just because there was not yet a market for Catalan jazz, but precisely because Tete had not yet forged that market through his musical practice.

Politically, too, the Franco dictatorship's reputation for brutal violence may have largely prevented Americans from exploring nuances related to the now suppressed linguistic and cultural diversity of Spain. As evidenced in this book's earlier discussion of Richard Wright's late-1950s memoir *Pagan Spain*, some in the United States could only conceive of Spain as a primitive, exoticized, bullfighting culture. Culturally speaking, beyond George Orwell's memoir *Homage to Catalonia* (1938)—which was itself only published in the United States in the early 1950s—the transnational market for products that acknowledged the existence of Catalan geography, language, and culture was practically nil. Tete himself addressed this in 1985, commenting on Americans' long-standing lack of knowledge regarding Catalonia: "En América saben lo que es Cataluña y que aquí se habla otra lengua distinta del español, gracias a mí. También he tratado de dar a conocer jazzísticamente temas del folklore tradicional catalán" (In America they know what Catalonia is and that a language distinct from Spanish is spoken here thanks to me. I've also worked to bring attention through jazz to songs from traditional Catalan folklore).[86]

Tete Montoliu's *Catalonian Folksongs* (1977) stands as an invitation to consider just how much transnational perceptions of Spain had changed since *Sketches of Spain* was released in 1960. The jazz market for Tete's post-dictatorial success in a sense relied on and in turn validated the willingness of consumers to acknowledge the existence of Catalonia, not to mention Barcelona's importance as a musical city. The inclusion of a number of Joan Manuel Serrat's compositions on the 1977 recording illustrates Tete's shared internalization of the Catalanist message of the *nova cançó*. The song list includes "Cançó de matinada," "Manuel," "Me embaix apeu," "Una guitarra," "Quin plan teniu Señor," and "Sota un cirerer florit." Tete also includes his own composition "Cigales al ven," which comes off as a paean of nature and its role in the broader cultural imaginary of Catalanism. As a further illustration of this point, as a closer the pianist includes the Catalonian anthem "Els Segadors" with few flourishes, thus letting the song's connection to Catalan identity take center stage.[87] The decision to not only record "Els Segadors" but to afford it a prominent place in closing the album serves as a reminder that popular song had long been a political statement—harkening back to a Jazz Age Barcelona forced to endure the 1920s regime of dictator Primo de Rivera.

While *Catalonian Folksongs* was originally released on the Dutch label Timeless in 1977, the liner notes that accompany the 1978 US release of the album on the Muse label are quite evocative from the perspective of Barcelona's claims to urban modernity. Moreover, they reinforce Jordi Pujol's description of Tete as the central point around which the cultural forces of Barcelona whirled. Noted jazz critic Frederick L. Bouchard approaches his liner notes in the form of diary entries dated July 11, September 5, September 6, September 7, September 8, December 9—all in 1977—and a final entry from October 15, 1978. These entries offer the promise of an exciting travel narrative driven by Bouchard's experiences journeying through Spain with his companion Sarah, and as such they play into the transnational narrative of Barcelona's fame as a cosmopolitan and global city.[88] Bouchard's propulsive narrative begins the moment he first hears Tete on the radio in Boston, due to the fact that "Deejay Steve Elman is doing a special on this Spanish pianist." Planning their trip, Fred and Sarah talk about the thrill of experiencing bullfights, sangria, and Gaudí's architecture. Arriving in Spain from across the Pyrenees in an iconic Spanish car (the SEAT), their journey includes such touristic highlights as drinking sherry in Jerez, seeing a flamenco show in Córdoba, and hearing Paco de Lucía's guitar licks in a Toledo record shop. Meanwhile, Bouchard daydreams: "The amiable specter of that hawk-faced, beshaded Catalonian keyboard genius huddled over the box in his favorite smokefilled taverna rose before me repeatedly." Arriving in Barcelona, they hear that Tete is in fact gone for the week, likely playing at the Montmartre in Copenhagen, "where he's been a regular with NHØ Pederson [sic] since 1961."

These liner notes highlight the dissolution of the repressive power of Spain's Francoist dictatorship. Bouchard notes that "[p]ost-Franco Spain may have loosened up a bit in some ways," and comments on how "Serrat combined his fine songs with Catalonian feelings for individual rights and a more liberal government in the waning days of the Generalissimo." The newfound cultural freedom enjoyed in Barcelona is palpable and channeled into urban symbolism, as Bouchard's text teems with mentions of street traffic, urban wandering, and iconic city sights from Las Ramblas, the Barrio Gotico, Plaça Catalunya, and Montjuich. But mostly there is Gaudí—Casa Milà/La Pedrera, Casa Batlló, and the Sagrada Familia. Against the background of Gaudí's spectacular urbanism, Tete's musical compositions are implicitly confirmed as equally powerful symbols of Catalan identity. Fred's text is certainly conscious of this effect, as when he writes: "When I see Sagrada Familia Cathedral, Gaudí's amazing though incomplete masterpiece, with its organic, crazy towers, 21st century dash and its mad profusion of supernatural ornament, my piano starts again. It is Tete at the keyboard, celebrating his beloved Barcelona in song." The propulsive narrative and content of

Bouchard's liner notes are important, as they demonstrate how economic, sociopolitical, and cultural considerations can all be grouped together as interconnected elements of a modern urban experience. The scene he delivers for readers and listeners is of a spectacular post-dictatorial Barcelona that is not unconnected from the rural experience implicit in greater Catalonia.

The interconnection of urban and rural references in this scene painted by the liner notes prompts other pertinent considerations. Perhaps one of the reasons that Tete is such a compelling figure within the landscapes of Iberian jazz is that, through music, he was able to overcome one of the key challenges to Catalan unity under Francoism. This problem was what Joan Ramon Resina refers to as the dictatorship's co-optation of Barcelonism as a tool in the fight against Catalanism. This co-optation rested on the differentiation between urban and rural forms of life. Resina writes that once the Francoists took control of Barcelona toward the end of the Spanish Civil War, the city no longer existed as it had before: "In its place there was now a provincial town inhabited by an alien spirit. But for a few years it was still possible to entertain the illusion that the countryside remained unchanged. Catalonia had taken refuge in the villages and small towns, where the state machinery was less obtrusive and tradition endured."[89] Odes to the natural world such as those on display in Tete's performance of "Cigales al ven," or in the *nova cançó* success of Raimon's "Al vent," for that matter, acquired new meaning under the dictatorship. As it had been under the rule of Primo de Rivera in the 1920s, in the postwar dictatorship of Franco, the cityscape became the first priority for the dictatorial war on deviations from "las buenas costumbres." Yet Tete also implicitly invokes links between the urban struggle against the repression of Catalan identity and the rural imaginary that sustains the latter by performing "Els Segadors" at the end of *Catalonian Folksongs*, a closing nod to rural labor within the context of jazz's urban circuits.

The urban-rural problematic under the Francoist regime began to shift somewhat as the initial euphoria of the post-dictatorship gave way to the further entrenchment of a neoliberal paradigm, however. This paradigm was, of course, already present under late Francoism, as the Spanish state in practice supported capitalist urban design. As Edgar Illas explores in *Thinking Barcelona* (2012), Catalan nationalism has historically allowed bourgeois interests to triumph over more radical forms of politics. While evident under the dictatorship, this tension became particularly strong in the post-dictatorial era as transnational neoliberalism was able to tighten its control over the urban built environment of Catalonia's capital city—one of many emerging pathways to capital accumulation.[90] While Tete Montoliu's musical production could neither resolve these evolving tensions nor be held responsible for them, his Catalan jazz work nonetheless provided an effective model for advancing an inclusive, urban-rural, pan-European Catalanism.[91]

Although Tete was a proud Catalanist, a Catalan nationalist, he stopped short of considering himself a separatist. He once stated in an interview that, "efectivamente, soy nacionalista, aunque no separatista, porque eso me parece un disparate" (indeed, I am a nationalist, but not a separatist, because to me that seems like nonsense).[92] Thus, it is important to keep in mind that, for Tete, jazz was a universal language. Despite his commitment and enduring connections to Catalanism, he transcends any attempts to subject Catalan jazz to a reductive definition or circumscribe its activities within a purely urban spatial context. In truth, his jazz work is not just a musical contribution or an urban contribution, but also a sociopolitical contribution to the transnational extension of the form. In jazz performance, the elements of Tete's Catalanism become a musical critique.

Despite early-career success in many other European countries, his political commitment and his sense of belonging to a broad community of Catalan speakers never wavered. Nor did this strong sense of community discourage him from exploring cultural and musical traditions that were not his own. It is significant that while Tete was grounded in both the urban culture of Barcelona and a wider Catalan cultural geography, he did not ignore or hide the Black American blues and jazz traditions on which bebop was constructed. Instead—as his performance at the Palau was intended to showcase, and as his entire professional career testifies—he foregrounded and even celebrated those traditions where others in the European jazz world might have sought to excise them or minimize their influence. His Catalan identity, his modern jazz sensibility, and the musical bridges he built throughout his career all reached a sort of harmony—perhaps the harmony of that very gathering in difference underscored by Fumi Okiji as a value of jazz.

4

Blues, Braille, and the Metanarrative
of Blindness

Tete Montoliu's transnational jazz reputation and congenital visual impairment make him a significant figure for the academic field and political project of disability studies. As Neil Lerner and Joseph N. Straus write, "Indeed, once one starts to think about music through the lens of disability, disability suddenly appears everywhere—in the bodies and minds of composers and performers, in the reception histories of musical works, and even in the works themselves, embedded there in the form of persistent narratives."[1] Outlining the intersections of disability and music can help us to understand certain paradoxes of ableism. Chief among these is an ableist society's tendency to explain musical talent away as something innate to the experience of impairment, while at the same time both exceptionalizing and denigrating musicians who do not meet the normative expectations of sighted culture. Just as crucial, this chapter responds to a simpler need: to acknowledge the contributions of those musicians who experience impairment to an ableist musical culture in which they are stigmatized. It is important to discuss where Tete Montoliu's visual impairment fits in a historical narrative of his musical education, while at the same time avoiding the traps analyzed by disability studies theorists.

The tendency is for disabled performers to be approached within ableist frameworks as either the "supercrip" who triumphs over adversity or as the "sadcrip" who is ultimately limited by an impairment. The challenge for music scholarship is to acknowledge a performer's visual impairment, but not to draw undue attention to it, nor to suggest it is the root of an exceptional musical skill. Unfortunately, this is precisely what occurs in common parlance. In Spain, as Roberto Garvía explores in *Organizing the Blind* (2017), the "'theory' (or prejudice)" that blind people "were particularly gifted at music because of a sort of sensorial compensation" became quite accepted around the turn of the twentieth century, and dates back to the "Tiresias stereotype" of pre-Christian times.[2] Any contemporary exploration of the intersection of disability and music necessarily takes place in the enduring historical context of such ableist understandings of impairment. While Tete's biography and career trajectory suggests that he was indeed gifted from a musical perspective, listeners must dispense with the thought that this gift was in any way related to his visual impairment. The inclusion of a brief bio of Tete Montoliu in Clifford E. Olstrom's *Undaunted by Blindness: Concise Biographies of 400 People who Refused to Let Visual Impairment Define Them* (2012) should be understood in two ways—as a testament to the pianist's international fame as a jazz artist, and as a response to the need to acknowledge the contributions of visually impaired musicians—but certainly not as part of a "supercrip" view that ties musical exceptionality to visual impairment.

There is little evidence to suggest that Tete himself felt his visual impairment was somehow related to his exceptional piano playing. Instead, he was passionate about modern jazz, and developed a corresponding artistic self-image early on through his amateur and professional jam sessions. He was often quite matter-of-fact about his visual impairment, stating in interviews, for example, that it kept him from being a football player and that he realized at a young age he would have to excel in music or sell charity lottery coupons for a living.[3] The latter is a reference to the formation, during the Spanish Civil War, of the Organización Nacional de Ciegos Españoles (National Organization of Spanish Blind Persons, or ONCE). To this day ONCE provides services for persons with visual impairment in Spain, and it employs people with an increasing range of disabilities. Although Tete became a member of ONCE on May 22, 1944, he did not attend the schools set up by the organization. He did, however, become the first visually impaired person in Catalonia, if not in Spain, to attend the Coneservatori Superior de Música de Barcelona using braille. He later commented on his strategy for reading sheet music in braille, saying, "Yo estudié la carrera de piano, los veinticuatro valses de Chopin y otras muchas partituras tocando, por ejemplo, con la mano izquierda, mientras con la derecha leía la partitura a través del Método Braille. Y viceversa" (I studied piano, the twenty-four waltzes by Chopin and many other scores, playing, for example, with the left hand, while with the right I read the score using the Braille Method. And vice versa).[4] Despite his early use of the braille system in mastering music lessons that were classical in nature—since jazz was not taught at the Conservatory—there are indications that Tete was later passed over for a position in the prestigious International Youth Orchestra (IYO) because his impairment was said to be an obstacle to sight-reading the orchestral arrangements. Here his disability—understood in the context of disability studies as a social relationship—can be meaning-fully distinguished from the material experience of his visual impairment.

This chapter draws from disability studies in analyzing the relationship of historical and cultural discourses of blindness to Tete's career. By introducing David Bolt's concept of the "metanarrative of blindness," it sets expectations for how readers might approach Tete's biography and explore his jazz legacy. This concept proves helpful in understanding how the pianist navigated certain social expectations of the ableist Spanish society in which he grew up and received his musical education. What is interesting in Montoliu's case is how these normative expectations overlapped in many ways with the social marginalization he experienced as a Catalan in dictatorial Spain. The metanarrative of blindness is also relevant to the later section of this chapter, which considers the visual marketing and reception of his jazz albums and performances. In the interim, an exploration of the musical history of American blues and jazz musicians who had visual impairments provides a necessary touchstone for understanding Tete's performances, recordings, marketing, and reception in transnational jazz contexts.

Disability, Impairment, and Tete's Musical Education

It has long been central to the methodology of disability studies that impairment is distinguishable from disability.[5] The term *disability* thus refers not to a specific individual body or a material experience of impairment but rather to a social relationship. As Tanya Titchkosky has written, "One cannot be disabled alone."[6] For instance, dyslexia only becomes associated with disability in a society defined by mass literacy demands.[7] Likewise, it is the planning of an urban built environment in accordance with the ableist imaginary that makes it necessary to advocate for ramp access to buildings.[8] In the same way, visual impairment becomes associated with disability in a society predicated on a culture of sightedness. Such a culture devalues, delegitimizes, and marginalizes those people who have visual impairments, fashioning a constructed norm that does not include them, and limiting the extent to which they control their own social and even artistic representation by others.

David Bolt's book *The Metanarrative of Blindness: A Re-reading of Twentieth-Century Anglophone Writing* (2016) complements other disability studies approaches to textual and cultural criticism in the humanities.

As such, it is best situated within a critical tradition that includes, for example, Martin Norden's *Cinema of Isolation: A History of Physical Disability in the Movies* (1994), David Mitchell and Sharon Snyder's *Narrative Prosthesis: Disability and the Dependencies of Discourse* (2000), Rosemarie Garland-Thomson's *Staring: How We Look* (2009), and Tobin Siebers's *Disability Aesthetics* (2010). For Bolt, the use of the term *metanarrative* is an acknowledgment that a certain social story exists "in relation to which those of us who have visual impairments often find ourselves defined, an overriding narrative that seems to displace agency."[9] The existence of this social metanarrative presents a twofold problem. First, he explains, there are recurrent tropes involving visual impairment that resonate across the literary, cultural, and, of course, social imaginations—one example would be "the blind beggar." Second, there is a corresponding lack of sufficiently informed criticism in the humanities engaging with those tropes.[10]

Because Bolt's book is concerned most of all with analysis of prose writing, some of the critical tools he develops are associated with that medium. One example is the process of nominal displacement, by which a character in a novel may be referred to not by name but rather by a disabling moniker such as "the blind man."[11] There is, in this relatively subtle displacement—one that remains quite common in literary prose—a residue of systemic ableist stigma. The fact that the names of characters may be so habitually substituted for by an impairment carries with it no shortage of dehumanization. The literary emphasis of Bolt's critical analyses, along with the metanarrative of blindness and the concept of ocularnormativism that sustains them, are more broadly applicable to all manner of cultural analysis. This includes the present approach to Tete Montoliu's pursuit of notoriety in the realm of musical production.

Ocularnormativism, which entails the systematic privileging of visuality over nonvisual forms of knowing, is a crucial support for the problematic metanarrative of blindness.[12] The ableist privilege reinforced by ocularnormative practices is supported by metaphor, social convention, and patterns of stigmatization that negatively equate visual impairment with lack. Metaphorical and symbolic ways of thinking tend to engage disability as a "sign for something else,"[13] a process in which there is no small degree of negation or conceptual violence. Thus, as Michael Bérubé writes, disability is "necessarily representational."[14] Ableist thinking cannot accept that impairment is simply just whatever it is without feeling the need to spectacularize and assimilate it. It is this collective act of representation that produces the stigma attached to visual impairment. Writings by people who experience visual impairment emphasize the social pressures induced by ocularnormativism. For example, in *The Difference that Disability Makes* (2002), Rod Michalko reflects on a time when "[p]assing as fully sighted became my strongest desire and I went about it with a devastating single-mindedness."[15] Here it is worthwhile to remark that sighted people tend not to recognize the distinctions between what Frances Koestler calls "total blindness, legal blindness, and functional blindness."[16] That is, as few as 10 percent of those people who are labeled as "blind" are completely without sight, such that the vast majority have some degree of residual vision.

Tete Montoliu was born with total visual impairment, in 1933, into a sighted culture where ocularcentrism, much less ocularnormativism, was unacknowledged. Due to the high degree of stigma attached to visual impairment, professional opportunities were virtually nonexistent. Given that playing football was not feasible, as he later joked, Tete thus understood from an early age that there were only two options for him to pursue in life. In his own words:

> Durant els anys quaranta a Espanya néixer cec implicava, a més, convertir-te irremeiablement en beneit perquè a ningú no se li acudia que un cec també podia ser intel·ligent i fer altres coses que quedar-se tancat a casa. Els pares eren els responsables d'aquella situació ja que vivien la ceguesa del seu fill com un càstig contra el qual no es podia fer res i preferien deixar el nen en un racó abans que preocupar-se de la seva possible educació. En meu cas vaig tenir dues opcions: o ser músic o vendre cupons. La meva sort va ser mostrar ràpidament qualitats per a la música, per a tocar el piano, de manera que ningú ja no va pensar més en el tema i em vaig deslliurar de vendre cupons.[17]

> (During the 1940s in Spain, to be born a blind person meant, moreover, that you were irredeemably blessed, because it didn't occur to anyone that a blind person might also be intelligent and do anything other than stay shuttered at home. The parents were deemed responsible, since they received the blindness of their child as a punishment about which they could do nothing and they preferred to leave the kid in a corner rather than worry about his possible education. In my case I had two options: either be a musician or sell lottery tickets. My luck was that I quickly demonstrated a talent for music, for playing the piano, such that no one thought about the matter any further and I was saved from having to sell lottery tickets.)

The word *beneit* (blessed) in this quotation deserves special mention. Here it carries the connotations of pathetic or deserving of pity, and should be taken in the context of a problematic historical discourse of charity that in Spain was one of the chief concerns of organized religion.[18] The discourse of pity, and the religious discourse of charity from which it stems, has been identified as one of the main obstacles to both disability rights movements and disability studies as an academic and political project. Tete's use of the word *beneit* here is seemingly an ironic invocation of that charitable discourse, and can be interpreted as drawing attention to and criticizing the religious basis of Spain's ocularnormative culture.

Tete has said that, in those days, being born without sight was most frequently taken to be a consequence of a parent's venereal disease, and that it was all too easy to associate this with popular judgments in circulation regarding skirt-chasing musicians.[19] Since his father was a professional musician, this was often the conclusion to which people would jump. However, medical testing established that the pianist's own visual impairment was congenital rather than disease-related.[20] It is interesting that some have sought to establish a link between success in popular music and those musicians experiencing congenital visual impairment, as opposed to adventitious impairment. For example, Terry Rowden writes that "[i]t is telling that almost all of the musical performers who have achieved significant popular success have been either congenitally blind or visually impaired from a very young age."[21] Though Rowden's speculation on how child psychology might support this observation is not uninteresting, in Tete's case such speculation seems unwarranted. After all, here was a child born into a family with a professional musician father and an amateur musician mother, into a household where American jazz was frequently played on vinyl records, and into a city whose streets still reverberated with echoes of its Jazz Age prominence. Moreover, Vicenç Jr. followed in his father's footsteps by attending the Barcelona Conservatory of Music. Given this context, it might have been more remarkable if Tete Montoliu had not in fact become a professional musician. And while it is indeed remarkable that he was recognized as the best jazz pianist in Europe, this success cannot be explained as a function of his visual impairment.

It is still necessary to note, as Rowden does, that popular music offered a potential path out of the poverty to which society has historically condemned those labeled as blind.[22] This was not a path that was easy to follow. In Spain, the association of visual impairment with oral and musical performance from the Middle Ages onward has been quite strong, and it is not difficult to find representations of this association in early modern and modern poetry, literary prose, and painting.[23] Nonetheless, as has been the case in all other societies subject to ocularcentrism, these examples affirm the stigmas of the sighted culture in which they have been produced. The musical culture of twentieth-century Barcelona was no less a sighted culture than any other, and in this context Tete's parents had to take action to ensure his musical education was beneficial.

At first, the Montolius placed their son in a school that enrolled students with visual, auditory, and vocal impairments. Yet after attending for only a short period, Tete did not want to return. Next, they managed to find a school devoted solely to children with visual impairments where he might feel more at home. This new school's director, Don Ramón Domínguez Sans, "era catòlic i catalanista" (was Catholic and Catalanist).[24] Most important was that the school employed a music teacher named Enric Mas, who played the piano, and who was also a person with visual impairment. Tete's proficiency with the instrument improved quite a bit under the tutelage of Mas, but when this arrangement naturally came to an end, the Montolius had to identify another teacher. The social stigma associated with their son's visual impairment very quickly became an insurmountable obstacle for many of the piano teachers they approached in the interest of furthering Tete's musical education. For example, when they mentioned the possibility to Frank Marshall, a teacher so famous he had the reputation of being a Catalan musical "institució" (institution) in his own right, he wouldn't even listen to Tete play before announcing his refusal to teach the youth.[25]

Eventually the Montolius approached Petri Palou, who had been the piano teacher for Tete's aunt.[26] Palou was impressed by Tete's abilities, but she was also concerned about his poor hand positioning and "la quantitat de tics acumulats durant els anys d'aprenentatge a l'escola per a invidents" (the quantity of tics accumulated during the years of studying at a school for the blind).[27] According to Jurado, "Palou tampoc no tenia experiència a fer classes a cecs i, al principi, s'hi va negar però després de sentir el petit Tete va decidir iniciar l'aventura" (Neither did Palou have experience imparting classes to the blind and, at first, she refused but after hearing the young Tete she decided to start the adventure).[28] The story is a bit more complicated than that, however, and it is interesting to consider why she might have changed her mind.

At this precise moment, in fact, none other than Joaquín Rodrigo, the Valencian composer of *Concierto de Aranjuez,* who was a musician with a visual impairment, was in Barcelona. While there, Rodrigo met with composer Frederic Mompou,[29] who happened to be a friend of Petri Palou's. It seems that in Mompou's conversations with Rodrigo, he mentioned Palou's reservations about taking Tete on as a piano student. Rodrigo reportedly said to Mompou, "Si el noi té condicions, que se'n faci càrrec. Ensenyar a un cec no és ni més fàcil ni més difícil, només requereix voluntat" (If the boy is good, he will take charge. Teaching a blind person is neither easier nor more difficult, it merely requires will).[30] Mompou relayed this message to Palou, and it seems that this encouragement from an eminent composer led her to accept Tete as a student. The young pianist continued to demonstrate increasing skill with the instrument through his many years with Palou, and they were able to sustain a friendship that continued well into Tete's most successful years as a jazz artist.[31]

After eventually completing his formal education at a school run by the Caja de Pensiones para la Vejez y de Ahorros on Rosselló Street, in 1946, his parents decided that their son should study at the Conservatori Superior de Música de Barcelona.[32] The student was quickly informed by the Conservatory's director, Joaquín Zamacois, that it was not a school for the blind.[33] Braille had never been used by a student enrolled in the Barcelona Conservatory, and it is possible that Tete's experience may have even been a first for Spain. There seems to be no doubt that it was a first for Catalonia.[34] At that time, the Conservatory only offered training in classical music, but Tete's intention to dedicate himself to jazz was unwavering.[35] Thus, there was a disconnect between his formal studies, which continued through his graduation, and his extracurriculars. He made a number of important connections at the school, including becoming friends with the saxophonist Ricard Roda, then-saxophonist and soon-to-be-singer Josep Guardiola, and the trombonist Jesús Peirón, and the small group of like-minded enthusiasts would meet surreptitiously between classes to play jazz. Tete remembered that they would have someone watch at the door to see if anyone was coming. If a teacher approached they would switch right into playing Bach.[36] As this anecdote conveys well, classical music was enforced as the school's single musical language.

By the late 1940s, jazz magazines had reappeared, the Hot Clubs were once again operating in Barcelona and Madrid, and the dictatorship had adopted a relatively jazz-tolerant posture.[37] However, anti-jazz attitudes remained entrenched in certain sectors of society. Understandably, given its historical links to classical music and its aspirations to high culture rather than popular forms, the Conservatory was one such place. In Tete's words, "Al Conservatori de Barcelona estava prohibit tocar jazz. No és que estigués mal vist, deien que no era música i simplement estava prohibit. Del que no s'adonaven és que, com que era una cosa prohibida, ens atreia encara més" (At the Barcelona Conservatory it was prohibited to play jazz. It isn't that it was badly seen, they said that it wasn't music and it was simply prohibited. What they didn't realize is that, since it was prohibited, we were drawn to it more).[38] In such an environment, one that was stifling to newer innovations in popular music, the stigma of jazz was deeply rooted and widespread. He remembers that those who heard him practicing on the piano would accuse him of playing the "música de putes i bordells" (music of whores and brothels).[39]

The conservatory's outright ban on jazz seems to have had much more to do with protecting time-honored notions of a privileged musical culture than with Spain's dictatorship per se. And yet the way in which Tete made sense of the ban acknowledged that at a deeper level there was, at least for him, a certain connection between the normative aspects of both contexts. Tete Montoliu understood music to be a language, and thus he believed jazz music was a minority language with respect to the hegemonic position held by classical music. Speaking on the subject of jazz and classical music at the Conservatory, he once stated, "Quan et vols expressar en un llenguatge has de fer-ho correctament, parlant bé aquell llenguatge. El que ja no és lògic és que per ensenyar un llenguatge es prohibeixin o menyspreïn els altres llenguatges" (When you want to express yourself in a language you must do so correctly, speak that language well. What is not logical is that in order to teach a language you prohibit or disparage other languages).[40] Here the implicit analogy Tete makes between jazz as a language and the Catalan language under the dictatorship is quite poignant, especially when one considers his fervent Catalanism and his long-sustained efforts to develop a Catalan modern jazz style. For the young musician growing up during the Franco dictatorship, jazz was to the Catalan language as classical music was to Castilian Spanish.

Even in this brief foray into Montoliu's musical education, the impact of the metanarrative of blindness is measurable. Stigmas and misperceptions that a child with visual impairment was abnormal, and even *tonto* (stupid), were pervasive in Tete's youth.[41] The negative reactions of those piano teachers his parents approached are more broadly representative of a sighted society believing that those with visual impairments had very little, if not in fact nothing at all, to contribute. Without Joaquín Rodrigo's affirmation that Tete had the agency to apply himself if he chose to do so, Petri Palou may not have been willing to take him on as a student. These challenges necessarily continued to some degree throughout his music career. One example is a televised interview conducted by Pablo Lizcano of RTVE on February 14, 1984, decades after he achieved national notoriety. Tete is asked certain questions that reveal the interviewer's complete ignorance of the fact that those who have visual impairments share with their sighted peers more commonalities than differences in their practical, social, sexual, and professional lives.[42] Lizcano also makes the error of invoking the myth of sensory compensation when he asks the pianist which compensatory abilities have emerged directly as the result of his visual impairment.[43]

It may be tempting to think that the devaluing of those with visual impairment is something that only sighted people do. Nevertheless, the metanarrative of blindness is a constructed discourse that pervades sighted culture and affects all who must live and work within it. On this point, the anecdote shared in chapter 2 concerning what happened when Montoliu first met saxophonist Rahsaan Roland Kirk in Copenhagen is instructive. Kirk, who was visually impaired from the age of two, had seemingly internalized the ocularnormativism of the sighted musical culture in which he had excelled. This was evident in his angry statement at the Jazzhus Montmartre in 1963 that he would not perform with Tete "because blind people did not know anything about music." Beyond the culture of musical performance, there is also the culture of music criticism to consider. It can be tempting for critics and scholars to overemphasize the importance of visual and nonverbal cues for performing jazz artists. Yet this argument, and certainly others like it, erroneously supports ocularcentric understandings of musical production and concertedly ignores the jazz work of artists like both Montoliu and Kirk.[44]

It is also important to acknowledge the ways in which those with visual impairments are able to identify, undermine, and take advantage of the metanarrative of blindness that sustains ocularnormativism. In interviews, Tete occasionally acknowledged a form of humor that can exist only among those labeled as blind by sighted society. One example is a humorous statement that Enric Mas made when he was teaching Tete as a child. During the piano lesson in question: "Mas em va dir molt seriós: 'Digues al teu pare que avui estic molt content perquè, per primera vegada, has llegit la lliçó a vista'" (Mas spoke to me very seriously: "Tell your father that today I am very happy because, for the first time, you have sight-read the lesson").[45] At home, Tete remembered, the Montoliu family laughed together hearing Enric's joke. This joke was funny precisely because it pushed back against the norms of a sighted culture that imagined it was only possible to learn music if one could visually read sheet music. Considering that, later on, Tete was not selected for the International Youth Orchestra ostensibly due to the requirement that the musicians were to sight-read Marshall Brown's arrangements, this form of humor may have contributed to his resilience in the face of the entrenched ocularnormativism he encountered in his life and jazz work. This consideration of a humor shared by, in Tete's words, "els cecs" (blind people), is important because it provides evidence that contradicts, to a small but nonetheless significant degree, the idea that "the issue of culture identification is not generally raised by blind persons."[46]

Another relevant anecdote concerns the fact that Tete won a thousand *pesetas* in a piano contest when he was twelve, even though he was open to the possibility that a woman at the end of her career had played better than him in the contest: "El premi es decidia per votació del públic i van veure el nen cec, que era maco, i tenia una cara com un piano . . ." (The prize was decided by a public vote and they saw the blind boy, who was handsome, and had a face like a piano . . .].[47] As Montoliu recalled, surely that woman needed the money more than his family did, but his visual impairment seemingly determined the decision. Here the social discourses of charity and pity, in his understanding, had doubtless played a role in the audience's selection of him as the contest's winner over someone more deserving.

One of the most interesting examples of taking advantage of the metanarratives of blindness that otherwise stripped Tete of his agency involved border officials in Spain. Miquel Jurado and Tete Montoliu had been in New York listening to music and buying large quantities of albums, as was the pianist's practice. As Jurado explains:

Vam arribar a Barcelona una mica acollonits. Encara vigilaven bastant les fronteres. I ens vam fer el cec: jo carregat amb les maletes i el Tete agafat de la meva mà, ensopegant amb tothom: "perdoni, és que és cec, deixi'ns passar" . . . I el guàrdia civil fins i tot ens va ajudar a portar la maleta.[48]

(We arrived to Barcelona and were warmly welcomed. They were still watching the borders quite a bit. And we "played the blind person": I was loaded with the suitcases and Tete was grabbing my hand, stumbling past everyone: "excuse me, it's that he is blind, let us through" . . . and the civil guard even helped us carry the suitcase.

The practice of "fer el cec" (playing the blind person) reaffirmed an in-group identity while turning stereotypical misperceptions back on the sighted society that produced them.

These anecdotes, of course, testify to the contradictory position that Tete occupied within the metanarrative of blindness. This social narrative constructed a sighted norm in relation to which he was judged at once to be not only different but, moreover, both stigmatized and exceptional. The religious discourse of charity and the social discourse of pity formed part of this narrative and stripped him of the agency that would have been habitually attributed to other sighted musicians and performers. Still, Tete's ability to forge his path as a musician, the advantages offered by his family's musical background, his day-to-day connections with jazz, and his musical education—in both formal and informal terms—were to make all the difference.

Blues Traditions, Sighted Culture, and Disability in Modern Music

Beyond Tete Montoliu and Rahsaan Roland Kirk, of course, there have been other successful popular jazz artists with visual impairment. The pianist Art Tatum is among the most well known. Given the ease with which Tete's style can be compared with Tatum's quick finger-work, he is an obligatory reference. Both Ray Charles and Stevie Wonder are also worthwhile points of reference given their popular success, the selection of the piano as their instrument of choice, and their prominence during the same decades in which Tete was at his peak. In the realm of European jazz, renowned Belgian-born guitarist Django Reinhardt—who was not visually impaired, but whose hand was severely burned in an accident—has also prompted scholars to consider the intersections between disability and jazz music.[49] Given the defining role of the blues in the forging of a US jazz tradition, it makes the most sense to begin by concentrating on the first half of the twentieth century, when the connections between visual impairment and the blues were quite strong in the public imagination.

The broader social context is important in any examination of the early twentieth-century blues traditions that influenced modern jazz. Disability studies scholar Rosemarie Garland-Thomson's book *Freakery: Cultural*

Spectacles of the Extraordinary Body (1996) points out that the popular tradition of "freak shows" reached its peak between 1840 and 1940.[50] This was a form of performance that hinged on normative visuality:

> The exaggerated, sensationalized discourse that is the freak show's essence ranged over the seemingly singular bodies that we would now call either "physically disabled" or "exotic ethnics," framing them and heightening their differences from viewers, who were rendered comfortably common and safely standard by the exchange. . . . A freak show's cultural work is to make the physical particularity of the freak into a hypervisible text against which the viewer's indistinguishable body fades into a seemingly neutral, tractable, and invulnerable instrument of the autonomous will, suitable to the uniform abstract citizenry democracy institutes.[51]

The freak show, understood as a popular tradition defined by patterns of normative spectatorship, is an obligatory historical point of reference for understanding the connection between performance and ableist attitudes.[52] Nonetheless, it is easy to entertain doubts about whether a given blues performer's visual impairment would seem to meet the levels sufficient for the "hypervisible text" that Garland-Thomson describes. For audiences who might have been primed for the sensationalized presentation of physical difference in such shows, the visual impairment of musicians is a comparatively less effective prompt for establishing the normalcy of sighted audiences. Scholars of disability and music such as Alex Lubet and George McKay have wondered whether visual impairment is even "an impairment at all when the musician . . . is actually making music."[53]

Visual impairment was also spectacularized in the marketing, career-building, and reception of selected musicians. One indication that the metanarrative of blindness shaped early twentieth-century blues performance can be found in the social conventions governing the naming of musical acts. Given Lubet and McKay's comments that visual impairment may not be "an impairment at all" when the musician is playing, the naming of the musical act thus acquires a heightened function in attracting audiences and conditioning their reception of blues music. As Terry Rowden explores in *The Songs of Blind Folk: African American Musicians and the Cultures of Blindness* (2009), "[i]t will quickly become apparent to anyone who casts even a cursory glance at writings on American blues music that in the first two decades of its recorded history, from approximately 1920 to 1945, the word 'blind' functioned as a professional surname for a startling number of African American musicians."[54] Examples include Blind Tom, Blind William Boone, Blind Willie McTell, Blind Lemon Jefferson, Blind Arthur Blake, Blind Boy Fuller, and Blind Willie Johnson. Here the descriptor "blind" does not serve to displace the name of the performer, but instead becomes fused with it. Although this infusion of disability into a performer's stage name is certainly not strong enough to draw parallels with performances staged under the banner of the freak show, it nonetheless exercises a certain exoticizing or exceptionalizing function. Rowden emphasizes how this naming practice owed more to the sighted musical industry than to the agency of individual performers: "It is important to remember that the tag 'blind' was more often than not placed on the performer by the record company and may not have reflected the singer's personal self-identification."[55]

Echoing the literary phenomenon of nominal displacement analyzed by Bolt, the usage of "blind" as a professional surname for these musicians evokes the contradictions at the core of the metanarrative of blindness. Thus, both a person and a perceived lack, both presence and absence, exceptionality and stigma, are packaged together for the able-bodied consumer's entertainment. Embedded in the performer's stage name, this contradictory appeal prepares listeners for the delivery of sensation along two overlapping categories. Here, musical spectatorship cannot be fully disentangled from ableist spectatorship, and the sensational element of ableist spectatorship turns on sighted culture's constructed "notion of the inherent musicality of blind people."[56]

Sighted culture's trope of "the blind musician" is very much an avatar of the "blind genius," one whose exceptional abilities confirm what is known as the "superstition of sensory compensation."[57] Rowden writes that "[n]o role has been more strongly linked to disability than musicianship has to blindness," and he reminds readers that "it has been the visibility of blind musicians and singers over millennia that has given music-making its exemplary status as 'the thing that blind people can do.' "[58] Collectively, blind blues acts of the 1920s through the 1940s forged an enduring association between the metanarrative of blindness and popular music. This association, in turn, would have an impact not merely on the marketing and consumption of popular music in the United States, through the trope of the blind Black blues musician, but also on the marketing and consumption of musical artists with visual impairment working in the American jazz tradition.

There are many parallels that can be established between Art Tatum and Tete Montoliu that go beyond their penchant for high-speed piano runs and playing in and out of tempo. From infancy, Tatum reportedly had "what was estimated to be approximately one-eighth of normal vision,"[59] and to a certain degree his own musical education anticipated Tete's. Tatum learned to play the piano from a young age, used the braille system, and later complemented his informal musical practice with formal training at the Toledo School of Music.[60] His teacher there, who also had a visual impairment, would have educated him in the classical tradition, rather than indulge the jazz forms for which Tatum became known. The pianist acknowledged the stride style of artists Fats Waller and James P. Johnson as a primary influence on his own. Tete, for whom Waller and Johnson were also influences, was similarly drawn to many of the tunes that Tatum had recorded. Examples are Waller's "Honeysuckle Rose" and Ellington's "Sophisticated Lady," although such common interests can equally be explained by the relative cohesion of the American jazz tradition's canon during the mid-twentieth century. The two performers indeed pertained to overlapping generations of the same transnational jazz world. To wit, in 1955, just before Montoliu performed with Lionel Hampton in Spain in 1956, Art Tatum recorded a splendid album in Los Angeles, California, with none other than Hamp on vibes and Buddy Rich on drums.[61]

A key difference between the pair of pianists was that Tatum was able to pass for sighted in some contexts, while Tete's total visual impairment made that impossible. Rowden writes that "Because of Tatum's ability to pass for sighted, there are many admirers of his work, even today, who are completely unaware of the fact that his visual impairment was so severe."[62] Passing as sighted in the realm of musical production can involve a number of elements, such as using lyrics related to visual experiences and the minimization of what are known as "blindisms." Because these elements offer little relevant evidence in the cases of Tatum and Montoliu, however, their explanation here is limited.

Generally speaking, as Rowden notes, there is a tendency for artists to avoid drawing attention to their visual impairments.[63] This resistance leads to the absence of autobiographical mention of visual impairment in their songwriting.[64] Yet in the blues there are nonetheless "instances in which a blind performer sings from and uses descriptive imagery seemingly indicative of the perspective of a sighted person."[65] It is difficult to investigate any such "lyrical passing"[66] in the realm of modern jazz, however. This is because modern jazz is a largely instrumental genre, one in which the instruments themselves take on a nonverbal form of narration, and in which autobiographical narrative is displaced by the creation of moods or the elaboration of concepts. Even in the case of jazz standards whose original lyrics might have been based in visual experience, the process of standardization itself effects a play with the notions of originality and authenticity that necessarily lessens the impact of any analysis seeking to explore the phenomenon of lyrical passing in jazz.

The term *blindism* carries in its very name sighted society's stigmatization of those who have visual impairment. Rowden explains this term's meaning using the concept of "'the illusion of privacy.' This is the difficulty that blind people have in remembering all the time that they can be seen,"[67] perhaps on display in Petri Palou's mention of the "tics" that reportedly concerned her in Tete's case. In sighted culture, those with visual impairment are given to understand—either implicitly, through experiences subsequently regarded as transgressive by those around them, or through explicit instruction—that the socially expected reaction to sighted norms is seemingly to control one's mannerisms.[68]

Art Tatum's desire to pass as sighted—what Rowden has referred to as "Tatum's performance of the role of sighted person"[69]—is echoed by selected elements of the marketing of his vinyl recordings. One of the first things informed contemporary consumers will note is that photographs of Tatum selected for album covers routinely show him without the dark glasses that have come to signify visual impairment. As opposed to more recent artists such as Ray Charles, Rahsaan Roland Kirk, Stevie Wonder, and Tete Montoliu, there is no indication Tatum even wore them. There are other ways to signify visual impairment, of course. The hallmark example is a photograph of early blues pianist Blind Tom Greene Bethune (1849–1908) that shows the artist seated at a desk, his eyes completely closed.[70] Art Tatum's vinyl marketing diverges also from the photography of the "blind musicians" in the blues tradition that Rowden covers in his book. On the album cover of his 1955 recording with Hampton and Rich, Tatum is seated at a piano, and seems to be playing with his eyes closed while his bandmates talk to one another. Yet due to the way the photograph is staged, and the particulars of the moment at which it was taken, it seems to lack any elements that would signify visual impairment. The solo image from *The Tatum Solo Masterpieces* similarly catches the artist with his eyes closed while at the piano, as if moved by inner concentration. On other albums, such as *Art Tatum: 20th Century Piano Genius*, *The Art Tatum Legacy*, and *The Essential Art Tatum*, for example, his image is artistically lit from behind or otherwise manipulated to accentuate the outline rather than the contours of his face. A rare example of a cover photograph that clearly shows Art's entire face can be found on the earlier Alamac release of *Art Tatum: Classic Piano Solos*. One of his eyes is misshapen. This visible injury, it should be noted, stems from a violent club incident and is not related to the original cause of the pianist's visual impairment. Still, by largely avoiding a clear presentation of his face and eyes, Art Tatum's artistic jazz representation tends to support, rather than challenge, the narrative that the pianist might have been sighted in his everyday life.

While Tatum desired to pass for sighted in the realm of jazz music, if not also in selected aspects of everyday life, Tete Montoliu did not possess sufficient residual sight to do so, and seemingly did not internalize the ocularnormative pressure to be anyone other than who he was.[71] In this sense, he can be compared to performer Stevie Wonder, who also had a congenital, total visual impairment. "Wonder has said, 'I never really wondered much about my blindness or asked questions about it, because to me, really, being blind was normal; since I had never seen it wasn't abnormal for me.'"[72] Stevie Wonder, however, nonetheless did demonstrate the desire "to avoid being seen in public with canes, guide dogs, or other prosthetic markers of blindness"—as did Ray Charles.[73] For his part, Charles went so far as to declare that there were three things he knew he never wanted to own: "a dog, a cane and a guitar."[74] The mention of the guitar in this statement, alongside two other items stereotypically associated with blind musicians, is quite intentional. It is crucial to remember that the guitar had been the instrument of choice for many visually impaired musicians. Ray Charles was thus rejecting more than just an instrument. That is, "Charles's valorization of Tatum, rather than any of the country blues artists, and his choice of the piano reflected his resistance to the stereotypical notions of blind people and blind musicians to which he had been exposed during his youth."[75]

Tete shares with both pianists the fact that he was known for wearing the iconic dark sunglasses that within sighted culture signified visual impairment. If Ray Charles is understood to have played a defining role in making those glasses "a standard part of the blind performer's public image"[76] in the United States, then Montoliu is his Iberian counterpart. Born only three years apart from one another, the pianists were part of the same musical generation. Already from a young age, Tete can be seen wearing dark glasses in the numerous photographs of him published in the books by Jordi Pujol Baulenas and Miquel Jurado. This includes everyday photographs from his childhood in the 1940s, but also album covers from the 1940s, 1950s, and

1960s. Tete wears dark glasses on the covers of 1965's *A tot jazz*, but also on *Tete Montoliu y su Quinteto* (1962), *Tete Montoliu y su Conjunto* (1958), and *Tete Montoliu y su Cuarteto* (1958), for example (see figure 4.1). One can see Tete wearing the dark glasses in a photograph taken of the members of El Conjunto Montoliu Jr. from the year 1947, and in many other images where he is engaged in a variety of activities beyond playing the piano.[77] If Tete's image had been included on the cover of Hamp's *Jazz Flamenco* (1956), in all likelihood he would have been sporting them there as well. Beyond the consistent use of dark glasses, however, Tete differs from Charles and Wonder in that he was seemingly not averse to posing for photographs that conveyed his interdependency. One such example is the cover photograph used on the 1981 release of *Catalonian Nights, Vol. 1*. There Montoliu clasps his long-standing bandmate and drummer Albert "Tootie" Heath's arm as the trio, including John Heard (bass), stand together in one of the iconic narrow streets of Barcelona's medieval urban core.[78]

Unlike the cases of Charles and Wonder, of course, it does not make much sense to consider Montoliu as an integral part of the 150-year legacy of US blues and jazz traditions that Rowden examines.[79] Yet neither does it make much sense to position Tete's jazz work within a tradition of visually impaired Spanish or even Catalan musicians, given that he sought to acknowledge Black American musical traditions and contribute to modern jazz from a position grounded in his own experiences of alterity. Whether we are concerned with the intersection of disability and music or the intersection of race

Figure 4.1 *Tete Montoliu y su cuarteto* (1958, Barcelona, Spain, SAEF, SP-1000), cover and 45 rpm disc, scan by the author.

and modern jazz, Tete Montoliu can only be understood as a transnational figure moved by the goal of gathering in difference with other jazz artists.

For some, this transnational positioning will be determined by his European, white privilege, the value of his contributions lessened as a possible consequence. Yet if European jazz is to be coded in simplistic terms as a white musical tradition—rather than a form inextricably linked to the Black American experience—then Tete challenges and even rejects that musical identification. Paul Austerlitz has written that "Euro-Americans are only partially aware of the privileges that they enjoy and of the black influences in their culture. Du Bois himself once discussed the 'Souls of White Folk,' noting that many whites identify with their skin color to a point of dehumanizing themselves."[80] This cannot be said of Tete Montoliu. Moreover, if one is willing to value his minoritized position as both a Catalan in Francoist Spain and a person who had total visual impairment navigating a sighted culture, it may then be possible to suggest the relevance of what W. E. B. Du Bois, in the Black American context, called "double consciousness" to an understanding of Tete's life and jazz work.[81] These considerations are crucial, because Tete's musical production cannot be considered in isolation from his embodied experience, his social attitudes, and his positioning in a musical space adjacent to that of Black American jazz.

Disability signifies also in the music he produced. Chapter 2 of this book emphasized a certain unevenness in Montoliu's jazz aesthetics, and related this quality to an urbanized modernity that had fractured social life, culture, and art in the twentieth century. Yet this same quality of his music can be understood within a disability framework. In truth, these two analytical frames in which we might approach musical production—one informed by the urban phenomenon, one by disability theory—are interlinked. George McKay, for example, underscores that the contemporary concept of disability arises with increasing late nineteenth- and early twentieth-century industrialization and the simultaneous emergence of popular music forms.[82] McKay's point is not unrelated to a central idea of Theodor Adorno's work. The same industrialized workplace that for the German thinker of popular music conditioned a musical tendency toward regularization also led to an increase in on-the-job injuries. "These shifts were due to the increasing visibility of disability—caused, in disability historian Henri-Jacques Stiker's view, by the increase in workplace accidents in the mechanized and pressured workplace of the later Industrial Revolution, and the large numbers of World War I disabled veterans."[83]

Joseph Straus notes the rise of rehabilitation discourse and programs post-WWI, also relying on Stiker's *A History of Disability*.[84] Most important, however, he also considers how these shifts accompanying modernization impacted musical production. As demonstrated in books such as *Extraordinary Measures* (2011) and *Broken Beauty* (2018), Straus is a scholar of classical music rather than more popular forms such as jazz. Still, his investigations are applicable to the category of modernist music as a whole, and it is thus not very difficult to apply his work to modern jazz. Straus argues that disability is a crucial category for understanding modernist music's predilection for "fractured forms, immobilized harmonies, conflicting textual layers, radical simplification of means in some cases, and radical complexity and hermeticism in others."[85] As mentioned in chapter 2, Montoliu's jazz work invites numerous analyses of this type; for example, on *Piano for Nuria*, Tete displays a penchant for fractured forms on the first track "Blues for Nuria"; there are two conflicting rhythms comprising the trio's version of "Stable Mates"; there are discordant and hermetic cacophonies that run through the entire second side of his solo piano album *Music for Perla*; and he frequently distorts his performances of Perry Robinson's "Margareta" on *Lush Life*. Consistent with Straus's analysis, the lack of forward motion demonstrated in Tete's frequent use of recursive or circular note patterns can also be understood as a musical disfigurement that distorts linearity in line with disabling propositions of modernist composition.[86]

What urban theorist Henri Lefebvre had identified as urban modernity's shattering of the tonal system in music echoes in Joseph Straus's discussion of disability and the "tonal problem."[87] As the musicologist relates, Austrian composer Arnold Schoenberg identified the tonal problem as "a musical event, often a chromatic note (i.e., a note from outside the principal scale) that threatens to destabilize the prevailing tonality (i.e., the sense of key)."[88] Straus convincingly analyzes how the notions of imbalance and unrest, which were crucial for Schoenberg's definition of the tonal problem, rely on a deeply rooted corporeal metaphor. "That these are both bodily states reveals the underlying physicality of Schoenberg's organicist orientation: a piece of music is a human body, and as such is susceptible to nonnormative stigmatized states, that is, disabilities. The normative and desirable bodily state (balance and rest) is understood in relation to a nonnormative and undesirable state (imbalance and unrest)."[89] The hallmark elements of Tete Montoliu's modern jazz work—unevenness, unrest, excessive speed, imbalance as expressed through the fractured aesthetics of nonsense phrasings, discord, and dissonance—can be explained through this corporeal metaphor in the same way that Straus uses it to explore the musical works of classical composers. What emerges from these considerations is an understanding that Tete's jazz work was nonnormative not merely in sociopolitical and national terms, but also with regard to the tonal aesthetics it shared with modern jazz.[90]

Album Covers and the Visual Business of Listening to Jazz

Parallel to Bolt's investigations of prose literary representations of the metanarrative of blindness, this section entertains the possibility that ocularnormativism can, and in fact does, figure in the production, reception, marketing, and consumption of social representations that take the form of images. The key distinction involved in this transposition is not inconsequential. It involves a shift of modalities from the verbal to the purely visual. The question is whether or not such a transposition from prose to image itself introduces new considerations that have not yet been sufficiently theorized. Can people who experience relatively low levels of visual impairment[91] be in a position to analyze and potentially also criticize visual representations of people who have total visual impairment? The previous section already introduced this sort of investigation in commenting on album cover photographs, but this section takes that premise further. Is there an image-specific, visual term that might correspond with Bolt's analysis of nominal displacement, for example? In what cases does an actual photograph become a trope, and what are the artistic, aesthetic, or design issues that enter into such a consideration? The other issue that comes up in the discussion of album cover art is artistic control and input. Did Tete Montoliu have much control over, input regarding, or interest in how his images were marketed and sold?[92]

Sufficient evidence is lacking to understand what Tete Montoliu thought, may have thought, or would have thought, about visual representations of his person. As scholars grounded in cultural studies methodology would assert, however, the thoughts of artists are not sufficient to determine how images of them function within a given cultural industry. It is possible to understand the sighted culture of jazz as an arena of cultural production in its own right, even if its contemporary visual representations have not yet been the subject of extensive analysis. Ultimately, the visual business of marketing jazz deserves critical attention as part of a sighted culture that, in certain cases at the very least, holds implications both for those who experience and for those who do not experience visual impairments.

The writings of Rod Michalko support this understanding. In *The Difference That Disability Makes*, the theorist describes how he began to realize that "sighted people also achieve themselves as sighted and did so in the same way as I did."[93] That is, as he remarks elsewhere, "[s]ightedness is socially achieved through language, gestures, customs, and the rest of the paraphernalia of a culture."[94] Sightedness is thus a cultural mode with performative expectations. Because both visual impairment and sightedness can be taken as different cultures with their own culturally specific norms,[95] this situation gives rise to a group of people who have visual impairments and who in practice must thus manage a diglossic cultural reality. In the juxtaposition to normative cultural expectations that this situation entails, it might also be described in terms of a double consciousness. The minoritized position of alterity to which people with visual impairments are assigned within sighted culture creates the opportunity for realizing a heightened awareness of the normative values of that sighted culture. Thus, Michalko writes, "[b]lindness 'showed' me that sightedness *could* be conceived as a culture with particular ways of 'looking and seeing,' understanding and knowing, and with particular ways of demonstrating this to sighted others."[96]

Here it is useful to distinguish the jazz market for vinyl recordings from the urban circuits of jazz performance. Certainly there are visual elements of jazz performance and jazz spectatorship, and there are visual materials that announce, mediate, or capture jazz performance for certain audiences, such that these areas can also be understood to form part of sighted culture. What the production and circulation of album covers offers as the subject of analysis is a concrete, relatively coherent, and certainly significant practice that is visual in nature. This cultural practice, which might be understood, as per Michalko, as the paraphernalia of sighted culture, was at its peak influence during the twentieth century. Yet it continues, nonetheless, in the twenty-first century as the demand for vinyl albums—new and re-released jazz recordings among them—remains strong indeed.

The most intriguing aspect of album covers is their multisensorial nature. They are a visual practice enacted by a sighted culture, constructed around an aural event, and mediated by tactile experience. The performer's image on album covers has long been a hallmark staple of this sighted cultural production. There is the notion that someone purchasing a jazz album and listening to the music etched into its grooves consumes the artist's live show or recording session at a remove. The vinyl record's grooves bear an indexical trace of that sonic performance. The album cover promises an iconic, visual connection to the performer, and as such is both a reaffirmation of the visual trappings of sighted celebrity and a visual contextualization of the music contained therein.

The jazz listening practice of the "blindfold test" confirms the significance of album covers for the sighted culture in which they are produced and consumed.[97] In this practice—which in truth does not seem to require that someone actually wear a blindfold—someone listens to a recording without being told beforehand any information about the artist or the album being played. The fact that an actual blindfold is not necessary to carry out the listening test provides evidence of David Bolt's point that the metaphorical significance and moral connotation of "blind" has triumphed over the practical considerations regarding visual impairment in sighted culture. The idea is that the listener—now unable to access and activate any connotations of prestige stemming from the jazz knowledge stimulated by the album cover and its named performance—should have a more objective and thus unbiased reaction to the musical track being played. Of course, to name the practice a "blindfold test" recapitulates the stigmatization that associates blindness with lack, and by extension seems also to legitimize the problematic forms of simulation by which those without visual impairments purport to sympathize with blindness by merely donning a blindfold. The musical "blindfold test" popularized by Leonard Feather through *DownBeat* magazine was also practiced in Spain, as evidenced in an issue of the very first year of the magazine *Revista Jazz Quàrtica* (April 1981). A superb example of how material culture can render visible the contradictory elements of the metanarrative of blindness, the cover for that issue of the magazine features a margin-spanning image of none other than Tete Montoliu. The test is referenced in the third item in the cover's listing of issue content, which is superimposed over the right-hand side of Tete's image in a pink-colored font: "RICARD RODA blindfold test."[98]

While analyses of the metanarrative of blindness in popular music album covers prove to be scarce, there are of course analyses of visual representations of visual impairment that are relevant. In *Blindness: The History of a Mental Image in Western Thought* (2001), Moshe Barasch analyzes representations of the blind in antiquity. Visual artists and literary authors alike have historically relied more frequently not on the eyes themselves, but on such depictions as a staff or a guide as an indicator that signifies blindness.[99] In painting, Barasch writes, the trope of "the outstretched hands," "the fumbling hand of the blind man, touching his way in a world he cannot see, has become an emblematic gesture that reappears in the art of all ages."[100] Similarly important in this regard is "posture, the specific position of the head. It is slightly raised, as if directing the blind eyes toward the sky or to some light above the head."[101] This posture is commonly encountered in painting and sculpture from antiquity through much later ages, and has been understood as signifying "the blind's inner life."[102] Of course, the use of the blindfold, a cap pulled over the eyes, or depiction of the eyes as narrow slits have also figured in visual representations.[103] Often depicted alone, the "solitary blind man" was imbued with a sense of dignity that conveyed his exceptional knowledge.[104]

What Georgina Kleege says about filmic representations of blind characters is relevant also to visual representations of musical performers with visual impairment. In *Sight Unseen* (1999), Kleege asserts that, "in fact, movies with blind characters are not about blindness at all. They are about sight."[105] Album covers can certainly be understood in a similar way. They are products of a sighted culture, intended for a sighted audience, and thus carrying the baggage of a sighted culture's misunderstandings and stigmatizations of visual impairment. Album covers differ significantly from films in that they are not narratives. This much is true whether one approaches cinematic narrative in either a fictional or a documentary mode. It is crucial to an understanding of disability representations in narrative film, just as in prose literature, to recognize that they may exercise a prosthetic function, delivering able-bodied spectators and readers to a catharsis that reaffirms normative ableist assumptions.[106] Yet the lack of narrative in a single visual image arrests this process. In place of narration we have thus the ontological assertion of photography.[107] The photograph narrates much less than it presents for contemplation. Even within this more narrow scope, however, photography is still subject to an aesthetic ambiguity. If, in the realm of cinema, "[t]he viewer contemplates the blind man on screen with both fascination and revulsion," as Kleege writes, then this is certainly still possible in the case of a single photograph.[108] Exploring a few representative album covers that feature Tete Montoliu's image can provide a way of assessing their situatedness vis-à-vis the norms of sighted culture.

Tete's SteepleChase releases, for example, are consistent with trends in jazz marketing. The covers of these albums show one or more featured artists in mid-shot or close-up, with Tete invariably wearing his characteristic dark glasses. The cover for *Tete!* (1974) is a paradigmatic example of this trend, and though it is tempting to search for elements that pander to sighted audiences, there is little evidence of that to be found. Here the jazz artist is shot in black-and-white and captured in profile, with his head and shoulders occupying a bit more than half of the cover itself. The remaining space is white background with no objects or detail whatsoever, beyond the album title. As a first consideration, it is important to attend to his posture, keeping in mind that the sighted representation of those who have visual impairments tends to incline upward, as if denoting an exceptional inner life or connection to transcendent forms of knowledge. Perhaps there is a slight incline here, but, all things considered, Tete appears to be looking directly eye-level. Even if the incline were more exaggerated, this would mean very little in the context of jazz album covers, which endeavor to portray all of their artists as exceptionally connected with a rich inner life and as purveyors of transcendental musical truths. For instance, guitarist Paco de Lucía assumes a strikingly upward-facing posture on the Philips US release of *Fuente y caudal* (1973), saxophonist John Coltrane is similarly photographed on his famous quartet's *Ballads* album featuring recordings from 1962, and bassist Ron Carter does the same on his celebrated *Yellow and Green* (1976), to name just a few examples.

Continuing with *Tete!* as a paradigmatic SteepleChase album cover, the fact that Montoliu's image is captured in close-up wearing his characteristic dark glasses seems unremarkable. First, it speaks to a general practice whereby the artist's image offers a visual and, by extension, seemingly personal introduction to his musical greatness for potential record buyers. Second, it can also be read as a matter-of-fact affirmation of his visual impairment. Music fans had already been primed to celebrate "blind" musicians by a long history that most recently included saxophonist Rahsaan Roland Kirk. This release contrasts with Stevie Wonder's *Talking Book* (1972), which "features a cover photograph of Wonder without the dark glasses that by then had become standard equipment for blind performers." As Rowden emphasizes in the case of *Talking Book*, "[t]his choice forces the viewer to look at or at least reflect upon Wonder's eyes."[109] The provocation of Wonder's album cover seems to be offered up as a challenge to sighted culture. By contrast, *Tete!* is quite unremarkable and has this in common with the many album covers with a similar design, from *Lush Life* (1971) to *Boston Concert* (1981). Such evidence contrasts with the case of Art Tatum, in that here representations of Tete cannot be considered as passing in terms of sighted culture. Even the trope of the "solitary blind man," while it seems to be relevant here, at least upon initial consideration, can be dispensed with once the context of professional musicianship is acknowledged. That is, the fact that Tete appears alone even on selected trio albums is merely evidence of the common practice of elevating the prestige of bandleaders at the expense of their bandmates, a fact that in context neither exceptionalizes nor stigmatizes the jazz artist.

In the example of *Catalonian Nights, Vol. 1* (1980) all three members of his trio are present, and Tete links his arm with that of drummer Albert "Tootie" Heath, seemingly demonstrating that he is not averse to being seen as a musician with a visual impairment. In the context of a career-spanning slate of somewhat unremarkable images, this one in particular conveys a sense of the man behind the image of the artist, somewhat similarly to Wonder's *Talking Book* cover, albeit in a different presentation. As Miquel Jurado has stated, "En Tete mai no va ser un cec autosuficient: des que era un nen es va acostumar a tenir algú al seu costat i a dependre d'aquella persona per a gairebé totes les accions normals de la vida quotidiana" (Tete was never a self-sufficient blind person: since he was a boy he was accustomed to having someone at his side and depending on that person for almost all of the normal acts of daily life).[110] On their travels together, Jurado was asked to describe for Tete how certain things looked, such as the Statue of Liberty in New York: "En Tete tenia curiositat per veure (una paraula que mai no podria ser més ben utilitzada) totes les coses, veure-les a través dels ulls del seu acompanyant per després poder crear-se la seva pròpia imatge interior" (Tete was curious to see [a word that could never be more well used] everything, see them through the eyes of his companion in order to subsequently be able to create his own internal image).[111] One way of understanding the cover of *Catalonian Nights, Vol. 1* is thus to say that it contrasts with the self-sufficient ideal propagated by representations of the "solitary blind man," thus questioning the association that this particular trope forges between visual impairment and solitude.

As it was with other jazz artists, there are many album covers where Tete is playing music either solo at the piano or with his bandmates. These tend to be unremarkable in the same sense alluded to above; that is, his dark glasses are the only element of the image that signifies he is a musician with visual impairment. The cover for the SteepleChase *Words of Love* release uses the body and the propped-open lid of a grand piano to frame him in mid-shot while he concentrates on the song he is performing. A variation on these unremarkable cover images is the SteepleChase release of *Catalonian Fire*, on

which Albert Heath and Niels-Henning Ørsted Pedersen converse in the
background, while in the foreground Tete smiles directly at the camera, cool,
collected, and confident.

In other cases, Tete's album covers feature abstract visual art, as did a
number of jazz releases. There are a number of album covers by pianist
Dave Brubeck, for example, that feature paintings: Neil Fujita in the case of
Time Out (1959), Joan Miró for *Time Further Out* (1961), and Franz Kline
for *Countdown: Time in Outer Space* (1962). In a similar vein, the case of
Vampyria, recorded by the duo Jordi Sabatés and Tete Montoliu, does not
feature an image of either jazz artist on the cover. In their place is a painting
whose three pale, gaunt, and vertically imbalanced human figures convey
a visual equivalent of the unusually haunting album title and musical aesthetic. This image itself offers itself to the thesis of Tobin Siebers in *Disability
Aesthetics* that disability's presence is the element that has allowed "the
beauty of an artwork to endure over time."[112] The accompanying liner notes
by Catalan writer Raimon Cuxart equally characterize the musical product
in terms that recall the disabling of modernist music advanced by Joseph
Straus. Cuxart begins with an epigraph by Charles Baudelaire, situates
Sabatés within "aquellos momentos culturales europeos que fueron cuna y
laberinto del arte contemporáneo" (those European cultural moments that
were the cradle and labyrinth of contemporary art), and punctuates his final
thoughts by attributing to the album an "atmósfera de belleza sutil y perversa"
(atmosphere of subtle and perverse beauty). The cover for the Tete Montoliu
Trio's free jazz experiment *Lliure jazz* (1969) boasts an abstract image that
appears to be a time-lapse photograph of swirling points of light. And for the
cover of *Carmina* (1984), Montoliu's collaborator and trio bassist John Heard
paints a warm and textured representation of Tete at a table, smoking and
conversing with the woman who inspired the album's title. The abstract art
covers, in particular, are intriguing—given the connections possible between
the rupture of ableism in the disfiguring characteristics of modernist composition and urban modernity's shattering of tonal aesthetics in music and of
perspective in painting.

Although not a visual aspect of album cover design per se, a quotation
from Tete himself that is incorporated into the liner notes for both *Boston
Concert* (1981) and the 1986 release of *Lush Life* (1971) recalls Rowden's assertion that "[b]lind people often find themselves in the position of having
to establish for the sighted what they themselves take for granted: their normality."[113] In the English-language quotation, Tete does just that—he asserts

his normality: "I am very normal, I think. I read a lot . . . Henry Miller, the South Americans. I like to smoke cigarettes. I'm not religious. . . . I am the best I can be." The fact that this is printed on the liner notes for not just one, but two album covers raises questions about the way in which vinyl record markets, as a product of sighted culture, may be anxious about how to represent performers with impairments.

A few of Tete's album covers stand out from the rest, given the way in which their visual design provokes some friction with the metanarrative of blindness. One of these is the cover for the original Spanish release of *Songs for Love*. The design at first may seem unremarkable. It is quite similar to other low-budget designs of the period that inherited an aesthetic of chromatic variation from pop art. Andy Warhol's brightly colored and iconic *Marilyn Monroe* (1967) was an exemplar of this principle of chromatic variation, where different versions of the same image, produced in different colors, were placed side by side. *Songs for Love* features six identical images of Tete Montoliu playing the piano in two rows. The top three images—yellow, orange, red—are rotated 180 degrees to constitute the bottom three images—light blue, purple, and deep blue. The individual image frames are not regular rectangles but rather a series of parallelograms, each with two obtuse and two acute angle corners. The design's central attribute is thus a visual distortion of sorts. While perhaps intended to evoke a sophisticated pop art aesthetic, the cover simultaneously represents the jazz artist through a form of conceptual violence. In the case of the Dave Brubeck Quartet's covers, the paintings by Fujita, Miró, and Kline suggested the existence of aesthetic parallels between modern visual art and modern jazz. In the case of Tete Montoliu's *Songs for Love* cover, however, it may play into the metanarrative of blindness that the trope of distorted vision is employed to represent the figure of a musician with visual impairment.

Another interesting example to consider is the cover art for *Tete Montoliu interpreta a Serrat*. The front and back of the album jacket are photographs of corrugated cardboard, a decision that heightens our understanding of the item as a musical product or commodity. On both front and back of the album at the very center of the visual cardboard texture there is a cut-out measuring 3¼″ square. The cut-out reveals a representational black-and-white pencil drawing on the paper insert that shows through the cover. On the front, but not the back cover, the cut-out square is a functional window, such that once the album cover is opened the front-facing 3¼″ square image is still visible. In this innovative structure, we thus find an artistic rendition of meta-representational album cover design; that is, an album cover that calls attention to its own role as packaging. Notwithstanding, it is the content of the penciled image that interests us here. It is a representation of Tete seated at the piano, characteristic dark glasses on his face, with his hands on the instrument's keys. The image on the back represents the same content, only from a different perspective—one situated above and behind Tete, and gazing over his back to see the piano keys. The individual piano keys themselves are easily identifiable. Yet the most remarkable aspect of the drawing is that this piano is not accurately drawn. It is clear that this piano could not be played by a trained pianist without some large degree of adaptation to its peculiar construction. The issue is with the placement of the black keys. Instead of representing the key sequence C, C#, D, D#, E, F, F#, G, G#, the order of keys is drawn as C, C#, D, D#, E, F, F#, E, F, F#, G, G#. An erroneous pattern is thus introduced. The error seems to be the product of a naïve artist who lacked sufficient familiarity with the instrument to draw it correctly. Even if this is an inconsequential error, the fact remains that it is a visual error to which Tete would not have had visual access. This case in particular raises the question about how much input or control the pianist had over the marketing of his albums.

One of the most curious album covers of all, and perhaps the one most indicative of the fact that a sighted culture sustains the market for vinyl releases, is *Lunch in L.A.* (Contemporary 1979). The design of this particular album cover might have once been called postmodern due to the way in which it incorporates geometrical shapes and pastel colors, and for its use of a playfully canted photo layout (see figure 4.2). This is not a conventional artist photograph or a scene of musicians performing. Instead, an intercalated photo portrays Tete seated in an upscale restaurant booth with what looks like a bottle of champagne chilling on ice to his right. On the back cover, a thank-you note to Bruce Vanderhoff of Le Restaurant informs readers as to the location where the photograph was shot. The most striking feature on the table is a strange flower-holder in the shape of a whimsical white frog-like animal, which is situated to Tete's left and is similarly facing the camera. The intended visual effect for sighted consumers is most likely lighthearted bemusement, perhaps specifically that bemusement befitting a well-deserved drunken celebrity lunch in the opulent culture of a global city like Los Angeles. Yet one question cannot be completely discarded: viewers may rightly wonder whether Tete is likely to have shared in the bemusement produced through the visual scene. Contemporary's cover art for *Lunch in L.A.* foregrounds the

Figure 4.2 *Lunch in L.A.* (1979, Los Angeles, USA, Contemporary 14004), cover, scan by the author.

matter of disability's social construction. The metanarrative of blindness is present through the images associations with whimsy, bemusement, and lack. If there is any humor in this cover, it is not the blind humor that Tete on occasion acknowledged, but instead a form of sighted humor, wherein visual impairment serves as the vehicle for the delivery of sensation to an able-bodied audience.

More than any other example, this cover allows us to adapt Georgina Kleege's previous statement on cinema to the context of album covers and say that, "in fact, [album covers] with blind [musicians] are not about blindness at all. They are about sight." Elsewhere, Kleege makes remarks that may potentially support the conclusion reached above in the visual reading of *Lunch in L.A.* Also in *Sight Unseen*, the scholar describes her experience visiting the Louis Braille Museum in France. Among the displeasing elements of her visit, she lists being informed that the museum is listed in the *Europe Off the Wall* guidebook, and the fact that the guide "evoked the familiar myth of [sensory] compensation."[114] She then notes, "Equally irksome was the sign at the end of the street, which read, 'Visitez la Maison Natale de Louis Braille' and pointed the way not with an arrow but with a hand holding a white cane. These things seemed tasteless jokes at blind people's expense, but I was probably being oversensitive and humorless—flaws often attributed to the blind."[115] Readers of Kleege's books—not merely *Sight Unseen* but also *More Than Meets the Eye: What Blindness Brings to Art* (2018)—are reminded that sighted researchers, certainly when uninformed by the work of visually impaired researchers like Kleege, often lack the conceptual tools to analyze representations of visual impairment. Yet if the cover art for *Lunch in L.A.* is any indication, it may indeed be necessary to develop these tools.

Epilogue

The Jazz Artist in Transnational Popular Culture

Tete Montoliu died of lung cancer. As Miquel Jurado has testified, he was active to the very end: "La malaltia d'en Tete va coincidir, precisament, amb una època de gran activitat" (Tete's illness coincided, precisely, with an era of great activity).[1] He played his last concert in Veruela, Saragossa, on June 30, 1997. On the way back to Barcelona he was not feeling well, and his wife, Montserrat García-Albea, took him to the hospital. It was to be his last admission there—he passed away on August 24, 1997.[2] Since then, the reputation he earned for modern jazz piano has continued to live on in the popular imagination. In this, he is somewhat of an archetypal figure. This epilogue thus continues to center on Tete's fame as a way of documenting the rise of jazz culture—not as a musical culture per se, but even more broadly as a popular culture whose impact goes beyond the narrow confines of jazz listenership. Here the twentieth-century jazz recording, understood simultaneously as a tangible musical object, finds its complement in a range of similarly tactile jazz products circulated in consumer markets.

The analysis of the culture peripheral to jazz leaves much to be desired with respect to its transnational extension. In the US context, Krin Gabbard's *Representing Jazz* (1995b) and its companion *Jazz among the Discourses* (1995a) sought to expand the interdisciplinary relevance and reach of the cultures surrounding the music. Notably, the bulk of Gabbard's first volume is made up of contributions that examine jazz in cinema and literature. It is crucial to recognize that the ties between jazz and its interdisciplinary resonance in, for example, literature and film are evident from the beginnings of the musical form itself, with no delay. The recording of jazz took off only in the 1920s, and already the musical form was consequential for literature.[3] Similarly, for example, both jazz and cinema developed in tandem through the first half of the twentieth century.[4] With this in mind, it is no surprise that the representation of the modern jazz artist continues to captivate readers and viewers. This much can be observed in a steady stream of biographical books and film releases, running from Ian Carr's *Miles Davis: The Definitive*

Biography (2006) to *Chasing Trane: The John Coltrane Documentary* (2016), directed by John Scheinfeld. Also of interest is the way that fiction and non-fiction alike have venerated the figure of the jazz performer as a cultural icon and social symbol. Tete Montoliu's legacy provides evidence of this broader phenomenon through the attention he has received not only in critical circles, but also in literary texts, television programs, films, and even comics.

Before turning to cultural representations of Tete himself, it is important to understand that the pianist was himself enchanted by the representation of Charlie Parker in literature. Montoliu consumed all manner of books voraciously: novels, drama, poetry, and more. He did so using the braille system. Tete prided himself on not having attended any schools run by ONCE, and although he saw the value of the organization's role in changing the perception that blind people were to be seen as charity cases (the *beneits* discussed in chapter 4), he complained in particular about their limited holdings of books in braille.[5] For an avid reader like Tete, this unfortunate circumstance seems to have played no small role in his judgment that, regarding his needs at the time, ONCE "era la cosa més horrorosa i depriment, trista. Els llibres que havíem de comprar eren '*ay María Madre mía*,' de religió. Saps perfectament que jo, per llegir llibres de Henry Miller, em gastava 20.000 pessetes perquè me'ls havia de fer copiar a sistema braille. Jo volia llegir coses que m'interessessin" (was the most horrifying and depressing, sad, thing. The books we had to buy were, "Ay María Madre mía" [Oh Mary, Mother of God], religious ones. You know perfectly well that, in order to read books by Henry Miller, I spent 20,000 *pesetas* because they had to be copied to the braille system. I wanted to read things that interested me).[6]

Montserrat has described Tete as a compulsive reader who made sure that he had two suitcases full of books in braille when he left for a tour.[7] In interviews, Tete mentioned his interest in Latin American authors such as Mario Benedetti and Gabriel García Márquez,[8] but he seems to have been most interested in the writing of Brussels-born Argentine author Julio Cortázar. The pianist particularly respected the prolific rate at which Cortázar wrote and published his books.[9]

Montoliu claimed that he wished he could have written Cortázar's story "El perseguidor" (The pursuer) (1959), which was based on one of jazz's greatest performers and personalities.[10] For readers of Spanish, and more than a few readers of English, in fact, "El perseguidor" became the archetypal piece of jazz fiction.[11] The story begins with a dedication—*In memoriam* Ch. P.—which refers, in no uncertain terms, to the world's loss of saxophonist Charlie

Parker, who had died in 1955. Its action centers on a jazz musician named Johnny Carter, though the parallels between the fictionalized Carter and the real-life Parker have been widely acknowledged. There is an interview from Spanish television in 1984 where, once Cortázar's short story is brought up in conversation, Tete Montoliu's reaction takes the shape of a characteristically wide smile. As he recounts with clear pleasure the dedication that precedes the story, he voices the letters C-H-P in Spanish in order to convey his knowledge of the jazz great that the protagonist Johnny Carter is truly intended to evoke. According to Robert Frankel, Cortázar's story inaugurates a new mode of storytelling for the author, one where history appears thinly veiled as literary fiction.[12] Many of the tragic details of Charlie Parker's life, including his death, are here compressed into a tightly organized tale whose density becomes the vehicle for transmitting sensation to the reader. Part of the story fictionalizes a real recording session from 1946 where Parker's performances were quite lousy overall and he left disgruntled. He later set fire to his hotel room, as the popular story goes, and was subsequently dragged naked into the hallway by a hotel employee. In the fictional version, the recording of a single song titled "Amorous" by Cortázar made the session worthwhile: "[T]here was what seemed to us a terrible beauty, the anxiety looking for an outlet in an improvisation full of flights in all directions . . . *Amorous* is going to stand as one of jazz's greatest moments," notes Cortázar's narrator.[13] In real life, the Parker recording in question was not titled "Amorous" but instead "Loverman," and Tete was among many listeners—including bassist Charles Mingus and jazz critic Ira Gitlin—who revered the broken beauty of that singular performance.[14] The Catalan pianist in fact recorded the tune himself frequently. His trio played it with Dexter Gordon at the Whisky Jazz in Madrid twice in 1964, it appears on the trio's release with Booker Ervin and Nuria Feliu (1965), on the album *Recordando a Line* (1972), on *Tootie's Tempo* (1976), and so on, through even the 1990s.[15] Listening to Tete play it, it is easy to imagine him smiling as his hands strike and run over the keys, a fusion of both Parker and Cortázar whirling in his literary-jazz imagination.

Montoliu was not immune from the enthralling effect of jazz as presented in literary prose. His enjoyment of jazz as a reader of literature was complemented, in at least one case, by his own appearance as a character.[16] It is no surprise for readers of Spanish literature that the instance in question should involve a work authored by Antonio Muñoz Molina—the contemporary novelist who has most consistently and thoroughly addressed jazz in his books and his journalistic writings (note that Muñoz Molina was also vice president of the Jazz Club of Granada when Tete passed away in 1997, and penned a brief reflection honoring the pianist). The intriguing, if passing, remark can be found in the author's self-reflexive novel *Como la sombra que se va* (2014)—translated into English as *Like a Fading Shadow*—that testifies to Montoliu's reputation in the jazz world. It is important that Muñoz Molina addresses Tete explicitly by name in his text, so that no interpretation by readers is necessary. Yet it is also quite interesting that the novelist portrays the pianist as socially distanced from his peers, and that he does this through reference not only to his visual impairment but also his Catalan identity. For the present purposes, the content of this passage itself is more important than an examination of the entirety of the literary context in which it appears:

> The other musicians, relieved after so many hours of focus and exertion, enjoyed their beers and relaxed, leaning back on their chairs, sharing stories and laughing. Tete remained still in his grey suit and tie, hands on the table, a confused smile, submerged in the only world he knew, yet eccentric to it, separated by his blindness and Catalan seriousness, hiding the fury that would later be unleashed on a piano without hesitation, without any warning, all at once.[17]

It is important to understand this reference within the context of a meta-literary work that reflects on the author Antonio Muñoz Molina's composition of his previous novel, the award-winning *El invierno en Lisboa* (*Winter in Lisbon*) (1987), which was itself devoted to the theme of jazz. As such, this passage can be read as autobiographical—it is reflective of the novelist's real encounter with Tete Montoliu. The importance of this passage stems from how Muñoz Molina describes the pianist. Here David Bolt's concept of the metanarrative of blindness from chapter 4 must be fused with the discussions of Catalan identity from chapter 3. That is, in representing the real pianist through the admittedly suspect and tired trope of the isolated, "solitary blind person," the Spanish novelist nevertheless also places his visual impairment on par with his "Catalan seriousness" as a marker of identity. Pairing these elements together folds both details into a social frame where they acquire the significance of social difference. The musician's Catalan identity becomes as essential for the reader as his visual impairment. Intriguingly, both markers of identity seem to be presented as the stores of a potential energy that will be released later in his characteristically impressive musical performance.

Visual media such as cinema and television were also crucial to expanding the national and transnational reach of jazz music. Jazz artists were courted by film directors, and some achieved a level of success in Hollywood film, for example, even if it came at a cost. The most emblematic case of this is the cinema work of jazz trumpeter and bandleader Louis Armstrong, or Satchmo, as he was known. It is of interest that a jazz club named Satchmo was once opened in Barcelona, honoring his foundational influence on American jazz but also demonstrating his international appeal. Armstrong appeared in a number of Hollywood movies from the late 1930s on, including *New Orleans* (1947), *High Society* (1956), and *Paris Blues* (1961). As Michael Meckna notes, these representations were not always favorable and involved no shortage of prejudice and racism toward Black musicians. White audiences of the time would have been primed to consume such images, and the fact was that "in many of these films Armstrong also plays a pivotal role in helping the white star overcome musical and/or personal difficulties."[18] This narrative context tended to imbue Satchmo's acting performances with a prosthetic function regarding the normative coding of white society—a form of cinematic representation not dissimilar to what happens with the representation of disability in film.[19]

Eva Woods Peiró's analysis of the connection between race and music in the popular genres of cinema under early Francoism, discussed in chapter 1, can be a helpful point of reference for beginning any understanding of Spanish cinema and jazz as popular music. The true complexity of how jazz representations would have functioned under the dictatorship becomes evident when we consider the case of the Spanish film *Raza*, released in the early 1940s at the peak of the regime's jazzphobia. *Raza* was actually written by dictator Francisco Franco himself, under the pseudonym Jaime Andrade, as Iván Iglesias notes. Given that the film's goal was to enshrine a normative construction of Spanishness—with all the propagandistic dictatorial intent that communicates—*Raza*'s cinematic portrayal of jazz was paradoxical, to say the least.[20]

When the moment comes for Tete's own debut in cinema during the late 1960s, it is very much in the form of a passing cameo. In the medium of fiction film, Tete appears as an actor and pianist in *Palabras de amor* (Words of love) (1968) by Antonio Ribas, and as a contributor of music composed by Joan Manuel Serrat in Jacinto Esteva's *Después del diluvio* (After the rain) (1970). The latter is particularly significant given Esteva's connection with the Barcelona school of filmmaking that emerged in the late 1960s as a cultural expression of Catalan identity. Tete is also the focus of a documentary by Pere Pons with dialogue in Catalan, Spanish, and English titled *Tete Montoliu: Una mirada* (Tete Montoliu: A look) (2007), thus cementing the pianist's enduring fame.[21] The emotional core of this documentary is formed by the testimonies we hear from those who knew Montoliu personally and professionally, his fellow musicians. Of course, Tete also appeared on television more and more frequently as his career progressed, in a combination of performances and interviews.

In the realm of comics and graphic novels, jazz in Europe has not been any less compelling as subject matter for audiences who are eager to consume stories of its history and greatest figures. Comics artist Jason Lutes's famous *Berlin* trilogy included lengthy visual considerations of the role of jazz and popular music in the Weimar Republic, including a sequence that can be considered one of the most powerful presentations of music in the visual art form. In *Berlin*, as the clarinetist from a Louisiana jazz band named the "Choco Kids" performs for a privileged white audience in the German city, his solo stretches out to span more than two pages of panels.[22] The varying sizes of the panel frames he uses communicate the varied length of the notes as well as the musical textures he weaves into his improvised performance. While this depiction is grounded in the artist's intention for some degree of historical accuracy, there have also been an increasing number of more transparently biographical publications dedicated to the musical lives of individual performers released in the medium of comics. Youssef Daoudi's *Monk!: Thelonious, Pannonica, and the Friendship behind a Musical Revolution* was published in 2018, and Paolo Parisi's *Coltrane* was released in 2012. Yet prior to both of these, there was *Montoliu Plays Tete* (2006), by Gani Jakupi and Miquel Jurado. The notion that Tete's comics representation preceded, and may have even helped to create, the market for comics releases on Thelonious Monk or John Coltrane is intriguing and deserves further investigation.

Jakupi and Jurado's graphic novel undeniably pays tribute to the pianist's legacy. Its tone is presentational and introductory, rather than critical or probing. It boasts an intricate aesthetic composition that can be compared to the pastiche and rhythmic playfulness of modern jazz. Rather than adopt a regularized panel format, much less the waffle-iron grid of the traditional comics page, the structure of *Montoliu Plays Tete* never settles on one particular page layout. Instead the pages oscillate unpredictably between margin-spanning images, rectangular landscape panels, and collage-style layouts that evoke the presentation of a photo album. This creates a compositional anxiety that mirrors the penchant of modern jazz musicians to play both in and out of rhythm. It also mixes together black-and-white drawings and photographs—or rather pieces of photographs—with patterns of color that are applied over and around the images as if constituting a distinguishable layer. Text appears both within and around images, and in variable fonts: from lettering in all caps, to typewriter style, to cursive script. Most frequently the panel frames are thin pencil lines that crosshatch at their corners, as if delivered upon the paper in the mode of a sketch rather than a final product. All of these decisions preserve those specific qualities—of spontaneity, propulsive movement, and ephemerality—that characterize the modern jazz music for which Tete was known.

Miquel Jurado's collaboration on the comic encourages the pursuit of accurate biographical details. Appearing throughout the project are references to such figures as Tete's piano teacher Petri Palou and his trio's drummer Peer Wyboris, for example. Also present are many of the same anecdotes found in Jurado's *Tete: Quasi-autobiografia*: the pianist was an avid reader via the braille system, he felt from a young age that he had only two options in life (be a musician or sell lottery tickets), Palou consulted with Joaquín Rodrigo via Frederic Mompou before taking Tete on as a piano student, he performed with Lionel Hampton, and so on. There are photographs of Tete with Niels-Henning Ørsted Pedersen, Chick Corea, and his second wife, Montserrat; drawings of George Coleman, Billy Higgins, and his first wife, Pilar; and sheets of musical notation employed decoratively as another component of the collage-style page design. While the graphic novel deserves to be analyzed in its own right, its intent to enshrine Tete as a legendary performer of modern jazz is evident enough from this brief description. There is no doubt that Tete's contributions to modern jazz will be remembered for some time, due in no small measure to these representations in literature, cinema, television, and comics. The fame of the figure of the jazz artist in all these popular cultural forms of course stems from that singular talent he demonstrated in his musical performances and recordings.

As a further testament to his impact, numerous celebrations and homages to the pianist were delivered on the occasion of his death in 1997 as well as on the tenth anniversary of his passing in 2007. In 1997, *Cuadernos de Jazz* published a series of reflections on Tete written by Joachim E. Berendt, Antonio Gamero, Johnny Griffin, José María Guelbenzu, Mike Hennessey, Herluf Kamp Larsen, Niels-Henning Ørsted Pedersen, Jordi Pérez

Vallmajor, Alex Riel, Miguel Sáenz, Jim Simpson, Martial Solal, and Yves Sportis. A musical tribute at Barcelona's 29th International Jazz Festival featured Johnny Griffin, Bobby Hutcherson, Cedar Walton, Niels-Henning Ørsted Pedersen, Billy Higgins, Horacio Fumero, and Peer Wyboris playing at the Palau de la Música on December 11 of the same year. Antonio Muñoz Molina penned a "Breve adiós a Tete Montoliu" (Brief goodbye to Tete Montoliu).[23] A cousin of Tete's wrote in a letter to *La Vanguardia* that "el insigne 'Mozart del jazz catalán' extendió el nombre de Cataluña y de Barcelona del norte al sur y del este al oeste del globo" (the famous "Mozart of Catalan jazz" spread the name of Catalonia and Barcelona from the north to the south and from the east to the west of the globe).[24] These and other such remembrances deliver the narrative of his accomplishments into a wider transnational geography that extends beyond Catalonia's capital city.

Superlatives were the rule rather than the exception during Tete's long career, and they were equally present as the jazz world mourned his loss. In 1997 the noted Spanish magazine *Ritmo* published a tribute titled "Tete Montoliu: Un homenaje al más grande pianista del jazz español" (Tete Montoliu: An homage to the greatest pianist of Spanish jazz).[25] In January 2008, an article published in the Mallorcan magazine *Lluc* begins by acknowledging that "Si hi ha un músic de jazz que hom està d'acord en considerar el més rellevant intèrpret del gènere que ha vist néixer el panorama musical nacional aquest és, sens dubte Tete Montoliu" (If there is a jazz musician that all agree can be considered the most important performer of the form that the national music scene has ever seen it must be, without a doubt, Tete Montoliu).[26]

Tete's legacy is also embedded in the fabric of urban spaces. For example, the town of Terrassa, where he played numerous times, posthumously honored him by changing the name of a street previously dedicated to Antoni Gaudí to the Passatge de Tete Montoliu.[27] The town of Sentmenat boasts Carrer Tete Montoliu, and the city of Granada has its own Calle Tete Montoliu. In Barcelona, the Tete Montoliu Gardens, on Carrer Sepúlveda 88–92, were dedicated to honor his legacy in 2007, and a plaque now hangs outside the pianist's lifelong residence at 83A Muntaner.[28] Nearby, on Carrer Sepúlveda, the Barcelona headquarters of ONCE features a permanent exhibit of some two hundred objects connected with his life and jazz work. Beyond Tete's own piano, his radio, his braille watch, numerous awards, posters, and original artwork dedicated to the pianist, the exhibit also features an expansive wall display of his album releases. Tete Montoliu's vinyl recordings remain, today, a particularly privileged component of his legacy.

As I wrote this book, I found myself reflecting on how Fumi Okiji, in her notion of jazz as critique, makes a key assertion concerning "the inadequacy and indispensability of jazz records," which is an apt title for her book's postscript. Certainly, jazz records are not the same thing as jazz work, but rather a reified instance of a musical practice that overflows the reified object.[29] And yet the history of jazz cannot be told without reference to jazz records.[30] The two are inextricably tied together. Okiji asks what the history of jazz music would be without the jazz recording, and she answers that it would be much less rich as a result.[31] She asks who Charlie Parker would have been without the Lester Young 78s whose listening informed his jazz work. In the same vein, I ask readers to imagine what a young Tete Montoliu growing up in Barcelona in the 1930s and 1940s would have been without his mother's Duke Ellington or Fats Waller vinyl records. His passion for buying and listening to records endured throughout his entire lifetime. Consider his statements such as this, reflecting on a visit with Miquel Jurado to New York in the summer of 1985, and on the pair's activities during the days leading up to Tete's performance at Carnegie Hall: "Sentíem jazz i compràvem discos, dia i nit compàvem discos i sentíem jazz" (We listened to jazz and we bought records, day and night we bought records and we listened to jazz).[32] Okiji sees in the jazz recording itself "an oral tradition for the twentieth century" and states definitively that "[l]istening to recordings is the first and primary activity in jazz musicians' 'self-pedagogy.' "[33] Taking these comments seriously means being willing to consider this oral tradition in its transnational dimension, as this book has done through emphasizing Tete's vinyl recordings.

One more comment is in order regarding research method. In this project I have been motivated by Theodor W. Adorno's work to immerse myself in nonregressive forms of listening. This project was predicated on the need to listen to vinyl records intensely, giving them my full concentration. I realized early on that although many recordings of Tete's music can be accessed online, these forms of listening just would not do. This can perhaps be all too easily unmasked as a scholarly conceit, but I have found too much enjoyment— consumeristic enjoyment, as is undoubtedly the case—in seeking to compile a Tete Montoliu vinyl record collection to dismiss that enjoyment outright. As a consequence, I have also known other emotions—the frustration of obtaining what turned out to be a less-than-stellar copy, for example—and I have long sat with the tragicomedy of pursuing vinyl when digital formats are so readily accessible. I have reached the emotional precipice required of those who contemplate paying far too much for an early recording only to back down, and I face lingering regret for having done so. Yet I have found enjoyment not merely in pursuing a Tete collection, but also in my concentrated listening practices. After so many hours logged listening to Tete on vinyl, I wonder whether it is even an exaggeration to say that Montoliu's style of playing itself—perhaps like that of others who are prone to crowd too many notes together at once—can function as an obstacle to regressive listening practices. Music of the density and intensity evidenced particularly in his recordings from the 1960s and 1970s commands the listener's attention. Even Tete's solo piano work is sufficiently dense, musically speaking, so as to disrupt the deconcentrated listening that might characterize the passive enjoyment of a bourgeois "cocktail hour." I have failed many times in my attempts to passively consume recordings of his jazz work, only to be brought back into the music by a key phrasing or a flurry of finger-work. I must reject the idea that his musical practice can be approached as a pure aesthetic realm detached from wider cultural meaning, or as a mere affirmation of the plodding mediocrity of modernity's culture industry.

It should not be forgotten that it is common for cultural and musical practices to shift and change over geography and over time. These changes prompt intriguing questions about the transnational contexts in which such shifting cultural forms re-emerge. New social, political, historical, and geographical contexts bring divergent meanings to cultural forms. Their enactment at a given place and time borrows selectively from existing traditions and exacerbates contradictions already embedded within those traditions. The idea that a cultural or a musical practice may be monolithic—bounded, internally homogeneous, and continuous through time—is thus a convenient fiction. In this spirit, previous scholarship has already explored a range of other musical practices that span Latin America, the United States, and Europe, such as samba, merengue, calypso, and tango, for example.[34] My hope is that this book's account of Tete Montoliu's legacy has provided a compelling argument that jazz is no exception to this rule.

Notes

Note on Theodor W. Adorno
and Jazz Criticism

1. Also, on the same page: "The relationship between jazz and black people is similar to that between salon music and the wandering fiddle players whom it so firmly believes it has transcended—the gypsies" ("On Jazz," Adorno 2002a, 477).
2. "The connection here is historically grounded; one of the horns used in jazz is called the Sousaphone, after the march composer" ("On Jazz," Adorno 2002a, 485).
3. Sousa (1854–1932) was born in Washington, DC.
4. "On Jazz," Adorno 2002a, 485. Adorno also linked the sax to French theater.
5. "Not only the saxophone has been borrowed from the military orchestra; the entire arrangement of the jazz orchestra, in terms of the melody, bass, *obbligati*, and mere filler instruments, is identical to that of a military band. Thus jazz can be easily adapted for use by fascism" ("On Jazz," Adorno 2002a, 485).
6. Marx's critique of alienation has been sufficiently extended by generations of critics who have focused on this precise period of postwar Europe. Most of all, readers might consult the extensive work by and about French philosopher Henri Lefebvre (1901–91). Lefebvre's theory plays into the discussions in chapter 2 of this book.
7. Adorno 2002b, 272.
8. Adorno 2002e, 391.
9. "Adorno frequently classifies all nonclassical music as jazz, evidently based on the dubious belief that jazz was the dominant and paradigmatic form of popular music during his lifetime. (Perhaps it did not occur to him that jazz was never synonymous with popular music and that with the emergence of bebop and later rock and roll, jazz became decidedly less popular.)" (Gracyk 1992, 527).
10. See remarks in Gracyk 1992, where the author updates and examines Adorno's remarks using the modern day record store's "classical" and "jazz" sections as illustration.
11. From "On the Fetish-Character," Adorno 2002d, 313.
12. Paddison 1996, 91–92.
13. Paddison 1996, 86–87, where Paddison cites from Rose's book *The Melancholy Science: An Introduction to the Thought of Theodor W. Adorno* (1978).
14. Paddison 1996, 88–89; Paddison writes of uncritical music as including "serious music of the past, now reduced to the level of museum exhibits or mere entertainment, as well as that 'modern' music which attempts some form of compromise for the sake of accessibility" (89). On the latter, see also Adorno's acknowledgment that

classical pieces may "have become objects of consumption for home decoration" (in *Philosophy of New Music*, 2006, 12).

15. See Paddison 1996, 90–91; Thompson 2018, 91.
16. "On the Social Situation of Music," Adorno 2002e, 421.
17. See "On the Social Situation of Music," Adorno 2002e, 421–22.
18. I refer readers to the original works of Henri Lefebvre, but also Andy Merrifield's presentation of Lefebvre's theory on this subject.
19. See also Witkin 1998, 162.
20. See Gracyk 1992, 530, 532; Witkin 1998, 174.
21. See "Farewell to Jazz," Adorno 2002a, 498; "On the Fetish-Character," Adorno 2002d, 313.
22. See "On Jazz," Adorno 2002a, 483; Witkin 1998, 167–68; and *New Philosophy of Music*, Adorno 2006, 188n24.
23. Adorno writes that the "immediacy," the "seemingly improvisational moments," and the "syncopation" of jazz are a "mask" or "pasted-on ornament meant to deceive us" about the music's commoditized identity ("On Jazz," Adorno 2002a, 473); "Even the much-invoked improvisations, the *hot* passage and *breaks* are merely ornamental in their significance, and never part of the overall construction or determinant of the form" (477); "The improvisational immediacy which constitutes its partial success counts strictly among those attempts to break out of the fetishized commodity world which want to escape that world without ever changing it, thus moving deeper into its snare" (478).
24. Also: "But then—and this explains the stereotypical quality—the rhythmic achievements of jazz are mere ornaments above a metrically conventional, banal architecture, with no consequences for the structure, and removable at will" ("Farewell to Jazz," Adorno 2002a, 498)
25. "On the Fetish-Character," Adorno 2002d, 306; the emphasis in the previous sentence, also from this page, is original.
26. "On the Fetish-Character," Adorno 2002d, 304.
27. "On the Fetish-Character," Adorno 2002d, 305.
28. During a brief reference to Adorno, Bermúdez (2018, 18) reaches a similar conclusion concerning "what Lacan would term enjoyment. Indeed if enjoyment is relevant to processes of social identity formation, it is also central to the consumption of music, and to the many pleasures we derive from it individually and collectively."
29. Benjamin 1985; Goffman 1984; Hannosh 1992.
30. Harvey 2009, 305–07; Lefebvre 2003, 1996; see also Mumford 1961, 448; 1970.
31. Merrifield 2002, 79.
32. "On Jazz," Adorno 2002a, 476.
33. "On the Fetish-Character," Adorno 2002d, 307.
34. "On the Fetish-Character," Adorno 2002d, 313.
35. "On the Fetish-Character," Adorno 2002d, 310.
36. "Adorno never learned to listen to jazz, and never credited either the autonomy of jazz players nor the high degree of social co-operation and reflexivity that was necessary to make good jazz. Adorno offers nothing in the way of a study of the culture of jazz

and jazz musicians nor an account or analysis of how they think concerning the business of making music" (Witkin 1998, 176).

37. See "On the Fetish-Character," Adorno 2002d, 308.
38. See "On the Fetish-Character," Adorno 2002d, 308.
39. "On the Fetish-Character," Adorno 2002d, 310; see also "On the Social Situation," Adorno 2002e, 419.
40. See Paddison 1996, 93.
41. Paddison 1993, 26.
42. See Paddison 1996, 94.
43. For example, Paddison 1996, 112; 1993: 205.
44. Paddison 1993, 100.
45. See Gracyk 1992, 527; Witkin 1998, 173.
46. Witkin 1998, 175; see also Gracyk 1992.
47. Witkin 1998, 177; see Gracyk 1992, whose argument Witkin recapitulates.
48. Garlitz 2007, 4.
49. , 173, also 162.

Introduction

1. Austerlitz 2005, x. Compare the state of jazz studies as framed by Buckner and Weiland 1991 with Gebhardt, Rustin-Paschal, and Whyton 2019. See also Whyton 2012.
2. Arribas García 2015, 55.
3. Tete is also mentioned in interviews with Marc Miralta Clusellas, bassist Javier Colina, who played with Tete, and Marcelino Galán Pérez (Michelone 2011, 143, 187, 63, 125). Gene Rizzo lists him as one of the best of all time (2005: 82–85).
4. Moreno Peracaula 2016, 85n117.
5. Moreno Sabogal 2012, 223. It should be understood that the use of superlatives is certainly not limited to this small sampling of judgments. One easily finds other examples of excessive praise being heaped on the jazz artist. Those who read only English, however, will have a slightly more difficult time of things, and it is to that very situation that the present book responds.
6. Atkins 2003b, xii.
7. The cultural studies landmarks exploring this period include Vilarós 1998, in Spanish, and Graham and Labanyi 1995, in English. Books such as Crumbaugh 2009 and Pavlović 2012 similarly represent crucial contributions to the English-language studies of the culture of this historical period. Book-length cultural studies approaches to the music of this period have generally lagged behind studies of its literature and film. The aforementioned volume *Spanish Cultural Studies*, edited by Graham and Labanyi, included a number of concise but insightful explorations of the musical culture of this period, but as the editors themselves acknowledged in their preface, "Spanish cultural studies are still in their infancy" (1995, v). La Movida, an explosion of cultural production in Madrid during the

post-dictatorship, emerged as a primary object of critical attention where music was understood to be crucial, along with film, performance, comics, and other forms of expression (echoed in the recent return to this topic in a volume by Nichols and Song [2014]). Yet English-language studies of popular music in Spain were advanced considerably with the special issue of the *Journal of Spanish Cultural Studies* on "Spanish Popular Music Studies," edited in 2009 by Silvia Bermúdez and Jorge Pérez.

8. This quotation comes from the "Preface" to Joan Ramon Resina's edited volume *Iberian Modalities* (2013, vii).

9. Francoism attempted to "eliminate the cultural and linguistic differences of these peoples" (Guibernau 2004, 36).

10. Bou and Subirana 2017, 5–6, from their introduction to *The Barcelona City Reader*.

11. From a chapter in of Bou and Subirana's collection authored by Alejandro Quiroga (2017, 164).

12. This is consistent with the framework outlined by Neil Lerner and Joseph N. Straus in *Sounding Off: Theorizing Disability in Music* (2006).

13. This humanities field was pioneered by figures such as Lennard J. Davis, Rosemarie Garland Thomson, David T. Mitchell, and Sharon L. Snyder, among others. See Davis 1997.

14. The historical literature on the Spanish Civil War is somewhat mountainous, and interested readers should consult books by Paul Preston (2012), Gerald Brenan, Helen Graham, and Stanley Payne, not to mention George Orwell's *Homage to Catalonia*.

15. Jurado 1998, 25–26, 28.

16. Jurado 1998, 27.

17. Jurado, in Jurado 1992, 11: "Va ser un dels músics més actius que va haver-hi a la Catalunya de la pre-guerra."

18. Jurado 1998, 34.

19. Jurado 1998, 35.

20. Tete, in Jurado 1998, 26.

21. Tete, in Jurado 1992, 20–21.

22. Tete, in Jurado 1998, 34.

23. Tete, in Jurado 1998, 26. Waller (1904–43) was born in New York, and Ellington (1899–1974) was born in Washington, DC.

24. He played this song with Dex during radio broadcasts on June 25 and August 20, 1964, from the Jazzhus Montmartre, Copenhagen; and at performances on November 30 and December 7, 1964, at Whisky Jazz in Madrid. See the lineup at http://www.jazz discography.com/Artists/Montoliu/tete-disc.php.

25. Hasse (2012) includes mention of numerous European countries in his essay on Ellington, but provides no evidence that the Duke played in or thought of playing in Spain from the 1930s through the end of the 1950s. Jordi Pujol Baulenas (2005, 332) describes an attempt to invite Ellington to Barcelona in 1958 that moved forward but ultimately fell apart due to disagreements in the city's jazz community.

26. On the joint performances of 1966, Iglesias 2013b, 109.

27. Quoted in Austerlitz 2005, ix; from Ellington 1976 [1973], 436.

28. Crouch 2006, 146. Reprinted from the critic's 1998 essay "Duke Ellington: Transcontinental Swing."

29. Jurado 1998, 140. Leonard Feather would eventually write, too, that "He swings as consistently as any pianist who ever grew up outside the native land of jazz" (ONCE, Jazz Review titled "Montoliu: Insight from the Outside," published in the *Los Angeles Times*).

30. See the foreword by Michel Lipskin in the book by Maurice Waller and Anthony Calabrese (1977, ix).

31. Gioia 2011, 94.

32. It should be remembered that when Tete was prompted by Miquel Jurado to select a personal top ten of his own album releases, the pianist chose *Tête a Tete* as his number one favorite. The pianist later reflected that even though "Catalan Suite" was unknown by both bassist Niels-Henning Ørsted Pederson and drummer Albert "Tootie" Health, the chemistry between the three of them was incredible and they recorded the extended piece in one take (Tete, in Jurado 1998, 257).

33. Burrows 2018, 417.

34. Lyttelton 1981, 31.

35. Lyttelton 1981, 44.

36. Lyttelton 1981, 45–46.

37. Jurado 1998, 37. Note of the song "Alligtor Crawl" that Fats Waller had originally titled it "Charleston Stomp" (Waller and Calabrese 1981, 89).

38. Jurado 1998, 38–39.

39. Tete, in Jurado 1998, 26.

40. This was one of the "programes infantils que presentava Gerardo Esteban" (Tete, in Jurado 1992, 15; see also Jurado 1998, 37).

41. Tete mentions elsewhere that "El piano m'arriva per nassos. Quan jo tenia tres o quatre anys ja hi havia el piano" (Tete, in Jurado 1992, 11).

42. The comments of Iván Iglesias on this period are mentioned later in this introduction.

43. This is a topic that is given further consideration in chapter 2. Chapter 3 delves more into Barcelona's reputation and history as a Jazz Age city.

44. Iglesias 2010c, 127: "En febrero y marzo de 1941, en pleno entusiasmo fascista, "Educación y Descanso" organizó en Barcelona dos "magnos Festivales de Jazz Hot," con algunos de los principales conjuntos de la capital catalana: las orquestas Martín de la Rosa, Gongo, Ramón Evaristo y Plantación, el dúo de piano Matas-Roqueta, el terceto Barreto, el Cuarteto Masmitjá, el Quinteto Hot Club, y las cantantes Conchita Leonardo y Rina Celi."

45. Tete, in Jurado 1998, 59.

46. Tete, in Jurado 1998, 57, 59. Tete later professed to have learned some English from jazz musicians (Jurado 1998, 59; Tete, in Jurado 1992, 36). Alfredo Papo was there that day with George Johnson: Tete was 12 and Papo was 21. Papo was one of those responsible for the Hot Club of Barcelona, and Tete mentions that he became aware that they had divergent tastes in jazz from that point onward (Jurado 1998, 59–60).

47. From "Las opiniones de un pianista," signed by Carlos Carrero, published in the *Tele-Expres* from January 1966 (ONCE).

48. Similarly, Tete stated that "la música es de los pocos lenguajes dignos que existen" (music is one of the few worthy languages that exist), quoted from Javier Rivera's interview piece "Tete Montoliu, una vida para el jazz," likely published in the early 1980s (ONCE).

49. Byas was born in 1912 in Muskogee, Oklahoma.

50. Iglesias 2013b, 103.

51. Jurado 1998, 61, 63. This was by the invitation of Alfredo Matas, director of the cine Windsor and responsible for the Copacabana.

52. Tete, in Jurado 1992, 22.

53. Jurado 1992, 20–21.

54. Pérez Vigo 2015, 270.

55. Jurado 1998, 64–65.

56. Jurado 1998, 65; see 63–68 for more on Byas.

57. Byas is referred to as a "segundo padre" (second father) to Tete in García Martínez 1997, 6. Byas returned to play with Tete's quartet in Barcelona at the Teatro Comedia on 5 May 1958.

58. Tete, in Jurado 1998, 74.

59. Tete, in Jurado 1998, 74–75.

60. Jurado 1998, 75. Jurado reports that the concert prompted a polemic about the new style of music, and members of the Hot Club of Barcelona who had set it up tried to defend the group without clearly supporting their musical style. Shortly after the concert, a brief interview with Ribera, Pérez, and Montoliu appeared in the "Ud. dirá" column of a local publication (March 26, 1952, ONCE).

61. The article's main title is "'Tete' Montoliu, El Gran Pianista de 'Jazz' Contrajo Ayer Matrimonio" (ONCE, *Diario de Barcelona*, April 6, 1956, p. 27, signed by Tomás Hernández).

62. Jurado 1998, 81–82. Also, "Reacciones y opiniones que revelaban una actitud racista por parte de la sociedad de aquellos años que no podía entender que Tete estuviera enamorado de una negra" (There were reactions and opinions that revealed a racist attitude on part of a society that in those years could not understand that Tete might be in love with a black woman) (Pujol Baulenas 2005, 299).

63. Tete, in Jurado 1998, 82. Also of interest, when an interview with Tete appeared in Barcelona's *La Vanguardia Española* soon after the concert with Lionel Hampton on March 24, 1956, the interviewer, who signed as Del Arco, noted Pilar's presence in a marked way from the outset: "Vicente es ciego de nacimiento. Me sorprende, al recibirme en su domicilio, con esta presentación: —Pilar Morales, mi prometida.— Estrecho la mano de una muchacha de color. Ella permanece al lado del músico mientras charlamos" (Vicente is blind from birth. He surprises me, upon greeting me at his home, with this presentation: —Pilar Morales, my fiancée.—I shake the hand of a young woman of color. She remains by the musician's side while we chat) (ONCE). Later in the published interview, Del Arco asks "¿Puedo preguntar qué es lo que les une?" (Can I ask what brings you together?).

64. "En Tete i la Pilar no actuaven junts en directe, però van gravar diversos discos de pedra de 78 revolucions amb el nom de Tete Montoliu y su Conjunto Tropical i un

repertori de boleros, mambos i *cha-cha-chás*" (Tete and Pilar did not play together live, but they recorded various 78-revolution stone records under the name of Tete Montoliu y su Conjunto Tropical and a repertoire of boleros, mambos and cha-cha-chas) (Jurado 1998, 82). The use of "pedra" (stone) in this quote refers to the practice of recording on records that were made of shellac and some mixture of mineral filler, many times from slate or limestone. Tete says they put him on the album because Pilar i Jorge Candela would sell better with his name: "Des de que tenia quinze anys el meu nom sempre ha venut" (Since I was fifteen years old my name has always sold) (Tete, in Jurado 1998, 84). Pilar and Tete did perform on a brief tour together at the end of 1956 (84), when they went to Zurich to play at the Café Terrasse. While there, Tete was able to see a performance at Congress Hall that included Lester Young, Miles Davis (even playing together), Bud Powell, and the Modern Jazz Quartet (86).

65. Tete, in Jurado 1998, 87. Also, regarding the decline of relationship with Pilar, "Si jo no hagués estat cec o, com a mínim, hagués estat més autònom, tot s'hauria acabat abans, però egoistament a mi ja m'anava bé. Vaig ser molt egoista en aquella època, ara ho veig clar però jo no ho puc arreglar" (If I hadn't been blind or, if at least I had been more self-sufficient, things would have ended sooner, but I was selfish and it was going well for me. I was very self-centered in those days, now I see it clearly, but I can't fix it) (151).

66. Tete and Montserrat García-Albea got married in Barcelona on April 20, 1995 (Jurado 1998, 223).

67. Jurado 1998, 95.

68. As related in García 2015, 387–88.

69. In this respect, there is a wealth of research that can be consulted on the historical links between the Christian Reconquest of the Iberian peninsula (711–1492) from North African Berber Muslims, the existence of slavery in medieval and early modern Iberia, and the Spanish Empire's Conquest of the Americas. See, for example, Phillips 2014 and Braun and Vollendorf 2013. As María Frías (2004, 141) begins her book chapter, "Historically, the blackening of Spain started in the eighth century when the Moors invaded the Andalusian region in the south. When this first period of black influence ended with the Moors being expelled by force at the end of the fifteenth century, the Moorish influence could be felt almost all over the country." In the context of discussing jazz, Paul Austerlitz attempts to distinguish Spain from other European empires: "As part of a larger Afro-Asian-Iberian nexus, Spaniards were primed for social and musical interaction with Africans when the two groups met in the Americas. Spaniards' previous exposure to Africa contrasts starkly with northern Europeans' geographic isolation, which inhibited the assimilation of African influences into English, Dutch, and French colonial culture" (Austerlitz 2005, 45–46; the differences between Spanish and North American slavery are discussed on p. 46). On the Iberian Atlantic see Moya 2013.

70. Bermúdez 2018, 7. "The processes and practices of imagining race are not new to Spain. Indeed, considering that the rise and expansion of European modernity rest heavily on the emergence of the colonial enterprises of the fifteenth and sixteenth centuries and on the articulation of racial differences 'to manage work,

reproduction, and the social organization of the colonized' (Lowe 2006, 204), Baltasar Fra-Molinero (2000) reminds us that early modern Spain and colonial Spanish America are initial contributors to the practices of racial hierarchization." See also Branche 2006, 3; Martín-Márquez 2008.

71. Cornejo-Parriego 2020b, 6.

72. Cornejo-Parriego 2020b, 6. See also in particular the chapters by M. Rocío Cobo-Piñero on the Jazz Age, Laurence E. Prescott and Rosalía Cornejo-Parriego on Josephine Baker, and Isabel Soto on Langston Hughes.

73. Montoliu's early experiences with jazz music unfold during the late 1930s and early 1940s, thus predating the enlightening example that Cornejo-Parriego (2020b, 5–6) gives of the musician Santiago Auserón, whose memories are used to date the arrival of Black music to Spain in the late 1950s and 1960s.

74. Hughes 1993, 315.

75. See Rogers 2016.

76. Hughes 1993n340. This anecdote is interesting from the perspective of theorist Fumi Okiji's notion of "gathering in difference," discussed in this book's initial note and later in this introduction.

77. Hughes 1993, 350–51. See also Soto 2020, 161.

78. Hughes 1993, 353. See also Collum 1992.

79. Soto 2017, 206.

80. Rogers 2016.

81. Rogers 2016, 167: "The blackness of Spain, however obscured, transfigured, or distorted over time, was apparent to W. E. B. Du Bois, for whom the 'black Spaniard' was part of the global battle for racial justice. Du Bois's journal *Crisis* pointed in a variety of articles to the hidden vitality of 'black Spain,' to its 'black madonnas,' even to Picasso and Gris as having come from 'Afro-Celtiberian Spain.' As neocolonialist ambitions in Spain and Italy cast new 'African shadows,' Du Bois exhorted an expanded range of 'black Spaniard[s]' to see their own implication in the struggle against capitalist imperialism and for an international black 'modern culture.'"

82. His perspective is not without its own complexity, as Isabel Soto (2020, 155) notes: "Hughes offers a distinctive perspective on the question of race on 20th century Spanish soil, cognizant of himself as black even as he projects a racialized construction onto Spaniards themselves."

83. Rogers 2016.

84. In the words of Rogers 2016, 198.

85. For example, Soto 2017; DeGuzmán 2005; Schmidt-Nowara 2001. "Wright is here in fact tapping into a history of negative exceptionalism which mobilizes the racial and affects Spain and Africa alike" (Soto 2017, 213). Schmidt Nowara explores the connection between "Wright's Black Atlantic and Spain's Black Legend" (2001, 150). See also the foundational study by Paul Gilroy (1993).

86. Wright 1995, 4.

87. Iglesias 2013b, 102. Also, "Després de la guerra, tot i que la música de jazz no estava específicament prohibida pel franquisme, estava sempre associada a un tipus de mentalitat més progressista, més esquerrana, i això estava mal mirat" (After the

war, although jazz music was not specifically prohibited by Francoism, it was always associated with a more progressive, more leftist mentality, and that was seen poorly) (Jurado, in Jurado 1992, 25). Bermúdez (2018, 29) mentions that "Spaniards consumed—as exotic objects—Afro-Cuban music and jazz during the 1930s and onwards," but since her book is concerned with the 1980s, 1990s, and beginnings of the 21st century, she does not explore the first half of the 20th century or the dictatorship with sufficient detail for our purposes here. See also Pedro 2016.

88. Iglesias 2013b, 102.

89. Iglesias 2010c, 125–26.

90. Quoted in Iglesias 2013b, 102: "By mid-1942, at the height of fascist enthusiasm, the Vice-Secretariat of Popular Education banned the broadcasting of 'the so-called black music, swing, or any other kind of compositions whose lyrics are in a foreign language.'" See also Iglesias 2013b, 110nn1–2 for original sources).

91. Iglesias 2013b, 103.

92. Iglesias 2010c, 130.

93. Iglesias 2013a.

94. Iglesias 2013b, 103.

95. This precise comparison of jazz's reception is also made in Holguín 2019, 185.

96. Iglesias 2010c, 125; also, Iglesias 2013a, 102; Thompson 2018.

97. Thompson 2018, 92–94; also xix, xiii. One must note, as Thompson does, that racializing discourse at the time suggested European composers were unable to reproduce the "insurmountable racial quality in African American jazz" (2018, xix). Yet as the scholar also points out, "This critical position, even when unintentional, is neither interesting nor worthwhile to pursue, as it obstructs analysis of the sociocultural, political, and aesthetic reasons for why German musicians either consciously adopted or outright avoided racialized black poses in the music itself. Germans wrote and played jazz. The critical difference lay not in whether German jazz composers heard nonnotational notes that African-Americans could hear, but rather how the German critical discourse surrounding jazz sought to manipulate that assumption to racist or antiracist ends" (xiii).

98. This characterization is supported by the examples provided in the "Note for the General Reader on Theodor W. Adorno and Jazz Criticism" that appears at the beginning of this book. Thompson 2018, 90.

99. "On Jazz," Adorno 2002a, 485. No doubt this is what occurred in Germany, a topic covered convincingly in the fourth chapter of Thompson's book, titled "The Music of Fascism: Adorno on Jazz" (Thompson 2018, 89–112).

100. Thompson 2018, xiii. Adorno's attempt to separate discussion of jazz music in Germany from US Blackness was thus part of a rhetorical move to expose the way in which this appropriation—the performance of "primitive" music by white Europeans—was itself racially charged. Yet even though Adorno may have demonstrated an awareness of how German fascism appropriated jazz to construct what was consumed as the musical object belonging to "a racially inferior culture," the philosopher did not go far enough: "Adorno is fully aware that the potential for fascism's appropriation of German jazz rests on the very hierarchical, discursive

logic fascists use to generate and condition belief in jazz as the product of a racially inferior culture. In removing African America from jazz history, Adorno seeks to critique fascism's claims to jazz without offering a corrective. In his jazz essays, Adorno is interested exclusively in attacking the culture industry as collusive with fascism, and after the war with totalitarianism more generally. He has no interest in speaking to race or the sociopolitical condition and cultural contribution of African Americans in Europe and America" (Thompson 2018, 93).

101. Thompson 2018, xxvi.
102. Okiji 2018, 6; see also Witkin 1998, 2000. Okiji works through claims that Adorno's view recognized and affirmed the African American origins of jazz, but that he saw any resulting challenge as anaesthetized by the culture industry (Buhler 2006). There is also the claim that the form of jazz—its presumed malleability and structuring through interchangeable parts, if not the ambivalent quality of improvisation itself—or rather the lack of form in jazz, is what allows it to become "but a tool of coercion and control" in service to capitalist ideology (Okiji 2018, 18).
103. Okiji 2018, 24.
104. This quotation is from "Entrevista con Tete Montoliu," by Julio Martínez, p. 104 (ONCE).
105. There is an appreciation here of the formal aesthetics of jazz music, one that has nothing at all to do with the staid and reductive structural view put forth by the author of "On Jazz."
106. Okiji 2018, 5. Here she departs radically from Adorno's simplistic binary that distinguished jazz from classical music and that attributed only to one of these two forms the possibility of being "critical."
107. Okiji 2018, 5.
108. Okiji 2018, 6.
109. Okiji 2018, 34.
110. Okiji 2018, 74.
111. Okiji 2018, 29–30.
112. Though this exact phrase does not itself appear in Okiji's book—it does appear on the back cover—this is a crucial characterization of her book's argument. I regard the preposition "in" as much more powerful than the phrase "gathering of difference," which does appear in the book, in the sense that difference should not be reified but instead conceptualized as a relation.
113. Okiji 2018, 5.
114. Okiji 2018, 32, 39–40. See also Du Bois 1996[1903].
115. This article was written by Ramón Sánchez Ocaña and published on February 28, 1969 (ONCE).
116. Consider also that an article from March 22, 1956, published in *Solidaridad Nacional*, notes of the coverage of Lionel Hampton's concert that month that "lo sorprendente es que gran parte de la Prensa no reflejara este entusiasmo y por otra parte tratase este hombre de manera un tanto descortés" (the surprising thing is that a great portion of the Press doesn't reflect this enthusiasm and moreover that

it treats this man (Hampton) in a somewhat impolite manner) (p. 19, ONCE). More on Lionel Hampton in chapter 1.

117. The friction given in Tete's transnational adaptation of jazz is not something that this book seeks to smooth out. I do not seek to comment on his felt associations with Blackness, for that matter. By no means do I want to suggest that Tete's musical production is synonymous with the expression of Blackness and the critique of US racial oppression launched through the music of African American jazz artists. To do so would be to ignore the reality of Tete's European social, racial, and musical context. Tete did talk frequently about the effort he put into playing jazz like the Black American musicians he listened to and played with, and he received approbation from Black American musicians who welcomed him with statements like (from Elvin Jones) "Toca usted como nosotros." For these examples, see Julio Coll's interview piece titled "Yo, Tete Montoliu," published in the "El jazz y todo lo demás" column of a print publication (ONCE).

118. Okiji 2018, 96–97. Commenting on the roots of the jazz form with Black American players, Tete once said, "[L]o cierto es que cuando uno de ellos sale bueno, es mejor que todos nosotros juntos. Es lo suyo. Es su música. La sienten de un modo especial. De un modo que ningún blanco puede sentirla" (What is certain is that when [a black American player] is really good, he is better than all us [Europeans] put together. It's his own. It's his music. They feel it in a special way. In a way that no white person can feel it) (ONCE, interview in "Crónica Ciudadana" section of a periodical, likely in the 1970s, signed by Ferrán Monegal).

119. This quotation comes from Joan Riambau's article "Una vida a tot jazz," published in *Avui* on August 25, 1997, p. 30, on the day after Tete's death (ONCE).

120. About Archie Shepp, with whom Tete played, Okiji writes: "Likewise, saxophonist Archie Shepp shared the belief that 'the Negro people . . . are the only hope of saving America, the political or the cultural America'" (in Okiji 2018, 50).

Chapter 1

1. This quotation is from the May 4, 1985, edition of *Mediterráneo*, where it appeared in an interview piece titled "Tete Montoliu: El músico catalán es del Barça y empieza cada vez que sube a un escenario" by Daniel Llorens (ONCE).

2. Nevertheless, Juan Zagalaz (2012b, 33) has offered ample evidence to the contrary in the *Journal of Jazz Studies*. As Zagalaz conveys, this remark appears frequently in criticism on jazz and Spain. Feather's view is echoed in the work of other jazz critics, for example in Maggie Hawthorn's statement that "Spain is hardly the cradle of jazz" (ONCE, from the *Seattle Post Intelligencer*, September 22, 1979). Also of interest is a "Music" column by Leonard Feather in the *San Francisco Chronicle* from October 14 to October 20, 1979, with the subheading "Enough real talent to justify the celebration" in which the critic wrote of Montoliu: "His background was supremely unlikely to equip him for a life in jazz. Like most citizens in totalitarian countries

he was almost completely deprived of exposure to jazz" (ONCE). This statement, as chapters in this book explore, cannot be taken seriously in the way Feather intends. He also writes there of how "the barren Spanish scene slowed Montoliu's acceptance." In a brief announcement from 1984 detailing the specifics of Tete Montoliu's upcoming performance with Sherman Ferguson and John Heard at the Reed Opera House in Salem on May 9, Feather is quoted as having written, "That a man with these handicaps, born and raised in a country where jazz was all but unknown, can achieve what he has is another of those inexplicable marvels that the art form comes up with every now and then" (ONCE). Spain does not appear in Leonard Feather's 1960 publication *The Encyclopedia of Jazz*, where in the section "Jazz Overseas" Feather mentions that "[m]ost experts have agreed that England, France, Sweden and Germany have produced the best jazz outside the United States" (1960, 486). Feather includes a brief entry on Montoliu in *The Encyclopedia of Jazz in the Seventies* (1976, 248), where he writes: "For many years Tete remained almost unknown, because of the lack of jazz activity in Spain."

3. Book-length studies such as José María García Martínez's *Del Fox Trot al Jazz Flamenco: El jazz en España: 1919–1996* (From the fox trot to flamenco jazz: Jazz in Spain 1919–1996) (1996), Jordi Pujol Baulenas's *Jazz en Barcelona, 1920–1965* (Jazz in Barcelona, 1920–1965) (2005), and Juan Giner, Joan Sardà, and Enric Vázquez's *Guía universal del jazz moderno* (Universal guide to modern jazz) (2006) are available for those who read Spanish; as are PhD dissertations and MA theses such as Iván Iglesias's "Improvisando la modernidad: El jazz y la España de Franco, de la Guerra Civil a la Guerra Fría (1936–1968)" (Improvising modernity: Jazz and Franco's Spain, from the Civil War to the Cold War [1936–1968]) (2010), Sandra Milena Moreno Sabogal's "Gestión del Jazz en la ciudad de Valencia" (The management of jazz in the city of Valencia) (2012), and Miguel Arribas García's "El Jazz en Barcelona durante la transición española (1975–1982)" (Jazz in Barcelona during the Spanish Transition [1975–1982]) (2015). Those who read Catalan may consult books like Alfredo Papo's *El jazz a Catalunya* (Jazz in Catalonia) (1985) or *Els 100 millors discos del jazz català* (The 100 best albums of Catalan jazz) (2012), coordinated by journalist and music critic Pere Pons i Martí Farré.

4. Cerchiari, Cugny, and Kerschbaumer 2012, vii: "The bibliography on regional histories and single musicians is quite a rich one, with more or less one hundred titles (among biographies are represented some of the most important European jazzmen ever—Django Reinhardt, Stéphane Grappelli, Martial Solal, Jean 'Toots' Thielemans, Jan Garbarek, George Shearing, Ian Carr, Joaquim Kühn, Albert Mangelsdorff, Gorni Kramer, Giorgio Gaslini, Enrio Rava, Jose Zawinul, Willem Breuker, Tete Montoliu)." Tete is mentioned specifically in a list of "single experiments consisting of new stimulating crossovers of jazz and ethnic roots" in Europe (xvii). Note, too, that the book suggests "the history of jazz in Europe has yet to be effectively written" (vii). See also Arndt 2012 and Cerciari 2012.

5. See Zagalaz 2012a, 2012b; Manuel 2016.

6. Quoted from the "Entrevista sincopada" signed by José Viñals and published in March 1962 (ONCE).

7. As Juan Zagalaz explores in the article "Los orígenes de la relación jazz-flamenco de Lionel Hampton a Pedro Iturralde (1956–1968)," in the mid-1960s, de Lucía had released a series of albums with evocative flamenco titles such as *12 Canciones de García Lorca para Guitarra* (Polygram Ibérica, 1965), *La fabulosa Guitarra de Paco de Lucía* (Polygram Ibérica, 1967), and *Fantasía Flamenca* (Universal Music Spain, 1967). See also Sevilla 1995.

8. In asserting that a market developed that gave attention to flamenco jazz in Spain, I am drawing also on the work of Juan Zagalaz, particularly in Zagalaz 2012b.

9. In Hispanic studies, this mode of scholarship has its equivalent in the work of Frances R. Aparicio and Susana Chávez-Silverman through their book *Tropicalizations: Transcultural Representations of Latinidad* (1997).

10. Bakriges 2003, 113.

11. See Austerlitz 2005, 42, also 50: "Jazz composer Jelly Roll Morton argued that 'Spanish tinges' were essential to jazz already in the early twentieth century." One notes that though this wording changes with time from "Spanish tinges" to "Latin tinges," they are nonetheless influences forged by Spanish colonization.

12. See also the comments on the historical context of this lexical choice in Washburne's "Latin Jazz, the Other Jazz": "At that time, 'Spanish' referred to music coming from any Spanish-speaking region" (Washburne 2001–2002, 414). In commenting on Jelly Roll Morton and the notion of a Spanish tinge, Juan Zagalaz notes that "el concepto 'español' en la Nueva Orleans de principios de siglo XX debe ser tomado con cautela" (2016, 96). On the ties with music in the black diaspora, see Abrahams et al. (2006, 30). See also Fernández 2006; González 2004; Roberts 1999; Suárez 1989.

13. See the listing at the end of Jurado 1998.

14. Note that, as one critic has mentioned, "[e]ven the 'Soleá' in his Sketches of Spain, although a languid rumination in Phrygian mode, has no distinctive flamenco features and is certainly not a soleá/soleares" (Manuel 2016, 51).

15. Rodrigo (1901–99) was born in Sagunto, Valencia, Spain. On the track's exceptionality, see Gioia 2011, 270.

16. Crouch 2006, 4. This reflection occurs in the critic's prologue.

17. Tete, in Jurado 1992, 17–18. Tete's statement in an interview that he disliked both Rodrigo's music and what he referred to as his fascism is also interesting, and just as interesting is his allusion to a Japanese release with a track where Montoliu quotes the melody of the "Concierto de Aranjuez" and afterward quickly turns to the improvisation of a blues tune (Tete, in Jurado 1992, 18). On the same page Tete also says: "*L'Aranjuez* . . . que jo he fet en el disc japonès no té res a veure amb l'original, és un trosset de la melodia i després hi improviso un blues. M'ho van imposar i jo no sabia què fer, amb això. A més, no sé tocar música clàssica" (The *Aranjuez* . . . that I did on the Japanese record has nothing to do with the original, it is a portion of the melody and afterwards I improvise a blues. They imposed it on me and I didn't know what to do with it. Also, I don't know how to play classical music). See also Cerchiari, Cugny, and Kerschbaumer 2012, xi, which mentions Miles Davis and Rodrigo's *Concierto de Aranjuez*.

18. One of the chief anchors for this reception is this inclusion of the "Concierto de Aranjuez," Aranjuez being a location directly south of Madrid and thus very close to the geographic center of the country, boasting a Royal Palace that is associated with the reigns of Kings Phillip II and Ferdinand VI. Other musical elements are discussed in the body text.

19. See Bakriges 2003, 107: "The marquis events that signal the change from 'jazz in Europe' to 'europaischer Jazz' emanate from the aftermath of the free movement of the sixties. It is in the wake of this period when the terms 'German jazz' or 'Italian jazz' come to the fore, as the perception of national jazz traditions are formed. These traditions are a result of the development of a jazz self-consciousness in Europe, a parallel, albeit later, development to the mainstreaming of a jazz tradition in America. Utilizing folk music traditions with musical improvisation and the jazz language (*Jazzbereich gefunden*) have served both to expand the borders of jazz, and to demarcate what many argue are distinctive national musical spaces in Europe."

20. Also relevant here are jazz critic Nat Hentoff's liner notes for *Sketches in Spain*, in which he relates the fact that Miles Davis and Gil Evans decided to record the piece because of a fortuitous encounter: it was in 1959 when one of Davis's friends played a recording of Rodrigo's composition for the renowned US trumpet player.

21. Manuel 2016, 40.

22. This quote by Hentoff is taken at face value and put to different use in a book chapter authored by a researcher from the Universidad de La Coruña, Spain (Frías 2004, 147).

23. Manuel 2016, 51.

24. Zagalaz 2016, 113.

25. Crouch 2006, 249; originally published in 1986 as "On the Corner: The Sellout of Miles Davis."

26. Iglesias 2013b, 109.

27. Labanyi 2003, 5.

28. Hayes 2009, 1.

29. See Hayes 2009, 29–37; Steingress 1998; and Holguín 2019, particularly part III, which is titled "Flamenco and the Franco Regime."

30. Steingress 1998, 167.

31. See García Gómez 1998, 194, 201. This includes landmarks in Spanish literature including *La Regenta*, and makes reference to the Concurso de 1922 where Fall and Lorca tied flamenco to the idea of Spain's national soul.

32. See Steingress 1998, 180.

33. See Guibernau 2004, introduction and chapters 2–3. "The triumph of the insurrectionists in the Spanish Civil War (1936–1939) represented the almost complete annihilation of the autonomous Catalan institutions (although some continued in exile) and the proscription of the country's language and culture" (1).

34. Steingress 1998, 180.

35. Woods Peiró 2012, 2.

36. Woods Peiró 2012, 20.

37. Note that because of their compositional similarities, these three recordings tend to be referenced together in jazz criticism. Two such examples occur in Crouch 2006, 54, 248.

38. Charnon-Deutsch 2003, 22.

39. Zagalaz 2016, 121. The quotation continues: "El necesario empleo de sonoridades frigias tiene tintes más *latinos* que propiamente *españoles*. Marca en cambio un hito histórico la entrada en escena de uno de los músicos de jazz españoles más importante de la historia: Tete Montoliu" (The necessary use of Phrygian sounds has more *latin* than truly *Spanish* overtones. It marks instead a historical milestone, this being the entry to the scene of one of the most important Spanish jazz musicians in history: Tete Montoiu).

40. Anderson, in preface to Ross 2003, ii, iii.

41. Hasse 2012, 189.

42. Hasse 2012, 189–90.

43. Hasse 2012, 190: "a European tour by the Ellington orchestra in the summer of 1933, sponsored by the British bandleader Jack Hylton."

44. Iglesias 2013b, 101.

45. Iglesias 2013b, 101.

46. Parsonage 2012, 167.

47. Iglesias 2013b, 101; Iglesias dates this opening to 1935, while Antoni Pizà and Francesc Vicens (2019, 11) date it to 1934.

48. Atkins (2003b, xiv) uses the phrase "U.S. economic interests and military muscle." See also Borge 2018.

49. Hampton (1908–2002) was born in Louisville, Kentucky.

50. Townsend 1959.

51. Zingg 1957.

52. See Gac 2005, also Iglesias 2013b.

53. See Iglesias 2013b, 105. Also, "Although the band was not sponsored by the Department of State, Hampton's tour went far to add to the musical bridge that American jazzmen and American music has built between other peoples of the world and ourselves" (Zingg 1957).

54. Quotation from Zingg 1957. Chapter 3 continues with this subject by considering an example from the 1920s.

55. Iglesias 2013b, 105: "Certainly, the visits of many leading American jazzmen and bluesmen to Barcelona starting in 1950, although facilitated by new Spanish-American relations, are primarily attributable to the efforts and negotiations of the Hot Clubs of Barcelona and Granollers: Willie 'The Lion' Smith, in 1950; Mezz Mezzrow, in 1951; Bill Coleman, in 1952; Dizzy Gillespie, 'Big Bill' Broonzy, and Jimmy Davis, in 1953; Lionel Hampton, Louis Armstrong, and Sidney Bechet, in 1955; Sammy Price and Count Basie, in 1956." See also Pérez Vigo 2015, 270.

56. See Jurado 1998, 89.

57. Tete, in Jurado 1998, 89. Elsewhere Tete relates a shorter version of this, see Tete, in Jurado 1992, 50.

58. Tete, in Jurado 1998, 90.

59. The column appeared in *La Vanguardia Española* and was signed by Del Arco (ONCE). It opens with the sentence: "Lionel Hampton ha declarado que Vicente Montoliu es el mejor pianista de jazz de España y le ha prometido llevárselo con él en su orquesta" (Lionel Hampton has stated that Vicente Montoliu is the best jazz pianist in Spain and has promised to bring him along with his orchestra).

60. Feather 1980, 119; also on this same page: "Few know that behind the façade is one of the world's wealthiest musicians, a socially and politically concerned citizen, a philanthropist and an ardent Republican who numbered the late Vice President Nelson Rockefeller among his closest associates."

61. Tete also notes that in Papo's book the author was very selective in his discussion of this pivotal event, omitting key details (Tete, in Jurado 1998, 90). After this recognition by Hampton, however, Papo suddenly wanted to be the pianist's friend.

62. Ted Gioia (2016, 259) opposes Milt Jackson's "softer, more relaxed manner" to "the note-filled cadenzas and ornamentation of Hampton's solo outings." "Few figures of the prebop era, with the obvious exception of Art Tatum (with whom the vibraphonist later jousted in a session of not-filled excesses), could squeeze more into a sixteen-bar solo than Hampton. In the battle of form versus content, the latter always won when this seminal figure was on stage" (Gioia 2011, 142).

63. This sort of comment is also replicated in somewhat later European press coverage, for example in a review of Tete's performance at Barcelona's Palau by Jaume Cleries published May 10, 1979, in the *Mundo Diario*, where the critic says that Tete was "víctima de su propia técnica" (victim of his own technique) (ONCE).

64. Tete, in Jurado 1998, 93; Tete, in Jurado 1992, 50.

65. Jurado 1998, 91–92.

66. The names of the members of "Hampton and the Flamenco Five" are not specified.

67. Jurado 1998, 92.

68. Jurado says that Tete played flamenco on Lionel Hampton's album and Tete responds, "Jo vaig tocar un tema que no té res a veure amb el flamenc. La història té molta gràcia" (I played a song that has nothing to do with flamenco. The story is quite amusing) (Tete, in Jurado 1992, 50).

69. Zingg 1957.

70. Zingg 1957.

71. Jurado 1998, 92. All this despite the fact that Hamp had been part of "the first interracial group in the history of jazz," Benny Goodman's quartet (which included Goodman, Gene Krupa, Hampton, and Teddy Wilson). This dynamic may have also continued through the rest of Tete's tour with Hampton. The pianist stated: "No vaig arribar a tocar en l'orquestra de Lionel Hampton perquè la seva dona no hi volia blancs" (I didn't get to play in Lionel Hampton's orchestra because his wife didn't want whites there) (Tete, in Jurado 1992, 50).

72. This album cover image is reproduced in Jurado 1998.

73. See Iglesias 2013b, 106: "Hampton recorded in Madrid an extravagant album entitled *Jazz Flamenco*, successfully distributed in the United States and in Spain by the RCA-Victor label. A *DownBeat* reviewer wrote that the diplomatic importance of Hampton's tour and recording undoubtedly exceeded the value of the music itself."

74. Jones was born in 1894 in Ohio, USA; Kahn was born in 1886 in Koblenz, Germany.

75. Juan Zagalaz (2016, 100) makes similar remarks on this aspect of the recording.

76. Despite André Hodeir's dismissal of Art Tatum's "genius" status, even he seems to regard Tatum's performance of "Tenderly" as worthy of acclaim. See Hodier 1962, 134.

77. Jurado 1998, 231–32.

78. In chapters 2 and 4, these aesthetic contradictions are approached within an urban and a disability framework, respectively.

79. Here both the Spanish and the English translation are taken from the liner notes on the re-release, which are also provided in French and German translation.

80. For more information on these performances, readers can consult the online discography at http://www.jazzdiscography.com/Artists/Montoliu/tete-disc.php.

Chapter 2

1. Atkins 2003b, xiii. "Jazz exists in our collective imagination as both a *national* and *postnational* music, but is studied almost exclusively in the former incarnation."

2. Young 1990, 1986; Jacobs 1992; Harvey 1996.

3. See Davidson 2009, 139, for examples of how journalists in Barcelona "heard" the sound of the city as influencing jazz music.

4. Even extended analyses with an explicitly urban framing do not delve into the nature of urban life, but rather tend to take it as a given. One example is *Shaping Jazz: Cities, Labels, and the Global Emergence of an Art Form* (2013) by Damon J. Phillips, which looks at sixty-seven cities in which jazz was recorded in the pre-1934 period and explores some intriguing interpretations regarding the music produced in what the author calls cities with a high degree of "disconnectedness."

5. Atkins 2003b, xiii.

6. Peretti 1994, 7. Note also Peretti's informative and concise discussion of the early blues origins of jazz in his chapter 1.

7. Witkin 1998, 160.

8. Tete's comments on this are brief and somewhat unspecific: "Vivíem en una residència just a sobre del piano bar, de manera que la Pilar, com que ja estava avorrida de sentir-me tocar i no teníem res a dir-nos, es quedava a casa i jo baixava sol. Allà vaig conèixer una senyora danesa de qui vaig estar molt enamorat. Per a ella vaig escriure el tema *Apartment 512*" (We were living in a flat right above the piano bar, and Pilar, who was already tired of hearing me play and since we had nothing to say to each other, stayed at home and I went down to get some sun. There I met a Danish woman with whom I fell very much in love. I wrote the song "Apartment 512" for her) (Tete, in Jurado 1998, 145).

9. He also played this song by Bronislau Kaper and Ned Washington on a few occasions. The performance data, as opposed to the recording data, comes from the valuable database JazzDiscography.com (http://www.jazzdiscography.com/Artists/Montoliu/tete-comp.php).

10. The song has been described as "a twin of Randle's Island" (Büchmann-Møller 2010, 309). Also, on the entire album, "Montoliu holds back, refraining from steamrolling the soloist with his outstanding technique" (Büchmann-Møller 2010, 309). Compare Stanley Crouch's dismissal of Tete's playing on this album as "mannered." Compared with Büchmann-Møller's assessment, Crouch seems to have no understanding of how well Tete is playing the role of accompanist. The critic writes: "But what impresses me most about Webster's continued dedication is his ability to create swing or cloudlike flotation even when held down by willing but unswinging European rhythm sections. Ten months before his death, Rooster Ben recorded *Did You Call?* Though the performances are slightly marred by the mannered piano of Tete Montoliu, Webster was in classic form" (Crouch 2006, 124). This is also testament to the US-European divide and the perception of European jazz as subpar.

11. Berish 2019, see also Berish 2012.

12. See Fraser 2015, chapter 1, titled "Why Urban Cultural Studies? Why Lefebvre?" On the themes of art and culture in Lefebvre, see Fraser 2015, chapter 3, and also, most importantly, Lefebvre 2006a, 1988.

13. This hallmark distinction is also the basis of the urban theory of Barcelona-based urban critic Manuel Delgado Ruiz. See Delgado Ruiz 2007b, 11; also Delgado Ruiz 2010, 2007a, 1999, 2002.

14. Understood as a relational process, the complexity of the urban requires forms of knowledge that push beyond the limitations of disciplinary specialization. See Lefebvre's comments in *The Urban Revolution* (2003, 57).

15. See Lefebvre 2006b, 2005, 2002, 1991.

16. Lefebvre 2006b, 21, 22.

17. Wirth 1938, 2.

18. Mumford 1970, 4, 191, also Mumford 1961; Lefebvre 2006b, 21. On the substantial differences in their understandings, see Fraser 2015, chapter 2.

19. See Jacobs 1992; also Fraser 2012 on the links between Jacobs, Lefebvre, and Delgado Ruiz.

20. Lefebvre 1996; Fraser 2015.

21. See Harvey 2006, 3; Cerdà 1867; Fraser 2011.

22. See Sennett 1992, also 1994, 2008.

23. Lefebvre 1996; Delgado Ruiz 2007a.

24. Mumford 1970, 149–50, 159; Lefebvre 1996, 177; 2007, 47, 134, 195; Harvey 1989, 24.

25. This inquiry differs somewhat from what Paul Austerlitz (2005) has called "jazz consciousness." See Harvey 1989.

26. Simmel 2010, 103, 106.

27. These shifts have to do with the uneven geographical development of the urban form. On uneven geographical development, see the foundational work Smith 1984. Also, as E. Taylor Atkins notes, "Jazz indeed jeopardized national unity and aggravated existing social tensions by sharpening awareness of the 'unevenness' of modernity . . . , the unequal distribution of its technologies and opportunities" (Atkins 2003b, xvi).

28. See Delgado Ruiz 1999, 208.

29. Delgado Ruiz 2007a, 11.

30. Berish 2019; Lott 1998, 461.

31. The effect is more subdued in the recording of "Come Sunday" on the solo piano album *Yellow Dolphin Street* (1977), where the left hand many times takes on the role of passive observer rather than detachment per se.

32. Consider that this rhythmic contrast is far less pronounced on the later album *Carmina* (1984) where Tete plays with John Heard on bass and Sherman Ferguson on drums.

33. The first two are from the defining concert released as *Tete Montoliu al Palau* (1979).

34. Tete shares this anecdote himself, and both Monk and Charles Mingus were in the audience (Tete, in Jurado 1992, 60). Thelonious also heard Tete play in Berlin and Copenhagen (Tete, in Jurado 1998, 131). Consider, too: "Un altre músic a qui en Tete va admirar profundament al llarg de tota la vida va ser Thelonious Monk" (Another musician whom Tete admired profoundly throughout his life was Thelonious Monk) (Jurado 1998, 131).

35. See, for example, the liner notes for *Piano for Nuria* (1968), written by Joachim E. Berendt.

36. There is also a worthy solo recording of "Blues for Nuria" on *The Music I Like to Play, Vol. II*.

37. Albert "Tootie" Heath was a long-standing member of the Tete Montoliu Trio—appearing on a great number of recordings with the pianist and Peter Trunk—yet this connection is often neglected by jazz scholars and even elided by Heath himself in interviews. For example, in one interview with Leonard Feather, Heath doesn't mention Tete, even though he has the opportunity: "Feather: You've spent quite a bit of the last decade in Scandinavia, haven't you? Albert: Yes, the last three or four years I've been in and out of Scandinavia. My base is there now, and I'll be back there soon. I'm traveling all over the world enjoying myself" (from a 1979 interview, published in Feather 1980, 91). Elsewhere, Ross (2003, 105) emphasizes Heath's performance with Dexter Gordon in Denmark: "Albert Heath, Stuff Smith, and Don Cherry all migrated in 1965. Heath and Smith moved to Denmark, and Cherry moved to France. Albert Heath performed with Dexter Gordon in Denmark, and with Kenny Drew in France." One might suppose that Ross and Heath alike could have imagined Tete to be unknown and therefore uninteresting to US readers.

38. Chapter 4 returns to this subject in using the work of Joseph Straus to bridge discussions of disability and modernist music.

39. This phrase of course comes from the 1925 essay by José Ortega y Gasset.

40. Lefebvre 1991, 25. See also Lefebvre 1995, 1988.

41. See Davidson 2009, chapter 3; for example, the fact that Gasch "engaged the notion of rhythm in very spatial terms. His treatments of modern architecture, the music hall revue, and the city's visual environment show how his critical application of *ritme* (rhythm) transcended jazz music and came to be both informed by and indicative of urban space and the practices associated with it" (2009, 69). Note that Gasch was also a supporter of Miró's work (see Davidson 2009, 70, 73, 80, 95, 110). On Gasch, Miró, and the wider context of the avant-garde, see Carmona 1995; a reference to Gasch also appears in Galasso 2018, 99.

42. Such perspectives linking jazz and visual art are no less common today, in fact. For example, see Eric Nisenson's statement that "Monk reworked harmony and form, producing an idiosyncratic, eerily displaced music filtered through a twisted and cracked prism, comparable to the great works of cubism" (1995, 23). On jazz and modernism see Harvey 1991.

43. Robinson and Wietzel 2002, 73.

44. Robinson and Wietzel 2002, 69.

45. In addition to Robinson and Wietzel 2002, see https://jazzdiscography.com/Artists/Robinson/index.php.

46. Robinson and Wietzel 2002, 69.

47. This club was different from the clubs in Barcelona at the time—as Miquel Jurado characterizes it: "Al Whisky es tocava jazz, fins i tot jazz molt modern" (In the Whisky jazz was played, even a very modern jazz) (Jurado 1998, 106). See also Pujol Baulenas 2005, 351.

48. Pujol Baulenas 2005, 354.

49. Tete on piano, Perry on clarinet, Vicho (from Chile) on tenor sax, Antonion Vidal on bass, and Luis Sangareay (from Portugal) on drums (Robinson and Wietzel 2002, 70). In Barcelona, Perry ate at Tete's parents' house every weekend.

50. Robinson and Wietzel 2002, 71.

51. This quotation comes from an interview titled "Tete Montoliu" and published in the "Crónica Ciudadana" section of a periodical that—I gather from the context—was published in the 1970s (ONCE). The interviewer signs Ferrán Monegal.

52. Jurado 1998, 105, who is writing about the Hot Club's classic jazz bias, specifically.

53. Iglesias 2010c, 122. Baltasar Samper's lectures from 1935 (Samper 2019) outline the distinction between *hot* and *straight* jazz.

54. Note that these clubs were of course themselves related to the transnational circulation of jazz music. See Cerchiari, Cugny, and Kerschbaumer 2012, xvi.

55. Papo 1985, 37.

56. Papo 1985, 28–34.

57. Papo 1985, 32.

58. Garnet Clark on piano could not travel to Barcelona from the United States (Papo 1985, 31–32).

59. Pizà and Vicens 2019, 14.

60. Papo 1985, 37.

61. Papo 1985, 41; on leftists, see also p. 34; Jurado 1998, 54.

62. Jurado 1998, 57.

63. Pujol Baulenas 2005, 297.

64. Pujol Baulenas 2005, 277.

65. Pujol Baulenas 2005, 285.

66. Papo 1985, 81.

67. Iglesias 2011, 47–48. See also Iglesias 2010a, 2016.

68. As discussed in chapter 1, this assessment of the 1952 concert is Miquel Jurado's. One might also consider a December 1949 concert at the Sala Mozart where the

Be Bop Trio formed by Montoliu, Jordi Pérez, and Juli Robera performed (Papo 1985, 64).

69. García Martínez 1997, 6.
70. Jurado 1998, 78.
71. Tete, in Jurado 1998, 77.
72. Tete, in Jurado 1998, 78. Also, "Cada dia m'enamorava d'una holandesa diferent" (Each day I fell in love with a different Dutch woman) (Tete, in Jurado 1998, 78).
73. Tete, in Jurado 1998, 80.
74. Jurado 1998, 105.
75. Pujol Baulenas 2005, 350.
76. Cited in Pérez Vigo 2015, 392; drawing on an interview with Claudio Cascales from September 20, 2014. "Burrull sí grabó en 1958 dos discos con cuatro temas cada uno, tocando con dos baquetas también, con el célebre Tete Montoliu, el primero se llamó 'Tete Montoliu y su Cuarteto' y el segundo 'Tete Montoliu y su Conjunto.' Estas fueron las formaciones: con cuarteto; Tete Montoliu (piano), Francesc Burrull (vibráfono), Eduardo García (batería) y Ramón Farrán (contrabajo), y con conjunto; Tete Montoliu (piano), Ricard Roda (saxo alto), Francesc Burrull (vibráfono), Eduardo García (batería) y Ramón Farrán (contrabajo)" (Burrull did record in 1958 two records with four songs on each, playing with two mallets, too, with the famous Tete Montoliu, the first was called "Tete Montoliu y su Cuarteto" and the second "Tete Montoliu y su Conjunto." These were the formations: with quartet; Tete Montoliu [piano], Francesc Burrull [vibraphone], Eduardo García [drums] and Ramón Farrán [double bass], and with ensemble; Tete Montoliu [piano], Ricard Roda [alto sax], Francesc Burrull [vibraphone], Eduardo García [drums] and Ramón Farrán [double bass]). Note that on the four songs included on "Volumen 1" of *Tete Montoliu y su cuarteto*, for example, Burrull does not play on "Bernie's Theme," "Walking," or "Fine and Dandy," and that the cover for that 7″ vinyl recording lists Farrán as the drummer, rather than the bassist, and García as the bassist, rather than the drummer.
77. Jurado 1998, 102.
78. Pujol Baulenas 2005, 335.
79. Moreno Sabogal 2012, 13–14.
80. Tete, in Jurado 1998, 106.
81. Jurado reports that from September 1961 to June 1962, Tete played at the Jamboree in Barcelona with a quintet that included Dick Spencer (sax), Alfonso Blesses (drums), Tete, Peter Trunk (bass), and Bent Säedig (sax). During this time the violinist Stéphane Grappelli also passed through, visiting from Paris (Jurado 1998, 109). Though other accounts date the opening of the Jamboree to 1959, an online article gives a later date: "Propietat de l'empresari Joan Roselló i amb els membres del Jubilee Jazz Club com a programadors, el Jamboree va obrir oficialment el 9 de gener de 1960 amb un concert a les sis de la tarda d'un quintet liderat per Tete Montoliu" (Owned by the businessman Joan Roselló and with members of the Jubilee Jazz Club as its programmers, the Jamboree opened officially the 9th of January of 1960

with a concert at six in the afternoon by a quintet led by Tete Montoliu) (http://www.
elpuntavui.cat/cultura/article/19-cultura/268409-50-anys-del-jamboree.html).

82. "Thanks mainly to a young blind pianist, Tete Montoliu, who was to become the
most international and influential Spanish jazz-man, so-called 'modern jazz' gradu-
ally abandoned its marginal position in Spain in the late 1950s and early 1960s"
(Iglesias 2013b, 103).

83. Tete, in Jurado 1992, 55.

84. The quotation continues: "In Portugal, also under a Fascist regime in the years following World War II, the situation was much the same" (*Eurojazzland*, Straka 2012,
193; endnote 11 in Straka 2012, 232, cites Christa Bruckner-Haring's presentation
"Jazz Research in Spain," at the 9th Jazz Research Congress, "Jazz and Jazz Research
in Europe," on May 17, 2009, in Graz).

85. Pujol Baulenas 2005, 339.

86. García Martínez 1997, 6.

87. Cerchiari, Cugny, and Kerschbaumer 2012, xii.

88. Jurado 1998, 112.

89. Jurado 1998, 113.

90. Tete, in Jurado 1998, 117–18; see also Tete, in Jurado 1992, 73–74.

91. Jurado 1998, 119–20.

92. See Jurado 1998, 118; Tete, in Jurado 1998, 119.

93. Tete, in Jurado 1992, 40.

94. Tete, in Jurado 1998, 114; Jurado 1998, 115.

95. Jurado 1998, 123.

96. One can get a sense of the band's avant-garde approach by listening to a recording
made of the performance at the Jazzhus on November 15, 1962, which did not feature Tete. See Shepp 1964 in the discography at the end of this book.

97. Jurado 1998, 114–15.

98. Interestingly, Ornette Coleman played at the Jamboree Jazz Club in Barcelona in in
October 1965 (Iglesias 2013b, 108).

99. Tete, in Jurado 1998, 114–15.

100. See, for example, Jurado 1998, 155.

101. The phrase "minds and emotions" is take from the album's liner notes, authored by
Martin Williams for Atlantic Records 1364.

102. Williams, liner notes to *Free Jazz*, emphasis in the original.

103. Cappelletti 2012, 130–31. See also Jost 1979, 2012.

104. Carles, Comolli, and Pierrot 2015, 12.

105. "Point of Contact: Discussion" *Downbeat Music '66: the 11th yearbook* (1966): 20.
Interestingly, Shepp is one of those US jazz artists who "conduct[ed] their recording
and performing careers almost exclusively in Europe" (Bakriges 2003, 100). Also,
"The story of American jazz musicians on a European sojourn is an old one. If there
were plenty of unremarkable jazz exiles in Paris and Copenhagen from the 1950s to
the 1970s who dined out on their American authenticity, there were also plenty of
advanced musicians who correctly surmised that the audience for jazz was small but
deep and essentially worldwide" (Ratliff 2003, E3).

106. On its appearance in France, "it did not only transgress most of the rules then held to be specific to jazz—it also purported to testify to the oppression of black Americans, to express their revolt, and even to play a role in their revolutionary struggle. In short, it was mixing the unmixable: music and politics" (Carles, Comolli, and Pierrot 2015, 3).

Chapter 3

1. Fernández 1995, 342.
2. Fernández 1995, 342–43. Fernández notes that "it was not till 1976 that the number of books published in Catalan per year reached the same figures as in 1936 (around 800 titles), and that the first newspaper in Catalan since the end of the war, *Avui*, appeared" (344).
3. Also relevant to this discussion is the way in which the Catalan question resurfaced along with working-class tensions in Barcelona during the second half of the sixties. See Molinero and Ysàs 2014, 21.
4. Pujol (2005, 490–95) puts Tete's work in the context of the *nova cançó*. See also Lluís Meseguer, "Escriptura lírica i cançó popular," *Catalan Review* 17, no.1 (2003): 79–91. Jurado (1998, 136) notes that Tete and Serrat played together in 1967 during a festival at the Palau de la Música, and that a Spanish tour with Joan Manuel Serrat followed the next year (139).
5. Tete, in Jurado 1998, 134.
6. While *nova cançó* singers such as Guillermina Motta and Joan Manuel Serrat can be tied to the group of artists known as the *gauche divine* in Barcelona's 1960s counter-culture, Tete's long stays outside of the city and his embrace of a Black American jazz form have perhaps led to his being passed over by critics. See Villamandos 2011, 19.
7. Davidson 2009, 26, 213.
8. Davidson 2009, 4, 9.
9. For a very readable, if detailed and comprehensive, look at Barcelona's connection with hallmark attributes of Catalan identity, readers should consult Hughes 1992. For how urban Barcelona and Catalan language and identity connects with artistic production in the post-dictatorship, see Fraser 2018b.
10. Pujol Baulenas 2005, 13.
11. See Davidson 2009, 11.
12. Pujol Baulenas 2005, 14.
13. Pujol Baulenas 2005, 14, 15.
14. Pujol Baulenas defines these as "orquestas formadas habitualmente por seis u ocho músicos negros norteamericanos, que practicaban una música sincopada y 'pintoresca,' completamente desconocida para los europeos" (orchestras usually made up of six or eight black American musicians, who produced a syncopated and "picturesque" music completely unknown to Europeans) (2005, 19).
15. Pujol Baulenas 2005, 21.
16. Pujol Baulenas 2005, 24.

17. Pujol Baulenas 2005, 26.
18. Atkins 2003b, xi
19. Atkins 2003b, xi.
20. See Davidson 2009, 29–30. Cobo-Piñero (2020, 54) discusses the dictatorship as well, but focuses on Madrid more than Barcelona; as do Prescott and Cornejo-Parriego (2020, 85–86).
21. Davidson 2009, 24.
22. Davidson 2009, 23.
23. Pujol Baulenas 2005, 27. As a sort of explanation, his text offers that at the time orchestras were not exclusively jazz oriented, they played all manner of popular music, and that "existía una profunda ignorancia y desinterés sobre lo que era y significaba el jazz verdadero" (there was a profound ignorance and lack of interest in what true jazz was and meant) (28).
24. Davidson 2009, 24.
25. Pujol Baulenas 2005, 33.
26. As Prescott and Cornejo-Parriego (2020, 73) explore, she had already debuted at the Teatro Metropolitano in Madrid on February 10, 1930.
27. See Pujol Baulenas 2005, 35–38. Davidson (2009, 49) mentions Josephine Baker's arrival in Barcelona. Prescott and Cornejo-Parriego (2020) comment on Baker's ambivalent reception in Spain.
28. Pujol Baulenas 2005, 40.
29. See also Papo's reflections on the 1920s, such as Papo 1985, 10.
30. Pujol Baulenas 2005, 41.
31. Pujol Baulenas 2005, 230.
32. Tete, in Jurado 1998, 123.
33. According to Miquel Jurado: "És anterior fins i tot al Festival de París o al de Montreux" (It predates even the Festivals of París or Montreux) (Jurado, in Jurado 1992, 60). Jurado also notes that "Barcelona va ser la primera ciutat d'Espanya que va tenir un festival de jazz, encara que sembli mentida" (Barcelona was the first city in Spain that had a jazz festival, even though it might seem untrue), followed by an explanation of why Sant Sebastià should be ruled out (59).
34. "Del 1951 al 1965 el jazz s'aferma a Catalunya" (From 1951 to 1965 jazz flourished in Catalonia) (Papo 1985, 75).
35. Papo 1985, 143.
36. The ONCE exhibit includes these awards, as well as many others, such as those from the city government of Granada in 1987, the city government of Villa de Chiva in 1989, the Asociación de Amigos del Jazz de Almería in 1993, the prize of the city of Barcelona in 1996, the city government of Madrid in 2000, the city government of Vigo in 2007, and many more.
37. Of course, as Tete himself has also said, "Me siento catalán en todas partes. Me siento catalán en la calle, en los bares. A cualquier hora y en cualquier sitio. Me siento catalán en las ganas que tengo siempre de tomar pan con tomate. A lo mejor es una tontería, pero Cataluña soy yo" (I feel Catalan everywhere. I feel Catalan in the street, in the bars. At any hour and in any location. I feel Catalan in the desire I always have

for bread with tomato. It is probably silly [to say this], but I am Catalunya) (ONCE, "Entrevista con Tete Montoliu," by Julio Martínez, p. 100).

38. Tete, in Jurado 1992, 40.

39. Tete, in Jurado 1992, 10.

40. Porta 2010 (http://www.elpuntavui.cat/esports/article/165344-les-jam-sessions-de-tete-montoliu.html).

41. Jurado 1998, 140.

42. Jurado 1998, 143; see also Jurado 1992, 52.

43. Jurado 1998, 125.

44. This quotation comes from the liner notes to the Concèntric release of *Elia Fleta con Tete Montoliu Trio*.

45. The duo also performed at the Waldorf Astoria, according to Jurado 1998, 127.

46. An interview from January 1966 confirms that Tete stuck to the less profitable arena of modern jazz despite offers to make more commercial music. He states, "Me gustaría que supiera las ofertas que me hacen aún a mí para que interprete música comercial. Son realmente tentadoras" (I'd like you to know the offers I still get asking me to play commercial music. They are really tempting) (ONCE, "Las opiniones de un pianista," by Carlos Carrero, in *Tele-Expres*).

47. See, for example, Abellán 1980; Labanyi 1995; Ruiz Bautista 2005; also Tusell 2011. In chapter 1 of the book *The Art of Pere Joan* (Fraser 2019a) I explore this context with reference to Catalan comics, specifically.

48. Jurado 1998, 134.

49. Regarding the importance of Spain's urban centers as producers of albums and recordings, it is notable but perhaps expected that Bakriges leaves Spain out of his list. "Between 1969 and 1981 over ninety record labels were established in Europe to document the new music" (Bakriges 2003, 100). Yet he does include Denmark and lists SteepleChase as one important example of this trend, as well as Timeless in Holland, both of which were labels that released and promoted Tete's jazz (102).

50. I draw here from Tete's comments in the liner notes for the album, where he responds to each track under the heading: "Perque he gravat aquest disc" (Why I have recorded this disc).

51. Elsewhere he performed and recorded other tunes by Gillespie, including "Groovin' High," "A Night in Tunisia," "Woody 'n' You," and "Blue 'n' Boogie."

52. The version in my possession is the vinyl reissue from 1989, which includes a gatefold sleeve with comments by both Mallofré and Montoliu himself. While I have not seen the liner notes for the 1965 version, the entry for the 1965 release on discogs mentions liner notes by Mallofré, and due to the content of the liner notes on the 1989 reissue, they appear to be the same. That is, there is no information that suggests a knowledge of Tete's career post-1965, and the collaborations, names, and influences mentioned (Rahsaan Roland Kirk, Dexter Gordon, Bill Evans, Miles Davis, etc.) would have all been known at the time of the album's first release.

53. According to Novell, the other two were Miquel Porter and Remei Margarit. See Novell 2009, 138, for more on the context. Carlos Aragüez Rubio (2006, 84–85) provides an alternate account of the event's participants.

54. Hughes 1992, 11.
55. Boyle 1995, 293–94. See also the immensely readable chapter 11 of Eude 2008, titled "I Come from a Silence: Catalan Music" (149–61), which gives detailed political portraits of the music and hits of both Raimon and Llach.
56. Ayats and Salicrú-Maltas 2013, 30.
57. Ayats and Salicrú-Maltas 2013, 28; see also Novell 2009, 137.
58. Ayats and Salicrú-Maltas 2013, 29; see also Novell 2009, 137.
59. Boyle 1995, 292. See also Aragüez Rubio 2006.
60. Ayats and Salicrú-Maltas 2013, 34.
61. Ayats and Salicrú-Maltas 2013, 34.
62. Criticisms that Serrat has sold out his Catalan identity in catering to Castilian markets and centrist politics have continued into the twenty-first century, as he has been an outspoken critic of the most recent chapter in the Catalan independence movement.
63. Jurado 1998, 134–35.
64. And also, "la Marina li va dedicar després una bella cançó titulada *Pianista de jazz*" (Marina later dedicated a beautiful song titled *Pianista de jazz* to him) (Jurado 1998, 134–35). Tete recorded "Les feuilles mortes," also known as "Autumn Leaves," with his trio, for example, on *Calafat* (1966) and *Tete Montoliu presenta Elia Fleta* (1966).
65. Tete, in Jurado 1998, 134. See also Jurado 1998, 133.
66. Tete, in Jurado 1998, 136.
67. On this subject, Tete has said that "encara que ell mai no ho dirà" (although he will never say so) (Tete, in Jurado 1998, 136).
68. The two songs from *Songs for Love* are labeled merely as "Two Catalan Songs" on the Marger vinyl release from 1975. The recordings themselves are from 1971.
69. Ayats and Salicrú-Maltas 2013, 34.
70. Ayats and Salicrú-Maltas 2013, 34.
71. The pianist once included this song in a discussion of the emotional resonance of "Els Segadors" and "Pel teu amor" (Rosó) (Tete, in Jurado 1998, 140–41).
72. See the online Tete Montoliu discography, at http://www.jazzdiscography.com/Artists/Montoliu/tete-disc.php. *Lliure Jazz* is discussed in chapter 2 of this book.
73. On the economic aspects of the aperture and cultural production during the late dictatorship see Crumbaugh 2009; Pavlović 2012.
74. Jurado 1998, 257.
75. Jurado 1998, 257.
76. His trio's *Catalonian Rhapsody* was recorded in 1992 in Spain, and to my knowledge released only on CD, never on vinyl.
77. "See Spain as Emerging Jazz Site" 1979, 46.
78. Tete's performance in the Alfred Morse Auditorium on the campus of Boston University the very next year also showcased a similar set of influences: starting with a "New England Blues"; swapping out the Monk influences for compositions by Charlie Parker ("Confirmation"), John Coltrane ("Giant Steps"), and Billy Strayhorn ("Lush Life"); retaining "Airegin" by Rollins and a brief reference to Ellington's "Come Sunday"; delving into jazz standards with "I Guess I'll Hang My Tears Out To Dry" (Cahn-Styne), "Have You Met Miss Jones?" (Rodgers-Hart), "Hot House"

(Dameron), "A Child Is Born" (Jones), and "When I Fall In Love" (Heyman & Young); and mixing in his own "Catalan Suite" and "Apartment 512."

79. This is the 1984 interview with Pablo Lizcano on RTVE (http://www.rtve.es/alaca rta/videos/autorretrato/autorretrato-tete-montoliu/4618827/), to which chapter 4 returns.

80. The notion that US jazz has its roots in percussive and blues practices of African American musical traditions has become so ingrained today that to deny this fact would quite understandably invite charges of racist bias and claims of revisionist history. Arguments that the blues are not an essential component of jazz, such as that put forward by European jazz critic André Hodeir, mistake the matter of identifiable blues influences being present in a specific jazz tune for the broader matter of historical influence. Simply put, in Tete's case, as in the case of so many other performers, jazz is a critique linked to and made possible by the transnational Black experience and anticipated by the blues tradition. This fact seems to have been front and center for Tete throughout his career, despite the fact that he was based in Europe. See Hodeir 1962, 62, where Hodeir also interestingly introduces the ableist metaphor of disability in his explorations of this topic.

81. See http://www.jazzstandards.com/compositions-2/airegin.htm.

82. Note that the album *Thelonious Alone in San Francisco* was one of Tete's favorites of all time (see the list at the end of Jurado 1998). "Blue Monk" opens that album. Note too that Tete played "Blue Monk" in a televised interview on RTVE.

83. Benet i Sanvicens 1994, 26.

84. To wit, an English-language review of the album in *Jazz Magazine* 3, no. 3 (Summer 1979) signed by Tom Piazza, begins: "You may be unfamiliar with Tete Montoliu's playing, as I was. I knew that he was a respected European pianist who had recorded with many American expatriates (he was a favorite of Ben Webster), but somehow I had missed hearing him until this beautiful album fell into my hands" (ONCE).

85. Fernández 1995, 343.

86. This quotation is from page 23 of the interview "Montoliu, tête-à-tête," published in *Dunia* 16 (1985), signed by Mayte L. Goicoechea (ONCE). For more on Catalonia see Eaude 2008.

87. On *Catalonian Folksongs* and "Els segadors," see Jurado 1998, 140–41.

88. See Balibrea 2017; Bou and Subirana 2017.

89. Resina 2017, 153; see also 108, where he argues that Barcelonism was a tool used by the dictatorship to combat Catalanism.

90. Illas 2012, 12–13.

91. See Font 2010 for remarks on homages to Tete Montoliu published in *Avui*. There is little doubt that Tete Montoliu is now regarded as an iconic and legendary performer of Catalan jazz in the broadest understanding of that descriptor. His connection with Barcelona is unquestioned: after all he inaugurated the Jamboree, his trio headlined the First Festival of Jazz in Barcelona, and he played the Palau de la Música.

92. Readers can consult the interview piece titled "Tete Montoliu se retira temporalmente por agotamiento físico y moral," by Carmelo Martín, published in *El País* on October 29, 1980 (ONCE).

Chapter 4

1. Lerner and Straus 2006, 1.
2. Garvía 2017, 10, 59. See also Straus 2011, 18.
3. See Jurado 1998, 31; also note that his maternal grandfather, Alfred Massana, was a founder of Barcelona FC and played center midfield.
4. This quotation is from an interview piece published in *Mundo-Revista* from August 19, 1979, titled "Tete Montoliu: 'Necesito improvisar'" (ONCE).
5. Note that in Fraser 2018a, I explored the productive ambivalence surrounding a certain return to the notion of impairment within the academic project of disability studies by examining Davis 2013 and Mitchell and Snyder 2015.
6. Titchkosky 2011, 5.
7. Titchkosky 2011, 21.
8. See Fraser 2019b, 22; Imrie 1996; Boys 2017.
9. Bolt 2016, 10.
10. Bolt 2016, 11.
11. Bolt 2016, 35.
12. Bolt 2016, 17.
13. See Straus 2018, 10, which draws on Berubé 2015, 154.
14. Berubé 2015, 154.
15. Michalko 2002, 9; referring also to Michalko 1998, 102–27. See also Kuusisto 1998.
16. Koestler 1976, 45, in Rowden 2009, 5; also congenital and adventitious blindness—see Rowden 2009, 6. Also the wide range of experiences in play, as Michalko notes: "Blindness, as it is defined legally and administratively, for example, ranges from 'total blindness' to 10 percent of 'normal vision'" (Michalko 2002, 60).
17. Tete, in Jurado 1998, 37.
18. Elsewhere, I discuss this religious discourse with reference to disability in Spain in an analysis of the novel *Angelicomio* by Salvador García Jiménez (Fraser 2013).
19. Jurado 1998, 29.
20. Jurado 1998, 29. Tete's grandson was also born blind.
21. Rowden 2009, 7.
22. "We must be wary of the tendency to endow blind people as a group with special characteristics" (Rowden 2009, 2); "While many blind people have been recognized for their significant contributions to society, for most of its recorded history, blindness has been more closely linked with poverty—not prodigious achievement or financial success" (3).
23. Madeline Sutherland-Meier (2015) explores this, as well as the history of ONCE, in an article published in *Disability Studies Quarterly*.
24. Jurado 1998, 43.
25. Jurado 1998, 46.
26. Tete, in Jurado 1992, 15.
27. Jurado 1998, 50.
28. Jurado 1998, 49.

29. For a concise and informed biographical sketch of Mompou (1893–1987), see Albet 1993, 47.

30. Jurado 1998, 50.

31. A photograph of Tete Montoliu and Petri Palou together appears in Jurado 1998, 203.

32. "El meu col·legi pertanyia a la Caja de Pensiones para la Vejez y de Ahorros, al carrer del Rosselló" (My school pertained to the Caja de Pensiones para la Vejez y de Ahorros, on Rosselló Street) (Tete, in Jurado 1992, 16). Jurado 1998, 51.

33. Tete, in Jurado 1992, 16.

34. See Tete, in Jurado 1992, 17.

35. Jurado 1998, 53.

36. Jurado 1998, 53–54.

37. This is discussed further in chapter 1with reference to Iglesias 2010c, 2013a, and 2013b.

38. Jurado 1998, 53–54.

39. Tete, in Jurado 1998, 53.

40. Tete, in Jurado 1998, 56.

41. This is voiced by Jurado as he attempts, in dialogue with Montoliu in the year 1992, to characterize how society has changed since Tete's childhood: "Però actualment un cec no és tractat com un tonto, sinó com una persona normal que té un dèficit. El que ha canviat és l'educació dels pares d'un cec, per evitar que el cec se'l tracti com si fos tonto, quan no ho és" (However, currently a blind person is not treated like a fool but rather as a normal person who has a deficit. What has changed is the education that the parents of a blind person receive, to prevent the blind person from being treated as a fool when he is not) (in Jurado 1992, 13).

42. See http://www.rtve.es/alacarta/videos/autorretrato/autorretrato-tete-montoliu/ 4618827/. Among others, Lizcano mentions Art Tatum, Bill Evans, and Thelonious Monk by comparison in introducing Tete for television spectators in Spain. While the interview (which is conducted in Spanish) begins somewhat unremarkably, it is not long before the questions reveal certain gaps in the formation of the interviewer, first of all related also to jazz music and jazz musicians, whom Lizcano seems inclined to regard as eccentrics, but later, and more importantly, misunderstandings rooted in sighted culture's construction of visual impairment. Regarding the latter one might start with the twenty-ninth minute of the interview.

43. This occurs in the thirtieth minute of the interview. Tete does not answer this question. Neither, it must be noted, is the interviewer's understanding of jazz music up to the task.

44. Bastien and Hostager's study overstates these issues and their importance for jazz in general, see Bastien and Hostager 1991, 152, also 154.

45. Tete, in Jurado 1998, 44.

46. Quoted in Rowden 2009, 8, from Safford and Safford 1996, 143; also French 1932, 3, where French writes that "to speak of blind people as such is to miss at the start one of the most fundamental characteristics of the group—their outstanding and sometimes overweening individualism" (also quoted in Rowden 2009, 8). See also the statement in Lubet 2011, 69, that "[t]he larger question asked here is whether there is a Blind

Culture analogous to the widely acknowledged Deaf Culture. I conclude this chapter by answering with a nuanced and provisional 'yes.'" Consider also Garvía 2017 and the cultural significance of ONCE in Spain.

47. Tete, in Jurado 1992, 15.
48. In Jurado 1992, 11–12.
49. Givan 2003, 22, discusses jazz guitarist Django Reinhardt.
50. Garland-Thomson 1996, 23.
51. Garland-Thomson 1996, 5, 10. See also Bogdan 1988, 2012; Fiedler 1978; Hevey 1992, 1993, 1997.
52. See also Rowden 2009, 15–17.
53. Lubet 2011, 43; see also McKay 2013, 13. "Making a virtue of necessity in their efforts to support themselves, blind performers of the 1920s and 1930s often naturalized their condition so thoroughly that their audiences and sighted peers sometimes had difficulty believing that a particular performer was 'really' blind" (Rowden 2009, 37).
54. Rowden 2009, 35. See also Lubet 2011, 71; McKay 2013, 13–14.
55. Rowden 2009, 36.
56. Rowden 2009, 12.
57. See Rowden 2009: 11, previously also the "vicariate of the senses" (Rowden 2009, 37). Perhaps no jazz musician has been labeled a "genius" more than Art Tatum: "However, even in a world in which the attribution of genius was so common, perhaps no other jazz performer has been as consistently accorded that title than the pianist Art Tatum" (Rowden 2009, 86–87). "From the very start of his career, Tatum's unparalleled technical virtuosity brought him lavish praise from almost all quarters of the jazz world" (Rowden 2009, 87). See also European jazz critic André Hodeir (1962, 127), who was not as convinced regarding Tatum's genius.
58. Rowden 2009, 11, 12.
59. Rowden 2009, 90.
60. See Arnold Laubich's liner notes on Tatum's *Pieces of Eight* release.
61. The album was released as part of the eight-LP Tatum Group Masterpieces by Pablo Records and also solo as *Tatum / Hampton / Rich*. The track "Toledo Blade" on which Tete and other local musicians played during the recording of Hamp's *Jazz Flamenco* (1956) is attributed to Lionel Hampton, but is also the name of the local newspaper in Toledo, Ohio, that reported on Art Tatum's many successes.
62. Rowden 2009, 90.
63. Rowden 2009, 42, 36.
64. Rowden 2009, 36.
65. Rowden 2009, 39.
66. The musical practice of "lyrical passing" has its complement in the communicative practice Rod Michalko analyzes as "verbal passing" (Michalko 2002, 151; Rowden 2009, 40).
67. Rowden 2009, 28, citing Hull, *On Sight and Insight*, 51.
68. "An especially significant aspect of the illusion of privacy that the congenitally blind are taught to recognize and control is the public display of those mannerisms that in blindness research have come, albeit problematically, to be called 'blindisms'"

(Rowden 2009, 28); these might be ridiculed by audiences, or else discounted or romanticized (in the case of Blind William Boone, see Rowden 2009, 32); "The rehabilitative removal of 'blindisms', then, amounts to the habituation of the construction of a blind person's social identity through the habitual imagining of what it means to see—specifically, of what it means to 'see blindisms'" (Michalko 2002, 139).

69. "As an almost blind man, Tatum's performance of the role of sighted person certainly entailed a degree of effort that no doubt prevented him from simultaneously performing the role of creatively evolving jazz genius with the intensity or flair of his sighted contemporaries like Charlie Parker and Thelonious Monk, or his blind successor Rahsaan Roland Kirk" (Rowden 2009, 90).

70. Rowden 2009, 16.

71. Rowden writes that "Tatum's ability to function independently, as an almost blind man in the highly communal world of 1930s and 1940s jazz, was much more limited than he would admit, perhaps even to himself" (2009, 88–89).

72. Quoted in Rowden 2009, 108; Wonder had retrolental fibroplasia.

73. Rowden 2009, 138.

74. See Rowden 2009, 99.

75. Rowden 2009, 98–99.

76. Rowden 2009, 97–98.

77. This photograph appears in Pujol Baulenas 2005, 230.

78. By contrast, Rowden writes, "Charles's resistance to stereotypical notions of what it meant to be a 'blind' person or a blind musician was never extreme enough to cause him to disavow his identity as a blind man, but, like many adventitiously blind people, throughout his life he displayed some degree of what blind activists call 'rejection of identification.' At its worst, this describes the behavior of 'the blind person who will have absolutely nothing to do with any other blind person'" (Rowden 2009, 97; citing from Cholden 1958, 97).

79. Rowden writes of how "the stories of blind and visually impaired African American musicians have mirrored the changes in America's image of African Americans and the social possibilities of the black community" (Rowden 2009, 1).

80. Austerlitz 2005, 15.

81. Rowden writes of those who might be considered his counterparts in the United States that "[t]he intersecting experiences of oppression that help explain the presence and particularity of blind black performers fundamentally negated their ability to live their lives as 'simply' black or 'simply' blind or, more drastically, 'simply' American, even if that was something to which a particular person may have aspired" (2009, 3–4). Rowden also suggests that the choice of playing jazz or blues may itself be yet another form of alterity when considered in tandem with visual impairment: "When blind performers have become prominent as jazz or rhythm and blues performers, they have had to face both the negative and the positive implications and effects of cultural narratives that position them as 'exemplary exceptions' more often than their peers in more folk-based forms" (2009, 85).

82. McKay 2013, 3, who relies on accounts from Henri-Jacques Stiker's *A History of Disability*.

83. McKay 2013, 3.
84. Straus 2018, 17–18.
85. Straus 2018, 1.
86. Straus 2018, 24.
87. Lefebvre 1991, 25; Straus 2011, 48.
88. Straus 2011, 48.
89. Straus 2011, 48–49.
90. While future scholarship might make a more extensive case that Straus's assertion is relevant to what might be called a disabling reading of jazz, this concise comment is sufficient in that it transposes a previously urban analysis to a disabling mode.
91. Prescription eyeglasses in my own case, for example.
92. This section does not reach many conclusions regarding these questions. Instead, it is content merely to offer them up for the reader's consideration, with the understanding that any precedent for this sort of analysis continues to be elusive. The work of Georgina Kleege is discussed below in this chapter, and is quite crucial for this endeavor, though she does not work with album covers or the visual business of musical production. Another intriguing work is Ledesma 2017, which explores visual impairment and filmmaking.
93. Michalko 2002, 45.
94. Michalko 1999, 109.
95. See Michalko 1999, 4.
96. Michalko 1999, 34, original emphasis.
97. Leonard Feather discusses the blindfold test briefly in *The Encyclopedia of Jazz in the Sixties*, where he writes, "It is the aim of the Blindfold Test to elicit the honest subjective reaction of the listener. Secondarily, the musician blindfolded usually attempts to identify the artists on each record, though it is always made clear before the interview that the evaluations are far more important than the guesswork" (1966, 20).
98. Roda is, of course, one of Tete's early friends, bandmates, and colleagues at the Conservatory. The inclusion of "blindfold test" in English in this Catalan-language publication is also significant, indicating that it was imported with American jazz traditions and maintained in the original English even after the resurgence of Catalan-language publishing markets in the post-dictatorship.
99. Barasch 2001, 39.
100. Barasch 2001, 41, 40.
101. Barasch 2001, 42.
102. Barasch 2001, 42, 43.
103. Barasch 2001, 141.
104. Corbin 2009, xi. See also Weygand 2009, 198, for more on representations of visual impairment.
105. Kleege 1999, 58.
106. See Mitchell and Snyder 2000.
107. See Roland Barthes 1982 on this property in photography.
108. Kleege 1999, 48.
109. Rowden 2009, 114.

110. Jurado 1998, 186.

111. Jurado 1998, 187.

112. Siebers 2010, 5.

113. Rowden 2009, 5.

114. Kleege 1999, 220.

115. Kleege 1999, 221.

Epilogue

1. Jurado 1998, 243; Jurado continues, saying: "Els seus concerts tot sol van alternar amb les actuacions en trio (sempres amb els seus inseparables Horacio Fumero i Peer Wyboris), duos amb Niels-Henning Orsted-Pedersen o concerts amb Mayte Martín per presentar el seu disc conjunt *Free Boleros* a tot Espanya" (Their concerts alone alternated with trio performances [always with their inseparable Hector Fumero and Peer Wyboris], duos with Niels-Henning Orsted-Pederson or concerts with Mayte Martín to present their joint album *Free Boleros* throughout Spain).

2. Jurado 1998, 245, 247.

3. See, for example, De Roche 2015; Borshuk 2006.

4. Sánchez 2016, 4.

5. Tete, in Jurado 1992, 16, see also 46.

6. Tete, in Jurado 1992, 14.

7. See Vidal 2017. "Era un lector compulsiu. Llegia llibres a una velocitat impressionant i, sempre que marxava de gira, ho feia amb dues maletes plenes de llibres en Braille. Llegia de tot: novel·la, teatre, poesia. . . . Li encantava Rodoreda, i també Cortázar, pel ritme que imprimia als seus textos" (He was a compulsive reader. He read books at an impressive speed and, whenever he went out on tour, he would pack two suitcases full of books in braille. He read everything: the novels, plays, poetry. . . . He loved Rodoreda, and Cortázar, too, for the rhythm with which his texts were printed).

8. Jurado 1992, 35.

9. See Tete, in Jurado 1992, 34.

10. Tete, in Jurado 1998, 234. See Cortázar 1964[1959].

11. Cortázar was also known for *Rayuela*, published in English as *Hopscotch*, which had the fame of being a novel whose chapters could supposedly be read in any order, replicating in literary form the improvisational qualities of the jazz form that inspired it. The author once said that "El perseguidor" was *Rayuela* in miniature. See Cortázar 1966 and Felkel 1979, 20.

12. A reading shared by many scholars of Cortázar's work, this is taken from Robert Felkel's 1979 article in the *Latin American Literary Review*.

13. See Felkel 1979, 23.

14. Felkel 1979, 23.

15. For more see http://www.jazzdiscography.com/Artists/Montoliu/tete-disc.php.

16. My belief is that a more thorough accounting would surely uncover further examples.

17. Muñoz Molina 2014, 104; the page number from the English translation cited here is 64.

18. Meckna 2006, 359.

19. See Norden 1994.

20. See Iglesias 2010c, 128. Jazz has been recuperated in several recent Spanish films that deserve mention; see Marvin D'Lugo's statement that "Fernando Trueba's Latin Jazz films *Calle 54* (2000) and *Chico y Rita* (2010) mark a significant point of convergence between music and film in which narrowly defined conceptions of Spanish national cinema are refigured in terms of a broader notion of identity politics shaped by the borderless cultural circulation of popular music" (D'Lugo 2015, 45).

21. On this, see the concise remarks on Tete Montoliu presented in Sánchez 2016, 29.

22. See Lutes 2008, 25–28.

23. This article is included in the compiled clippings at ONCE.

24. This quotation is from a letter written by Joan Capmany Montoliu published on the opinion page of *La Vanguardia*, p. 20, presumably in 1997 (ONCE).

25. García Martínez 1997, 5.

26. Vicens Vidal 2008, 40.

27. Readers can consult the article "Terrassa tiene ya un pasaje dedicado al fallecido pianista Tete Montoliu," by Pamela Navarrete, in the *Diari de Terrassa*, March 7, 1998, p. 12 (ONCE).

28. Readers can consult the article "Una placa recuerda a Tete Montoliu en la casa donde vivió y murió" in *El País* from December 13, 1998 (ONCE).

29. Okiji writes of the process of "transforming jazz work into an object" (Okiji 2018, 89) and emphasizes that "[j]azz work is not what is reproduced in the records" (90).

30. "The history of jazz is inextricably tied to the history of the jazz record. . . . To talk about the history of jazz is really to talk about the history of the jazz record" (Okiji 2018, 87).

31. "While it may be a stretch to suggest that jazz would not have developed at all without records, it is surely indisputable that it would have taken on a markedly different, and less rich, character" (Okiji 2018, 88).

32. Jurado 1998, 20.

33. Okiji 2018, 88, 90.

34. Respectively, Vianna 1999; Austerlitz 1997; Guilbault 2007; Savigliano 1995.

References

Abellán, Manuel L. 1980. *Censura y creación literaria en España (1939–1976)*. Barcelona: Península.

Abrahams, Roger D., with Nick Spitzer, John F. Szwed, and Robert Farris Thompson. 2006. *Blues for New Orleans: Mardi Gras and America's Creole Soul*. Philadelphia: University of Pennsylvania Press.

Adorno, Theodor W. 2006. *Philosophy of New Music*. Translated, edited, and introduced by Robert Hullot-Kentor. Minneapolis: University of Minnesota Press.

Adorno, Theodor W. 2002a. *Essays on Music*. Edited by Richard Leppert, translated by Susan H. Gillespie. Berkeley: University of California Press.

Adorno, Theodor W. 2002b. "The Curves of the Needle." In *Essays on Music*, edited by Richard Leppert, new translation by Susan H. Gillespie, 271–76. Berkeley: University of California Press.

Adorno, Theodor W. 2002c. "The Form of the Phonograph Record." In *Essays on Music*, edited by Richard Leppert, new translation by Susan H. Gillespie, 277–82. Berkeley: University of California Press.

Adorno, Theodor W. 2002d. "On the Fetish-Character of Music and the Regression of Listening." In *Essays on Music*, edited by Richard Leppert, new translation by Susan H. Gillespie, 288–317. Berkeley: University of California Press.

Adorno, Theodor W. 2002e. "On the Social Situation of Music." In *Essays on Music*, edited by Richard Leppert, new translation by Susan H. Gillespie, 391–436. Berkeley: University of California Press.

Adorno, Theodor W. 2000. "The Perennial Fashion—Jazz." In *The Adorno Reader*, edited by Brian O'Conner, 267–79. Oxford: Blackwell.

Adorno, Theodor W. 1989–90 [1936]. "On Jazz." Translated by Jamie Owen Daniel. *Discourse* 12, no. 1: 45–69.

Albet, Montserrat. 1993. "Frederic Mompou." *Catalonia Culture* 32 (January): 46–47.

Anderson, Kirk. 2003. "Preface." In *African-American Jazz Musicians in the Diaspora*, edited by Larry Ross, ii–iv. Lewiston, NY: Edwin Mellon Press.

Aparicio, Frances, and Susan Chávez-Silverman, eds. 1997. *Tropicalizations: Transcultural Representations of Latinidad*. Hanover, NH: University Press of New England.

Aragüez Rubio, Carlos. 2006. "La nova cançó catalana: Génesis, desarrollo y trascendencia de un fenómeno cultural en el segundo franquismo." *Pasado y Memoria: Revista de Historia Contemporánea* 5: 81–97.

Arndt, Jürgen. 2012. "European Jazz Developments in Cross-Cultural Dialogue with the United States and Their Relationship to the Counterculture of the 1960s." In *Eurojazzland: Jazz and European Sources, Dynamics, and Contexts*, edited by Luca Cerchiari, Laurent Cugny, and Franz Kerschbaumer, 342–65. Lebanon, NH: Northeastern University Press.

Arribas García, Miguel. 2015. "El Jazz en Barcelona durante la transición española (1975–1982)." MA thesis. Valladolid: Universidad de Valladolid.

Atkins, E. Taylor, ed. 2003a. *Jazz Planet*. Jackson: University Press of Mississippi.

Atkins, E. Taylor. 2003b. "Toward a Global History of Jazz." In *Jazz Planet*, edited by E. Taylor Atkins, xi–xxvii. Jackson: University Press of Mississippi.

Austerlitz, Paul. 2005. *Jazz Consciousness: Music, Race, and Humanity*. Middletown, CT: Wesleyan University Press.

Austerlitz, Paul. 1997. *Merengue: Dominican Music and Dominican Identity*. Philadelphia: Temple University Press.

Ayats, Jaume, and Maria Salicrú-Maltas. 2013. "Singing against the Dictatorship (1959–1975): The *Nova Cançó.*" In *Made in Spain: Studies in Popular Music*, edited by Sílvia Martínez and Héctor Fouce, 28–41. New York: Routledge.

Bakriges, Christopher G. 2003. "Musical Transculturation: From African American Avant-Garde Jazz to European Creative Improvisation, 1962–1981." In *Jazz Planet*, edited by E. Taylor Atkins, 19–40. Jackson: University Press of Mississippi.

Balibrea, Mari Paz. 2017. *The Global Cultural Capital: Addressing the Citizen and Producing the City in Barcelona*. London: Palgrave.

Barasch, Moshe. 2001. *Blindness: The History of a Mental Image in Western Thought*. New York and London: Routledge.

Barthes, Roland. 1982. *Camera Lucida: Reflections on Photography*. New York: Hill and Wang.

Bastien, David T., and Todd J. Hostager. 1991. "Jazz as Social Structure, Process and Outcome." In *Jazz in Mind: Essays on the History and Meanings of Jazz*, edited by Reginald T. Buckner and Steven Weiland, 148–65. Detroit: Wayne State University Press.

Benet i Sanvicens, Sebastià. 1994. "Music in Catalonia Today." *Catalonia Culture* 39 (October): 26–29.

Benjamin, Walter. 1985. *Charles Baudelaire: A Lyric Poet in the Era of High Capitalism*. Translated by Harry Zohn. London: Verso.

Berish, Andrew. 2019. "Space and Place in Jazz." In *The Routledge Companion to Jazz Studies*, edited by Nicholas Gebhardt, Nichole Rustin-Paschal, and Tony Whyton, 153–62. New York: Routledge.

Berish, Andrew. 2012. *Lonesome Roads and Streets of Dreams: Place, Mobility, and Race in Jazz of the 1930s and '40s*. Chicago: University of Chicago Press.

Bermúdez, Silvia. 2018. *Rocking the Boat: Migration and Race in Contemporary Spanish Music*. Toronto: University of Toronto Press.

Bermúdez, Silvia, and Jorge Pérez, eds. 2009. "Spanish Popular Music Studies." Special issue, *Journal of Spanish Cultural Studies* 10, no. 2: 127–262.

Berubé, Michael. 2015. "Representation." In *Keywords for Disability Studies*, edited by Rachel Adams, Benjamin Reiss, and David Serlin, 151–55. New York: New York University Press.

Bogdan, Robert. 1988. *Freak Show: Presenting Human Oddities for Amusement and Profit*. Chicago: University of Chicago Press.

Bogdan, Robert, with Martin Elks and James A. Knoll. 2012. *Picturing Disability: Beggar, Freak, Citizen, and Other Photographic Rhetoric*. Syracuse, NY: Syracuse University Press.

Bolt, David. 2016. *The Metanarrative of Blindness: A Re-reading of Twentieth-Century Anglophone Writing*. Ann Arbor: University of Michigan Press.

Borge, Jason. 2018. *Tropical Riffs: Latin America and the Politics of Jazz*. Durham, NC: Duke University Press.

Borshuk, Michael. 2006. *Swinging the Vernacular: Jazz and African American Modernist Literature*. New York: Routledge.

Bou, Enric, and Jaume Subirana, eds. 2017. *The Barcelona Reader: Cultural Readings of a City*. Liverpool: University of Liverpool Press.

Boyle, Catherine. 1995. "The Politics of Popular Music: On the Dynamics of New Song." In *Spanish Cultural Studies: An Introduction*, edited by Helen Graham and Jo Labanyi, 291–94. Oxford: Oxford University Press.

Boys, Jos, ed. 2017. *Disability, Space, Architecture: A Reader*. London and New York: Routledge.

Branche, Jerome C. 2006. *Colonialism and Race in Luso-Hispanic Literature*. Columbia: University of Missouri Press.

Braun, Harald E. and Lisa Vollendorf, eds. 2013. *Theorising the Ibero-American Atlantic*. Leiden and Boston: Brill.

Büchmann-Møller, Frank. 2010. *Someone to Watch over Me: The Life and Music of Ben Webster*. Ann Arbor: University of Michigan Press.

Buckner, Reginald T., and Steven Weiland. 1991. "Introduction." In *Jazz in Mind: Essays on the History and Meanings of Jazz*, edited by Reginald T. Buckner and Steven Weiland, 13–18. Detroit: Wayne State University Press.

Buhler, James. 2006. "Frankfurt School Blues: Rethinking Adorno's Critique of Jazz." In *Apparitions: New Perspectives on Adorno and Twentieth-Century Music*, edited by Berthold Hoeckner, 103–30. New York: Routledge.

Burns, Ken, dir. 2001. *Jazz*. 10-episode PBS Miniseries. Arlington, VA: Public Broadcasting Service.

Burrows, George. 2018. "Transatlantic Re-soundings: Fats Waller's *London Suite* and the Jazz Atlantic." *Atlantic Studies* 15, no. 3: 417–30.

Cappelletti, Arrigo. 2012. "Across Europe: Improvisation as a Real and Metaphorical Journey." In *Eurojazzland: Jazz and European Sources, Dynamics, and Contexts*, edited by Luca Cerchiari, Laurent Cugny, and Franz Kerschbaumer, 123–40. Lebanon, NH: Northeastern University Press.

Carles, Philippe, Jean-Louis Comolli, and Gregory Pierrot. 2015 [1971]. *Free Jazz/Black Power*. Jackson: University of Mississippi.

Carmona, Eugenio. 1995. "From Picasso to Dalí: 'Arte Nuevo' and the Spanish Masters of European Avant-Garde Painting." In *The Spanish Avant-Garde*, edited by Derek Harris, 97–109. Manchester, UK: Manchester University Press.

Carr, Ian. 2006. *Miles Davis: The Definitive Biography*. New York: Da Capo Press.

Cerchiari, Luca. 2012. "Introduction." In *Eurojazzland: Jazz and European Sources, Dynamics, and Contexts*, edited by Luca Cerchiari, Laurent Cugny, and Franz Kerschbaumer, vii–xviii. Lebanon, NH: Northeastern University Press.

Cerchiari, Luca, Laurent Cugny, and Franz Kerschbaumer. 2012. *Eurojazzland: Jazz and European Sources, Dynamics, and Contexts*. Lebanon, NH: Northeastern University Press.

Cerdà, Ildefons. 1867. *Teoría general de la urbanización*. 2 vols. Madrid: Imprenta Española.

Charnon-Deutsch, Lou. 2003. "Travels of the Imaginary Spanish Gypsy." In *Constructing Identity in Contemporary Spain: Theoretical Debates and Cultural Practice*, edited by Jo Labanyi, 22–40. Oxford: Oxford University Press.

Cholden, Louis S. 1958. *A Psychiatrist Works with Blindness: Selected Papers*. New York: American Foundation for the Blind.

Cobo-Piñero, M. Rocío. 2020. "Jazz and the 1920s Spanish Flappers: 'Las sinsombrero.'" In *Black USA and Spain: Shared Memories in the 20th Century*, edited by R. Cornejo-Parriego, 52–72. New York: Routledge.

Collum, Danny Duncan, ed. 1992. *African Americans in the Spanish Civil War: "This Ain't Ethiopia, but It'll Do."* New York: Hall.

Corbin, Alain. 2009. "Preface." In *The Blind in French Society from the Middle Ages to the Century of Louis Braille*, edited by Zina Weygand, translated by Emily-Jane Cohen, x–xiii. Stanford, CA: Stanford University Press.

Cornejo-Parriego, Rosalía, ed. 2020a. *Black USA and Spain: Shared Memories in the 20th Century.* New York: Routledge.

Cornejo-Parriego, Rosalía. 2020b. "African Americans and Spaniards: 'Caught in an Inescapable Network of Mutuality.'" In *Black USA and Spain: Shared Memories in the 20th Century*, edited by R. Cornejo-Parriego, 1–19. New York: Routledge.

Cortázar, Julio. 1964 [1959]. "El perseguidor." *Las armas secretas*, 249–313. Buenos Aires: Sudamericana.

Cortázar, Julio. 1966. *Rayuela.* Buenos Aires: Sudamericana.

Crouch, Stanley. 2006. *Considering Genius: Writings on Jazz.* New York: Basic Books.

Crumbaugh, Justin. 2009. *Destination Dictatorship: The Spectacle of Spain's Tourist Boom and the Reinvention of Difference.* Albany: State University of New York Press.

Daoudi, Youssef. 2018. *Monk!: Thelonious, Pannonica, and the Friendship behind a Musical Revolution.* New York: First Second.

Davidson, Robert A. 2009. *Jazz Age Barcelona.* Toronto: University of Toronto Press.

Davis, Lennard. 2013. *The End of Normal: Identity in a Biocultural Era.* Ann Arbor: University of Michigan Press.

Davis, Lennard. 1997. "Introduction: The Need for Disability Studies." In *The Disability Studies Reader*, edited by Lennard Davis, 1–10. New York: Routledge.

DeGuzmán, María. 2005. *Spain's Long Shadow: The Black Legend, Off-Whiteness, and Anglo-American Empire.* Minneapolis: University of Minnesota Press.

Delgado Ruiz, Manuel. 2010. "La ciudad levantada: La barricada y otras transformaciones radicales del espacio urbano." In "Hacia un urbanismo alternative." Special issue, *Architectonics, Mind, Land & Society* 19, no. 20: 137–53.

Delgado Ruiz, Manuel. 2007a. *La ciudad mentirosa: Fraude y miseria del "modelo Barcelona."* Madrid, Catarata.

Delgado Ruiz, Manuel. 2007b. *Sociedades movedizas: Pasos hacia una antropología de las calles.* Barcelona: Anagrama.

Delgado Ruiz, Manuel. 1999. *El animal público.* Barcelona: Anagrama.

De Roche, Linda. 2015. *The Jazz Age: A Historical Exploration of Literature.* Santa Barbara, CA: Greenwood.

D'Lugo, Marvin. 2015. "Fernando Trueba: Rewriting the Pedagogy of Spanish Transnational Musical Narratives." *Journal of Spanish Cultural Studies* 16, no. 1: 45–60.

Du Bois, W. E. B. 1996 [1903]. *The Souls of Black Folk.* New York: Penguin.

Eaude, Michael. 2008. *Catalonia: A Cultural History.* Oxford: Oxford University Press.

Ellington, Duke. 1976 [1973]. *Music Is My Mistress.* New York: Da Capo.

Feather, Leonard. 1980. *The Passion for Jazz.* New York: Horizon Press.

Feather, Leonard. 1976. *The Encyclopedia of Jazz in the Seventies.* New York: Horizon Press.

Feather, Leonard. 1966. *The Encyclopedia of Jazz in the Sixties.* New York: Horizon Press.

Feather, Leonard. 1960. *The Encyclopedia of Jazz.* New York: Horizon Press.

Felkel, Robert W. 1979. "The Historical Dimension in Julio Cortázar's 'The Pursuer.'" *Latin American Literary Review* 7, no. 14: 20–27.

Fernández, Josep-Anton. 1995. "Becoming Normal: Cultural Production and Cultural Policy in Catalonia." In *Spanish Cultural Studies: An Introduction*, edited by Helen Graham and Jo Labanyi, 342–46. Oxford: Oxford University Press.

Fernández, Raúl A. 2006. *From Afro-Cuban Rhythms to Latin Jazz*. Berkeley: University of California Press.

Fiedler, Leslie. 1978. *Freaks: Myths and Images of the Secret Self*. New York: Simon & Schuster.

Font, Raquel. 2010. "50 anys del Jamboree." *Avui*, January3, 2010. http://www.elpuntavui. cat/cultura/article/19-cultura/268409-50-any.

Fra-Molinero, Baltasar. 2000. "Ser mulato en España y América: Discursos legales y otros discursos literarios." In *Negros, mulatos, zambaigos: Derrotos africanos en los mundos ibéricos*, edited by Berta Ares Queija and Alessandro Stella, 123–47. Seville: Escuela de Estudios Hispano-Americanos, Consejo Superior de Investigaciones Científicas.

Fraser, Benjamin. 2019a. *The Art of Pere Joan: Space, Landscape and Comics Form*. Austin: University of Texas Press.

Fraser, Benjamin. 2019b. "Obsessively Writing the Modern City: The Partial Madness of Urban Planning Culture and the Case of Arturo Soria y Mata in Madrid, Spain." *Journal of Literary and Cultural Disability Studies* 13, no. 1: 21–37.

Fraser, Benjamin. 2018a. *Cognitive Disability Aesthetics: Visual Culture, Disability Representations, and the (In)Visibility of Cognitive Difference*. Toronto: University of Toronto Press.

Fraser, Benjamin. 2018b. "The Public Animal in Barcelona: Urban Form, the Natural World and Socio-Spatial Transgression in the Comic "Un cocodril a l'Eixample" (1987) by Pere Joan and Emilio Manzano." *Journal of Spanish Cultural Studies* 19, no. 1: 89–110.

Fraser, Benjamin. 2015. *Toward and Urban Cultural Studies: Henri Lefebvre and the Humanities*. New York: Palgrave.

Fraser, Benjamin. 2013. *Disability Studies and Spanish Culture: Films, Novels, the Comic and the Public Exhibition*. Liverpool: Liverpool University Press.

Fraser, Benjamin. 2012. "The 'Sidewalk Ballet' in the Work of Henri Lefebvre and Manuel Delgado Ruiz." In *The Urban Wisdom of Jane Jacobs*, edited by Diane Zahm and Sonia Hirt, 24–36. London and New York: Routledge.

Fraser, Benjamin. 2011. *Henri Lefebvre and the Spanish Urban Experience*. Lewiston, PA: Bucknell University Press.

French, Richard Slayton. 1932. *From Homer to Helen Keller: A Social and Educational Study of the Blind*. New York: American Foundation for the Blind.

Frías, María. 2004. "Nights of Flamenco and Blues in Spain: From Sorrow Songs to *Soleá* and Back." In *Blackening Europe: The African American Presence*, edited by Heike Raphael-Hernandez, 141–55. New York: Routledge.

Gabbard, Krin, ed. 1995a. *Jazz among the Discourses*. Durham, NC: Duke University Press.

Gabbard, Krin, ed. 1995b. *Representing Jazz*. Durham, NC: Duke University Press.

Gac, Scott. 2005. "Jazz Strategy: Dizzy, Foreign Policy, and Government in 1956." *Americana: The Journal of American Popular Culture 1900 to Present* 4, no. 1. http:// www.americanpopularculture.com/journal/articles/spring_2005/gac.htm.

Galasso, Regina. 2018. *Translating New York: The City's Languages in Iberian Literatures*. Liverpool: Liverpool University Press.

García, Hugo. 2015. "Barbarians, Telescreens, and Jazz: Reactionary Uchronias in Modern Spain, ca. 1870–1960." *Utopian Studies* 26, no. 2: 383–400.

García Gómez, Génesis. 1998. "Volksgeist y género español." In *Flamenco y nacionalismo: Aportaciones para un sociología política del flamenco*, edited by Gerhard Steingress and Enrique Baltanás, 193–206. Seville: Fundación Machado, Universidad de Sevilla, Fundación El Monte.

García Martínez, José María. 1997. "Tete Montoliu: Un homenaje al más grande pianista del jazz español." *Ritmo* 692: 5–8.

García Martínez, José María. 1996. *Del fox trot al jazz flamenco: El jazz en España: 1919–1996*. Madrid: Alianza Editorial.

Garland-Thomson, Rosemarie. 2009. *Staring: How We Look*. Oxford: Oxford University Press.

Garland-Thomson, Rosemarie, ed. 1996. *Freakery: Cultural Spectacles of the Extraordinary Body*. New York: New York University Press.

Garlitz, Dustin Bradley. 2007. "Philosophy of New Jazz: Reconstructing Adorno." MA diss., University of South Florida, Department of Humanities and American Studies. https://scholarcommons.usf.edu/cgi/viewcontent.cgi?referer=https://www.google.com/&httpsredir=1&article=3182&context=etd.

Garvía, Roberto. 2017. *Organizing the Blind: The Case of ONCE in Spain*. London and New York: Routledge.

Gebhardt, Nicholas, Nichole Rustin-Paschal, and Tony Whyton, eds. 2019. *The Routledge Companion to Jazz Studies*. New York and London: Routledge.

Gilroy, Paul. 1993. *The Black Atlantic: Modernity and Double-Consciousness*. Cambridge, MA: Harvard University Press.

Giner, Juan, Joan Sardà, and Enric Vázquez. 2006. *Guía universal del jazz moderno*. Barcelona: Ma Non Troppo.

Gioia, Ted. 2016. *How to Listen to Jazz*. New York: Basic Books.

Gioia, Ted. 2011. *The History of Jazz*. 2nd ed. New York: Cambridge University Press.

Givan, Benjamin. 2003. "Django Reinhardt's Left Hand." In *Jazz Planet*, edited by E. Taylor Atkins, 19–40. Jackson: University Press of Mississippi.

Goffman, Erving. 1984 [1959]. *The Presentation of Self in Everyday Life*. Hammondsworth, UK: Penguin.

González, Fernando. 2004. "What Latin Jazz? Moving beyond Jazz-with-Congas." *JAZZIZ* 21, no. 9: 46–47.

Gracyk, Theodore A. 1992. "Adorno, Jazz, and the Aesthetics of Popular Music." *Musical Quarterly* 76, no. 4: 526–42.

Graham, Helen, and Jo Labanyi, eds. 1995. *Spanish Cultural Studies: An Introduction: The Struggle for Modernity*. New York: Oxford University Press.

Guibernau, Montserrat. 2004. *Catalan Nationalism: Francoism, Transition and Democracy*. London and New York: Routledge.

Guilbault, Jocelyne. 2007. *Governing Sound: The Cultural Politics of Trinidad's Carnival Musics*. Chicago: The University of Chicago Press.

Harvey, David. 2009 [1973]. *Social Justice and the City*. Athens, GA: University of Georgia Press.

Harvey, David. 2006. *Paris, Capital of Modernity*. London and New York: Routledge.

Harvey, David. 1996. *Justice, Nature and the Geography of Difference*. London: Blackwell.

Harvey, David. 1989. *The Urban Experience*. Baltimore: Johns Hopkins University Press.

Harvey, Mark S. 1991. "Jazz and Modernism: Changing Conceptions of Innovation and Tradition." In *Jazz in Mind: Essays on the History and Meanings of Jazz*, edited by Reginald T. Buckner and Steven Weiland, 128–47. Detroit: Wayne State University Press.

Hasse, Edward John. 2012. "'A New Reason for Living': Duke Ellington in France." In *Eurojazzland: Jazz and European Sources, Dynamics, and Contexts*, edited by

Luca Cerchiari, Laurent Cugny, and Franz Kerschbaumer, 189–213. Lebanon, NH: Northeastern University Press.

Hayes, Michelle Heffner. 2009. *Flamenco: Conflicting Histories of the Dance.* Jefferson, NC: McFarland.

Hevey, David. 1997. "The Enfreakment of Photography." In *The Disability Studies Reader,* edited by Lennard J. Davis, 332–47. New York and London: Routledge.

Hevey, David. 1993. "From Self-Love to the Picket Line: Strategies for Change in Disability Representation." *Disability, Handicap & Society* 8, no. 4: 423–29.

Hevey, David. 1992. *The Creatures Time Forgot: Photography and Disability Imagery.* London and New York: Routledge.

Hodeir, André. 1962. *Toward Jazz.* Translated by Noel Burch. New York: Da Capo Press.

Holguín, Sandie. 2019. *Flamenco Nation: The Construction of Spanish National Identity.* Madison: University of Wisconsin Press.

Hughes, Langston. 1993. *I Wonder as I Wander: An Autobiographical Journey.* 2nd ed. New York: Hill and Wang.

Hughes, Robert. 1992. *Barcelona.* New York: Alfred A. Knopf.

Hull, John M. 1997. *On Sight and Insight: A Journey into the World of Blindness.* Oxford: Oneworld Publications.

Iglesias, Iván. 2016. "Performing the 'Anti-Spanish' Body: Jazz and Biopolitics in the Early Franco Regime (1939–1957)." In *Jazz and Totalitarianism,* edited by B. Johnson, 157–173. New York: Routledge.

Iglesias, Iván. 2013a. "Hechicero de las pasiones del alma: El jazz y la subversión de la biopolítica franquista (1939–1959)." Trans: Revista Transcultural de Música 17.

Iglesias, Iván. 2013b. "Swinging Modernity: Jazz and Politics in Franco's Spain (1939–1968)." In *Made in Spain: Studies in Popular Music,* edited by Sílvia Martínez and Héctor Fouce, 101–12. New York: Routledge.

Iglesias, Iván. 2011. "'Vehículo de la mejor amistad': El jazz como propagandanorteamericana en la España de los años cincuenta," *Historia del presente* 17: 41–54.

Iglesias, Iván. 2010a. "Improvisando aliados: El jazz y la propaganda franquista de la Segunda Guerra Mundial a la Guerra Fría." In *VII Encuentro de Investigadores sobre el Franquismo,* edited by Ana Cabana Iglesia, Daniel Lanero Táboas, and Victor Santidrián Arias, 529–40. Santiago de Compostela, Spain: Universidade de Santiago de Compostela.

Iglesias, Iván. 2010b. *Improvisando la modernidad: El jazz y la España de Franco, de la Guerra Civil a la Guerra Fría (1936–1968).* PhD diss., Universidad de Valladolid.

Iglesias, Iván. 2010c. "(Re)construyendo la identidad musical española: El jazz y el discurso cultural del franquismo durante la segunda guerra mundial." *Historia Actual Online* 23: 119–35.

Illas, Edgar. 2012. *Thinking Barcelona: Ideologies of a Global City.* Liverpool: Liverpool University Press.

Imrie, Rob. 1996. *Disability and the City: International Perspectives.* London: Paul Chapman.

Jacobs, Jane. 1992. *The Death and Life of Great American Cities.* New York: Vintage.

Johnson, Bruce, ed. 2016. *Jazz and Totalitarianism.* New York: Routledge.

Jost, Ekkehard. 2012. "The European Jazz Avant-Garde of the Late 1960s and Early 1970s: Where Did Emancipation Lead?" In *Eurojazzland: Jazz and European Sources,*

Dynamics, and Contexts, edited by Luca Cerchiari, Laurent Cugny, and Franz Kerschbaumer, 275–97. Lebanon, NH: Northeastern University Press.

Jost, Ekkehard. 1979. "Über den Anfang vom Ende des Epigonentums und über die Überwindung der Kaputtspielphase im westdeutschen Free Jazz." *Neue Zeitschrift für Musik* 140, no. 3: 237.

Jurado, Miquel. 1998. *Tete: Quasi autobiografia.* Barcelona: Pòrtic, Proa.

Jurado, Miquel. 1992. *Tete Montoliu. Diàlegs a Barcelona.* Barcelona: Ajuntament de Barcelona.

Jurado, Miquel, and Gani Jakupi. 2006. *Montoliu Plays Tete.* Barcelona: DISCMEDI/BLAU.

Kleege, Georgina. 2018. *More Than Meets the Eye: What Blindness Brings to Art.* New York: Oxford University Press.

Kleege, Georgina. 1999. *Sight Unseen.* New Haven, CT: Yale University Press.

Koestler, Frances. 1976. *The Unseen Minority: A Social History of Blindness in the United States.* New York: David McKay.

Kuusisto, Stephen. 1998. *Planet of the Blind: A Memoir.* New York: Delta.

Labanyi, Jo. 2003. "Introduction: Theorizing Culture in Modern Spain." In *Constructing Identity in Contemporary Spain: Theoretical Debates and Cultural Practice,* edited by Jo Labanyi, 1–21. Oxford: Oxford University Press.

Labanyi, Jo. 1995. "Censorship or the Fear of Mass Culture." In *Spanish Cultural Studies: An Introduction: The Struggle for Modernity,* edited by Helen Graham and Jo Labanyi, 207–14. New York: Oxford University Press.

Ledesma, Eduardo. 2017. "The Blind Gaze: Visual Impairment and Haptic Filmmaking in João Júlio Antunes' *O jogo/ The Game* (2010)." *Studies in Spanish and Latin American Cinemas* 14, no. 1: 23–39.

Lefebvre, Henri. 2007. *Everyday Life in the Modern World.* Translated by Sacha Rabinovich. 11th paperback ed. New Brunswick, NJ: Transaction.

Lefebvre, Henri. 2006a. *La presencia la ausencia: Contribución a la teoría de las representaciones.* Translated by Øscar Barahona and Uxoa Doyhamboure. Mexico City: Fondo de Cultura Económica

Lefebvre, Henri. 2006b. *Rhythmanalysis.* Translated by S. Elden and Gerald Moore. London and New York: Continuum.

Lefebvre, Henri. 2005. *Critique of Everyday Life.* Vol. 3. Translated by Gregory Elliott. London and New York: Verso.

Lefebvre, Henri. 2003 [1970]. *The Urban Revolution.* Translated by Robert Bononno. Minneapolis: University of Minnesota Press.

Lefebvre, Henri. 2002. *Critique of Everyday Life,* Vol. 2. Translated by John Moore. London and New York: Verso.

Lefebvre, Henri. 1996[1968]. *The Right to the City: Writings on Cities.* Edited and translated by E. Kofman and E. Lebas, 63–181. Oxford: Blackwell.

Lefebvre, Henri. 1995. *Introduction to Modernity.* Translated by John Moore. London and New York: Verso.

Lefebvre, Henri. 1991. *Critique of Everyday Life, Vol. 1.* Translated by John Moore. London and New York: Verso.

Lefebvre, Henri. 1988. "Toward a Leftist Cultural Politics: Remarks Occasioned by the Centenary of Marx's Death." Translated by David Reifman. In *Marxism and the*

Interpretation of Culture, edited by Lawrence Grossberg and Cary Nelson, 75–88. Chicago: University of Illinois Press.

Lerner, Neil, and Joseph N. Straus. 2006. "Introduction: Theorizing Disability in Music." In *Sounding Off: Theorizing Disability in Music*, edited by Neil Lerner and Joseph N. Straus, 1–10. New York and London: Routledge.

Lott, Eric. 1998. "Double V, Double-Time: Bebop's Politics of Style." In *The Jazz Cadence of American Culture*, edited by Robert G. O'Meally, 457–68. New York: Columbia University Press.

Lowe, Lisa. 2006. "The Intimacies of Four Continents." In *Haunted by Empire: Geographies of Intimacy in North America*, edited by Ann Laura Stoler, 191–212. Durham, NC: Duke University Press.

Lubet, Alex. 2011. *Music, Disability and Society*. Philadelphia: Temple University Press.

Lutes, Jason. 2008. *Berlin: City of Smoke*. Montreal: Drawn and Quarterly.

Lyttelton, Humphrey. 1981. *The Best of Jazz II: Enter the Giants, 1931–1944*. New York: Taplinger.

Manuel, Peter. 2016. "Flamenco Jazz: An Analytical Study." *Journal of Jazz Studies* 11, no. 2: 29–77.

Martínez, Sílvia, and Héctor Fouce, eds. 2013. *Made in Spain: Studies in Popular Music*. New York: Routledge.

Martin-Márquez, Susan. 2008. *Disorientations: Spanish Colonialism in Africa and the Performance of Identity*. New Haven, CT: Yale University Press.

McKay, George. 2013. *Shakin' All Over: Popular Music and Disability*. Ann Arbor: University of Michigan Press.

Meckna, Michael. 2006. "Louis Armstrong in the Movies, 1931–1969." *Popular Music and Society* 29, no. 3: 359–73.

Merrifield, Andy. 2002. *Metromarxism: A Marxist Tale of the City*. London: Routledge.

Meseguer, Lluís. 2003. "Escriptura lírica i cançó popular." *Catalan Review* 17, no. 1: 79–91.

Michalko, Rod. 2002. *The Difference That Disability Makes*. Philadelphia: Temple University Press.

Michalko, Rod. 1999. *The Two-In-One: Walking with Smokie, Walking with Blindness*. Philadelphia: Temple University Press.

Michalko, Rod. 1998. *The Mystery of the Eye and the Shadow of Blindness*. Toronto: University of Toronto Press.

Michelone, Guido. 2011. *El jazz habla español: 63 entrevistas con músicos de jazz, blues, world, tango-jazz, latin-jazz, flamenco-jazz*. Milan: EDUCatt, Università Cattolica.

Mitchell, David T., with Sharon L. Snyder. 2015. *The Biopolitics of Disability: Neoliberalism, Ablenationalism, and Peripheral Embodiment*. Ann Arbor: University of Michigan Press.

Mitchell, David T., and Sharon L. Snyder. 2000. *Narrative Prosthesis: Disability and the Dependencies of Discourse*. Ann Arbor: University of Michigan Press.

Molinero, Carme and Pere Ysàs. 2014. *La cuestión catalana: Cataluña en la transición española*. Barcelona: Planeta/Crítica.

Moreno Peracaula, Xavier. 2016. "*Nuevo Flamenco*: Re-Imagining Flamenco in Post-dictatorship Spain." PhD diss., Newcastle University.

Moreno Sabogal, Sandra Milena. 2012. "Gestión del Jazz en la ciudad de Valencia." MA diss., Universidad Politécnica de Valencia.

Moya, José C. 2013. "The Iberian Atlantic, 1492–2012." In *Theorising the Ibero-American Atlantic*, edited by Harald E. Braun and Lisa Vollendorf, 51–73. Leiden and Boston: Brill.

Mumford, Lewis. 1970 [1938]. *The Culture of Cities*. New York: Harcourt Brace Jovanovich.

Mumford, Lewis. 1961. *The City in History*. New York: Harcourt, Brace & World.

Muñoz Molina, Antonio. 2014. *Como la sombra que se va*. Barcelona: Seix Barral.

Muñoz Molina, Antonio. 1989 [1987]. *El invierno en Lisboa*. Barcelona: Seix Barral.

Nichols, William, and H. Rosi Song. 2014. *Toward a Cultural Archive of la Movida: Back to the Future*. Madison: Fairleigh Dickinson University Press,

Nisenson, Eric. 1995. *Ascension: John Coltrane and His Quest*. New York: Da Capo Press.

Norden, Martin F. 1994. *Cinema of Isolation: A History of Physical Disability in the Movies*. New Brunswick, NJ: Rutgers University Press.

Novell, Pepa. 2009. "Cantautoras Catalanas: de la *nova cançó* a la *nova cançó d'ara*: El paso y el peso del pasado." *Journal of Spanish Cultural Studies* 10, no. 2: 135–47.

Ockelford, Adam. 2006. "Using a Music-Theoretical Approach to Explore the Impact of Disability on Musical Development: A Case Study." In *Sounding Off: Theorizing Disability in Music*, edited by N. Lerner and J. Straus, 137–55. New York and London: Routledge.

Ogren, Kathy. 1991. "'Jazz Isn't Just Me': Jazz Autobiographies as Performance Personas." In *Jazz in Mind: Essays on the History and Meanings of Jazz*, edited by Reginald T. Buckner and Steven Weiland, 112–27. Detroit: Wayne State University Press.

Okiji, Fumi. 2018. *Jazz as Critique: Adorno and Black Expression Revisited*. Stanford, CA: Stanford University Press.

Olstrom, Clifford E. 2012. *Undaunted by Blindness: Concise Biographies of 400 People who Refused to Let Visual Impairment Define Them*. 2nd ed. Watertown, MA: Perkins School for the Blind.

Orwell, George. 1938. *Homage to Catalonia*. London: Secker and Warburg.

Paddison, Max. 1996. *Adorno, Modernism and Mass Culture: Essays on Critical Theory and Music*. London: Kahn & Averill.

Paddison, Max. 1993. *Adorno's Aesthetics of Music*. Cambridge: Cambridge University Press.

Papo, Alfredo. 1985. *El jazz a Catalunya*. Translated by Josep Alemany. Barcelona: Llibres a l'abast 207.

Parisi, Paolo. 2012. *Coltrane*. New York: Random House.

Parsonage, Catherine Tackley. 2012. "Benny Carter in Britain, 1936–1937." In *Eurojazzland: Jazz and European Sources, Dynamics, and Contexts*, edited by Luca Cerchiari, Laurent Cugny, and Franz Kerschbaumer, 167–88. Lebanon, NH: Northeastern University Press.

Pavlović, Tatjana. 2012. *The Mobile Nation: España Cambia de Piel (1954–64)*. Bristol, UK: Intellect Publishers.

Pedro, Josep. 2016. "'The Purest Essence of Jazz': The Appropriation of Blues in Spain during Franco's Dictatorship." In *Jazz and Totalitarianism*, edited by B. Johnson, 174–90. New York: Routledge.

Peretti, Burton W. 1994. *The Creation of Jazz: Music, Race, and Culture in Urban America*. Urbana: University of Illinois Press.

Pérez Vigo, Rafael. 2015. "El vibráfono en el jazz: El vibráfono jazzístico en España." Phd diss., Departamento de Comunicación Audiovisual, Documentación e Historia del Arte, Universitat Politècnica de València.

Phillips, Damon J. 2013. *Shaping Jazz: Cities, Labels, and the Global Emergence of an Art Form*. Princeton, NJ: Princeton University Press.

Phillips, William D. 2014. *Slavery in Medieval and Early Modern Iberia*. Philadelphia: University of Pennsylvania Press.

Pizà, Antoni, and Francesc Vicens. 2019. "L'estigma alarmant del cabaret." In *Música de jazz: Confèrenies de 1935*, by Baltasar Samper, edited by A. Pizà and F. Vicens, 7–32. Palma: Lleonard Muntaner.

Pons, Pere, and Martí Farré, eds. 2012. *Els 100 millors discos del jazz català*. Valls, Spain: Cossetània.

Porta, Frederic. 2010. "Les 'jam-sessions' de Tete Montoliu." *El Punt Avui*, May 3, 2010. http://www.elpuntavui.cat/esports/article/165344-les-jam-sessions-.

Prescott, Laurence E., and Rosalía Cornejo-Parriego. 2020. "Josephine Baker in Spain: The Ambivalent Reception of an African American Female Superstar." In *Black USA and Spain: Shared Memories in the 20th Century*, edited by R. Cornejo-Parriego, 73–94. New York: Routledge.

Preston, Paul 2012. *The Spanish Holocaust: Inquisition and Extermination in Twentieth-Century Spain*. London: Harper.

Pujol Baulenas, Jordi. 2005. *Jazz en Barcelona, 1920–1965*. Barcelona: Almendra Music.

Quiroga, Alejandro. 2017. "Football and Identities in Catalonia." In *The Barcelona Reader: Cultural Readings of a City*, edited by Enric Bou and Jaume Subirana, 163–84. Liverpool: University of Liverpool Press.

Ratliff, Ben. 2003. "Jazzmen Pay Homage to Catalonia: Barcelona Embraces American Musicians Building Careers." *New York Times*, January 7, 2003.

Resina, Joan Ramon. 2017. *Josep Pla: Seeing the World in the Form of Articles*. Toronto: University of Toronto Press.

Resina, Joan Ramon, ed. 2013. *Iberian Modalities*. Liverpool: University of Liverpool Press.

Rizzo, Gene. 2005. *The Fifty Greatest Jazz Piano Players of All Time: Ranking, Analysis, and Photos*. Milwaukee, WI: Hal Leonard.

Roberts, John Storm. 1999. *Latin Jazz: The First of the Fusions, 1880s to Today*. New York: Schirmer.

Robinson, Perry, and Florence Wietzel. 2002. *Perry Robinson: The Traveler*. San Jose, CA: Writers Club Press.

Rogers, Gayle. 2016. *Incomparable Empires: Modernism and the Translation of Spanish and American Literature*. New York: Columbia University Press.

Rogers, Gayle. 2016. *Incomparable Empires: Modernism and the Translation of Spanish and American Literature*. New York: Columbia University Press.

Rose, Gillian. 1978. *The Melancholy Science: An Introduction to the Thought of Theodor W. Adorno*. London: Macmillan.

Ross, Larry. 2003. *African-American Jazz Musicians in the Diaspora*. Lewiston, NY: Edwin Mellon Press.

Rowden, Terry. 2009. *The Songs of Blind Folk: African American Musicians and the Cultures of Blindness*. Ann Arbor: University of Michigan Press.

Ruiz Bautista, Eduardo. 2005. *Los señores del libro: propagandistas, censores y bibliotecarios en el primer franquismo*. Gijón, Spain: Trea.

Safford, Philip L., and Elizabeth J. Safford. 1996. *A History of Childhood and Disability*. New York: Teachers College Press.

Samper, Baltasar. 2019. *Música de jazz: Confèrenies de 1935*. Edited by Antoni Pizà and Francesc Vicens. Palma: Lleonard Muntaner.

Sánchez, Roberto. 2016. *El jazz y el cine español: Las conexiones entre el jazz y el cine en España*. Saarbrücken, Germany: Editorial Académica Española.

Savigliano, Marta. 1995. *Tango and the Political Economy of Passion*. Boulder, CO: Westview Press.

Sax, David. 2016. *The Revenge of Analog: Real Things and Why They Matter*. New York: Public Affairs.

Scheinfeld, John, dir. 2016. *Chasing Trane: The John Coltrane Documentary*. New York: Abramorama.

Schmidt-Nowara, Christopher. 2001. "'This rotting corpse': Spain between the Black Atlantic and the Black Legend." *Arizona Journal of Hispanic Cultural Studies* 5: 149–60.

"See Spain as Emerging Jazz Site." 1979. *Billboard*, September 22, 46.

Sennett, Richard. 2008. *The Craftsman*. New Haven, CT: Yale University Press.

Sennett, Richard. 1994. *Flesh and Stone: The Body and the City in Western Civilization*. London and New York: W. W. Norton.

Sennett, Richard. 1992. *The Conscience of the Eye: The Design and Social Life of Cities*. New York and London: W. W. Norton.

Sevilla, Paco. 1995. *Paco de Lucía: A New Tradition for the Flamenco Guitar*. San Diego: Sevilla Press.

Siebers, Tobin. 2010. *Disability Aesthetics*. Ann Arbor: University of Michigan Press.

Simmel, Georg. 2010. "The Metropolis and Mental Life." In *The Blackwell City Reader*, edited by G. Bridge and S. Watson, 103–10. Malden, MA: Wiley-Blackwell.

Skovgaard, Ib. 1974. Liner Notes to *Catalonian Fire* by Tete Montoliu Trio. SteepleChase SCS-1017.

Smith, Neil. 1984. *Uneven Development: Nature, Capital and the Production of Space*. Oxford: Basil Blackwell.

Soto, Isabel. 2020. "'Negroes Were Not Strange to Spain': Langston Hughes and the Spanish 'Context.'" In *Black USA and Spain: Shared Memories in the 20th Century*, edited by R. Cornejo-Parriego, 153–72. New York: Routledge.

Soto, Isabel. 2017. "Black Atlantic (Dis)Entanglements: Langston Hughes, Richard Wright, and Spain." *Zeitschrift für Anglistik und Amerikanistik: A Quarterly of Language, Literature and Culture* 65, no. 2: 203–17.

Steingress, Gerhard. 1998. "Ideología y mentalidad en la construcción de la identidad cultural (casticismo, ideal andaluz y psicología cotidiana en el flamenco)." In *Flamenco y nacionalismo: Aportaciones para un sociología política del flamenco*, edited by Gerhard Steingress and Enrique Baltanás, 165–91. Seville: Fundación Machado, Universidad de Sevilla, Fundación El Monte.

Stiker, Henri-Jacques. 2000. *A History of Disability*. Ann Arbor: University of Michigan Press.

Straka, Manfred. 2012. "Cool Jazz in Europe." In *Eurojazzland: Jazz and European Sources, Dynamics, and Contexts*, edited by Luca Cerchiari, Laurent Cugny, and Franz Kerschbaumer, 214–34. Lebanon, NH: Northeastern University Press.

Straus, Joseph N. 2018. *Broken Beauty: Musical Modernism and the Representation of Disability*. Oxford: Oxford University Press.

Straus, Joseph N. 2011. *Extraordinary Measures: Disability in Music.* Oxford: Oxford University Press.

Suárez, Virgil. 1989. *Latin Jazz.* New York: W. Morrow.

Sutherland-Meier, Madeline. 2015. "Toward a History of the Blind in Spain." *Disability Studies Quarterly* 35, no. 4. http://dsq-sds.org/article/view/4039/4113.

Townsend, Irving. 1959. Liner notes to *Golden Vibes,* by Lionel Hampton with Rhythm and Reeds. Columbia CS-8110.

Thompson, Mark Christian. 2018. *Anti-Music: Jazz and Racial Blackness in German Thought between the Wars.* Albany: State University of New York Press, 2018.

Titchkosky, Tanya. 2011. *The Question of Access: Disability, Space, Meaning.* Toronto: University of Toronto Press.

Tusell, Javier. 2011. *Spain: From Dictatorship to Democracy, 1939 to the Present.* Translated by Rosemary Clark. Chichester, UK: John Wiley and Sons.

Vianna, Hermano. 1999. *The Mystery of Samba: Popular Music and National Identity in Brazil.* Chapel Hill: University of North Carolina Press.

Vicens Vidal, Francesc. 2008. "Tete Montoliu i Mallorca: En el desè aniversari de la seva mort." *Lluc: Revista de Cultura i d'Idees* 861 (January–February): 40–47.

Vidal, Guillem. 2017. "Les coses del Tete." *El Punt Avui,* March 29, 2008. http://www.elpuntavui.cat/cultura/article/19-cultura/1105619-les-c.

Vilarós, Teresa M. 1998. *El mono del desencanto: Una crítica cultural de la transición española (1973–1993).* Madrid: Siglo XXI.

Villamandos, Alberto. 2011. *El discreto encanto de la subversión: Una crítica cultural de la gauche divine.* Pamplona, Spain: Laetoli.

Waller, Maurice, and Anthony Calabrese. 1977. *Fats Waller.* Foreword by Michael Lipskin. New York: Schirmer Books.

Washburne, Christopher. 2001–2002. "Latin Jazz, the Other Jazz." *Current Musicology* 71–73: 409–26.

Weygand, Zina. 2009. *The Blind in French Society from the Middle Ages to the Century of Louis Braille.* Translated by Emily-Jane Cohen. Stanford, CA: Stanford University Press.

Whyton, Tony. 2012. "Europe and the New Jazz Studies." In *Eurojazzland: Jazz and European Sources, Dynamics, and Contexts,* edited by Luca Cerchiari, Laurent Cugny, and Franz Kerschbaumer, 366–80. Lebanon, NH: Northeastern University Press.

Wirth, Louis. 1938. "Urbanism as Way of Life." *American Journal of Sociology* 44, no. 1: 1–24.

Witkin, Robert W. 2000. "Why Did Adorno 'Hate' Jazz?" *Sociological Theory* 18, no. 1: 145–70.

Witkin, Robert W. 1998. *Adorno on Music.* London: Routledge.

Woods Peiró, Eva. 2012. *White Gypsies: Race and Stardom in Spanish Musicals.* Minneapolis: University of Minnesota Press.

Wright, Richard. 1995 [1957]. *Pagan Spain.* New York: HarperCollins.

Young, Iris Marion. 1990. *Justice and the Politics of Difference.* Princeton: Princeton University Press.

Young, Iris Marion. 1986. "The Ideal of Community and the Politics of Difference." *Social Theory and Practice* 12, no. 1: 1–26.

Zagalaz, Juan. 2016. "Los orígenes de la relación jazz–flamenco: De Lionel Hampton a Pedro Iturralde (1956–1968)." *Revista de Investigación sobre Flamenco: La Madrugá* 13: 93–124.

Zagalaz, Juan. 2012a. "Flamenco-Jazz: Una perspectiva analítica de sus orígenes: La obra temprana de Jorge Pardo, 1978–1981." In *Congreso las fronteras entre los géneros: Flamenco y otras músicas de tradición oral*, edited by José Migue Díaz-Báñez, Francisco Javier Escobar Borrego, and Inmaculada Ventura Molina, 39–50. Seville: Universidad de Sevilla.

Zagalaz, Juan. 2012b. "The Jazz-Flamenco Connection: Chick Corea and Paco de Lucía between 1976 and 1982." *Journal of Jazz Studies* 8, no. 1: 33–54.

Zingg, David Drew. 1957. Liner Notes for *Jazz Flamenco*, by Lionel Hampton and His Orchestra. RCA LPM-1422.

Discography and Further Listening*

*Dates here are of the album release, not necessarily the album recording.

Bennett, Tony, and Bill Evans. 1975. *The Tony-Bennett-Bill Evans Album*. Fantasy F-9489.

Brubeck, Dave. 1959. *Time Out*. Columbia CS-8192.

Brubeck, Dave. 1961. *Time Further Out*. Columbia CS-8490.

Brubeck, Dave. 1962. *Countdown: Time in Outer Space*. Columbia CL-1775.

Burton, Gary, and Chick Corea. 1973. *Crystal Silence*. ECM-1024-ST.

Byas, Don. 1972. *Don Byas 1945*. Alamac QSR 2447.

Carter, Ron. 1976. *Yellow and Green*. CTI-6064-S1.

Coleman, Ornette. 1960. *Free Jazz*. Atlantic LP-1364.

Coltrane, John. 1961. *My Favorite Things*. Atlantic SD-1361.

Coltrane, John. 1961. *Olé Coltrane*. Atlantic LP-1373.

Coltrane, John. 1962. *Ballads*. Impulse! A-32.

Coltrane, John. 1964. *Crescent*. Impulse! A-66.

Coltrane, John. 1966. *Live at the Village Vanguard, Again!* Impulse! A-9124.

Coltrane, John. 1995. *A Love Supreme*. Impulse! GR-155.

Corea, Chick. 1976. *My Spanish Heart*. Polydor PD-2-9003.

Davis, Miles. 1959. *Kind of Blue*. Columbia CS-8163.

Davis, Miles. 1959. *Porgy and Bess*. Columbia CS-8085.

Davis, Miles, and Gil Evans. 1957. *Miles Ahead*. Columbia CL-1041.

Davis, Miles, and Gil Evans. 1960. *Sketches of Spain*. Columbia CK-65142.

Di Meola, Al, John McLaughlin, and Paco de Lucía. 1981. *Friday Night in San Francisco*. Columbia EC-37152.

Ellington, Duke. 1958. *Black, Brown and Beige*. Columbia CS-8015.

Evans, Bill. 1961. *The Village Vanguard Sessions*. Milestone 47002.

Garner, Erroll. 1955. *Concert by the Sea*. Columbia CL-883.

Garner, Erroll. 1964. *Errol Garner Plays Gershwin and Kern*. EmArcy Records 826-224-2.

Garner, Erroll. 1968. *One More Time!* Harmony HS-11268.

Gordon, Dexter. 1963. *Our Man in Paris*. Blue Note BST-84146.

Hampton, Lionel. 1959. *Golden Vibes*. Columbia CS-8110.

Hawkins, Coleman. 1978. *Body and Soul*. Pickwick QJ-25131.

Iturralde, Pedro. 1967. *Jazz Flamenco*. HHS-11-128.

Iturralde, Pedro. 1968. *Jazz Flamenco, Vol. 2*. HHS-11-151.

Jarrett, Keith. 1975. *The Köln Concert*. ECM-2-1064.

Llach, Lluís. 1976. *Barcelona: Gener de 1976*. Movieplay S 32783.

Monk, Thelonious. 1952. *Genius of Modern Music, Vol. 2*. Blue Note 5009.

Monk, Thelonious. 1965. *Solo Monk*. Columbia CL-2349.

Monk, Thelonious. 1965. *Thelonious Alone in San Francisco*. Riverside RS 9312

Morales, Pilar, and Fernando Orteu's Orchestra. 1961. *Pilar Morales y el conjunto de Fernando Orteu*. SAEF SAP-55037.

Ørsted Pedersen, Niels-Henning, and Sam Jones. 1976. *Double Bass.* SteepleChase SCS 1055.

Parker, Charlie. 1966. *Yardbird.* Pickwick PC-3054.

Raimon. 1976. *El recital de Madrid.* Movieplay S 65014/15.

Robinson, Perry. 1962. *Funk Dumpling.* Savoy MG-12177.

Rollins, Sonny. 1978. *Green Dolphin Street.* Pickwick Records QJ-25181.

Shepp, Archie. 1964. *Archie Shepp and the New York Contemporary Five.* Storyville 6017004.

Tate, Buddy 1960. *Tate-a-Tate.* Swingville SVLP-2014.

Tatum, Art. 1974. *The Art Tatum Legacy.* Olympic Records 7120.

Tatum, Art. 1981. *Pieces of Eight.* The Smithsonian Collection R029.

Tatum, Art, Lionel Hampton, and Buddy Rich. 1955. *Tatum—Hampton—Rich.* Pablo 2310-720.

Waller, Fats. 1973. *The Fats Waller Legacy.* Olympic Records 7106.

Waller, Fats. 1976. *Fats Waller Plays Fats Waller.* Everest FS-319.

Index